THE CULT OF ST GEORGE
IN MEDIEVAL ENGLAND

T0366457

The Cult of St George in Medieval England

Jonathan Good

THE BOYDELL PRESS

First published 2009
The Boydell Press, Woodbridge
Paperback edition 2015

ISBN 978 1 84383 469 4 hardback
ISBN 978 1 78327 063 7 paperback

The Boydell Press is an imprint of Boydell & Brewer Ltd
PO Box 9, Woodbridge, Suffolk IP12 3DF, UK
and of Boydell & Brewer Inc.
668 Mt Hope Avenue, Rochester, NY 14620–2731, USA
website: www.boydellandbrewer.com

The publisher has no responsibility for the continued existence or accuracy
of URLs for external or third-party internet websites referred to in this book,
and does not guarantee that any content on such websites is,
or will remain, accurate or appropriate

A CIP record for this book is available
from the British Library

This publication is printed on acid-free paper
Edited and typeset by
Frances Hackeson Freelance Publishing Services, Brinscall, Lancs

Contents

Illustrations

Acknowledgements

Many people and institutions have helped with this project, and I am happy to acknowledge them here. In England, I benefited from conversations with and kindnesses from John Barron, Jonathan Bengston, Paul Blyth, Jonathan Canning, Michael Clanchy, Jonas Cleary, John Gillingham, Christopher and Caroline Hallpike, Alasdair Hawkyard, David and Laurie Herman, Shelagh Mitchell, Emily O'Brien, Nicholas Orme, Marie-Hélène Rousseau, and Nigel Saul. In London, the staffs at the British Library, the Institute for Historical Research, the Warburg Institute, the Courtauld Institute, and the National Archives were all very helpful, as was the staff at the Bodleian Library at Oxford. At the University of Minnesota I learned much from Barbara Hanawalt, Ruth Mazo Karras, Rebecca Krug, Stanford Lehmberg, Lachlan Mead, Oliver Nicholson, Katherine Reyerson, and J.B. Shank. The staff at Minnesota's Wilson Library was particularly helpful. Ron Akehurst, Laura Dale Bischof, Sarah-Grace Heller, and David Oosterhuis helped with translations, and D'A.J.D. Boulton, Kevin Harty, John Kennedy, and the late Charles T. Wood provided useful references. My editor at Boydell and Brewer, Caroline Palmer, has been unfailingly cheerful throughout, and the anonymous reader offered many useful suggestions. Of course, while all these people contributed to this project in so many ways, its faults and errors remain mine alone.

I am grateful for the financial support of the Social Sciences and Humanities Research Council of Canada, the History Department of the University of Minnesota, the Wimmer Trust at the University of Minnesota, and the Faculty Development Committee at Reinhardt College.

Parts of Chapters 2 and 3 have appeared as "*Argent, a Cross Gules*: The Origins and English Use of the Arms of Saint George," in *The Coat of Arms* 213 (Spring 2007): 9–18 and as "Richard II and the Cults of Saints George and Edward the Confessor," in *Translatio, or the Transmission of Culture in the Middle Ages and Renaissance*, ed. Laura Hollengreen (Turnhout: Brepols, 2008), 161–78. I am grateful for the publishers for permission to reproduce the material here.

Finally, I must acknowledge the support of my family: my parents Ron and Sandra Good, my brother Christopher, and my parents-in-law Dan and Ruth Mattson. Without the support and encouragement of my wife, Anne, this project would never have seen completion, and I dedicate it to her, and to our daughter Susanna.

Abbreviations

AASS	*Acta Sanctorum quotquot tota orbe coluntur.* Paris: V. Palmé, 1863–
BL	London, British Library
CCR	Calendar of Close Rolls
CChR	Calendar of Charter Rolls
CLR	Calendar of Liberate Rolls
CPR	Calendar of Patent Rolls
EETS	Early English Text Society
HMSO	His/Her Majesty's Stationery Office
MGH	*Monumenta Germaniae Historica*
PL	J.-P. Migne, ed. *Patrologiae Cursus Completus … Series Latina.* 221 vols. Paris: 1844–64.
PRO	London, National Archives (Public Record Office)
REED	Records of Early English Drama

Introduction

This book is about St. George in medieval England, in particular about the process by which he became the national patron in the fourteenth and fifteenth centuries. St. George was not of English origin himself – if he ever even existed, he would most likely have been one of the many Christians martyred for their faith in the Eastern Roman Empire sometime in the third or early fourth centuries. Thereafter, for various reasons, he became a patron of agriculture, of the Byzantine army, of crusading against non-Christians, and of the medieval ideal of chivalry (the main reason why he came to be portrayed in legend and image as a dragon-slayer). Some or all of these qualities were appealing to any number of people across the Christian world, who thereby adopted him as their patron – the Genoese, Moscovites, and Ethiopians being only a few. Certainly the idea of crusading, or at least of "just war," was also appealing to the kings of England, starting with Edward I (1272–1307), who deployed St. George to justify their own wars with Wales, Scotland, and France. This usage was shortly taken by many in the English political community to mean that St. George was the patron, not only of the king, but also of the realm, in which they had a stake. Some reasons for this transference will be suggested below; suffice it to say that while it did not completely displace other meanings of his cult in late medieval England, it was clearly the most important, and the major reason why the saint survived the Reformation as a national symbol.

If anything served to diminish this status, therefore, it was not religious but political. Parliamentary union with Scotland in 1707 largely succeeded in subsuming "England" into the new political idea of "Britain," thereby producing a new panoply of symbols like the Royal Union Banner or the classical allegorical figure of Britannia. St. George was never entirely forgotten as a patriotic symbol, but his importance was diminished – until recently. With devolution – the creation of separate assemblies for Wales, Scotland and Northern Ireland, granted the right to pass certain types of legislation without recourse to Westminster – the United Kingdom has become less united. Although England has not received the same level of devolved political power, the English, viewing the drifting-away of the so-called Celtic fringe and the potential "break-up of Britain," have in general become more aware of their older, English identity. St. George, English since the late Middle Ages, has thus been making a comeback: his red-cross flag flies where once the Union Jack did, and his feast day of 23 April receives more attention every year.

As part of this revival, numerous books on St. George have also appeared.[1] By far the best has been Samantha Riches's *St George: Hero, Martyr and Myth* (2000).[2] Riches, an art historian, uses a corpus of over one hundred images of the saint, supplemented by literary evidence and historical records, to analyze the meanings of St. George's cult over the course of its existence. Riches examines his status as a long-suffering martyr, as a patron of chivalry (including an association with the Blessed Virgin Mary), as a military saint and patron of England, and as a dragon-slayer. The richly illustrated book has gone a long way toward reintroducing the English to their patron saint. The present study, however, differs from Riches's work in a number of ways. While covering some of the same ground, it is more historical than art-historical, leaning heavily on manuscript and printed record sources. It also focuses much more on George's status as a national patron in the fourteenth and fifteenth centuries, the main reason why he is undergoing a revival today. In this way it takes after Jonathan Bengtson's 1997 article "Saint George and the Formation of English Nationalism,"[3] although explores the topic in much greater depth, including enumerating specific ways that the political and devotional cults of St. George actually overlapped. It therefore also represents a contribution to the study of premodern English nationalism, suggesting some ways that the idea of England was constituted for those beyond court and parliament.

Chapter 1 explores medieval saints' cults and medieval nationalism, including English nationalism, situating St. George in both. Chapter 2 deals with the cult's origins in the ancient Near East, its development (including St. George's accumulated statuses of martyr, warrior, crusader, and knight), and arrival in England. Chapter 3 details the deployment of St. George by the kings of England starting with Edward I and ending with Henry VII, and how this usage was shared with both the baronial class and the army,

[1] Christopher Stace, *St George, Patron Saint of England* (London: Triangle, 2002); Giles Morgan, *St George: Knight, Martyr, Patron Saint and Dragonslayer* (Edison, N.J.: Chartwell, 2006).
[2] Samantha Riches, *St George: Hero, Martyr and Myth* (Stroud, Glos.: Sutton, 2000).
[3] Jonathan Bengtson, "Saint George and the Formation of English Nationalism," *Journal of Medieval and Early Modern Studies* 27:2 (1997): 317-40.

both to the kings' benefit – and detriment. Chapter 4 explores some manifestations of the popular cult of St. George, including guilds of the saint, many of which embodied a uniting of political with devotional piety. Chapter 5 traces the vicissitudes of St. George in England from the Reformation to the present.

It was by no means inevitable that St. George should have become the patron of England. Understandably, most national patrons are connected in some way with their nations: the saints had been members of the nation while alive, or had ministered to it in some way, or their principal shrines were located within the nation's territory. England had plenty of such saints, many of whom fulfilled all three criteria. St. George fulfilled none of them, yet became England's patron. Why? As chance would have it, "good" kings venerated St. George, while "bad" kings did not, establishing a positive connection between the saint and the nation. George also had a number of advantages over his competitors, among them the fact that he was more chivalrous (and thus compelling), and a more powerful intercessor, than any native saints. His foreignness may have aided him, in fact, since he did not favor any particular area of the country over any other, and since he was the sort of saint to command respect on the international stage. Once established as a national patron, he represented an England that was hierarchical, but inclusive, with everyone having a proper role to play, and his chivalry reflected well on the English, regardless of their actual station. This latter fact is the main reason why St. George has remained a symbol of England to the present day.

1

George the Saint, England the Nation

The process by which St. George came to be the patron saint of England was convoluted and owed a great deal to chance. It also came relatively late in the day: other European polities had their patrons from as early as the tenth century, but the earliest possible mention of St. George being the "special protector" of the English came in 1351, and he did not replace any other saint in this category. In order to discuss why this was the case, some preliminary discussion of sainthood, and nationhood, in the late Middle Ages will be useful.

Although popular, St. George was by no means the only saint in late medieval England. To a degree difficult to imagine today, saints were ubiquitous: their names bestowed on children, churches, ships, and even bells; their feasts commemorated throughout the liturgical year; their shrines the object of pilgrimage; their images sculpted and painted in churches and homes; their stories told and retold, publicly and privately. From the second century AD, Christians had held certain deceased members of their faith in particular esteem. The posthumous title "holy" (Latin *sanctus*, hence "saint") was originally reserved for those who had maintained their faith in the face of torture and execution, although with the conversion of the Roman Empire in the fourth century the category of saint was expanded to include ascetic holy men and women, learned or well-loved ecclesiastics, and successful missionaries and other servants of the faith, and was retroactively attributed to most people in the New Testament who had had direct contact with Jesus. A day was set aside to commemorate the saint, usually the date of his or her death (i.e. "heavenly birth") although saints' days could be strategically placed to compete with pagan holidays. Originally a saint was acclaimed locally, and even after the papacy reserved for itself the sole right to canonize saints in the eleventh century, the sustained enthusiasm of a local cult was an essential ingredient in a successful drive for canonization. Saints served as moral examples for living Christians, and the various genres of hagiography produced about them attested to their holiness in life and steadfastness in the face of death. More importantly, however, saints also served as heavenly intercessors for living Christians. God may have been ineffable, but saints, who for their merits were now with God in heaven, had once been human and knew something about the burdens borne by the average Christian in the course of his or her daily life. They were therefore ideally suited to hear prayers and pass them along to God; even to act as his deputies.[1] This conception of heaven as a sort of imperial court is only obliquely sanctioned by the canonical works of the New Testament, but it clearly fulfilled a need to humanize the divine, and remained a distinctive feature of Catholic Christianity throughout the Middle Ages.

From at least the fourth century it was believed that saints were especially receptive to prayers in the presence of their earthly remains. These relics could be elaborately entombed and the destination of people who might travel long distances on pilgrimage to seek the saint's miraculous and especially curative power.[2] Such a practice is not sanctioned by the New Testament either, but it evidently has its origins in the Christian doctrine of the resurrection of the dead, foretold in the book of Revelation and endorsed in the Nicene Creed – the saint would someday, perhaps very soon, come to reclaim his bones. Relics thus became a conduit between heaven and earth, and the Christian community that possessed them would enjoy the saint's constant protection and be especially devoted to him. A saint's patronage, however, could operate in other ways than by the proximity of relics (which could, in any case, be subdivided and shared, even stolen).[3] Saints (or at least the better-known

[1] See, *inter alia*, Stephen Wilson, "Introduction," in *Saints and their Cults: Studies in Religious Sociology, Folklore and History*, ed. Stephen Wilson (Cambridge: Cambridge University Press, 1983), 1–53; Eamon Duffy, *The Stripping of the Altars: Traditional Religion in England 1400–1580* (New Haven and London: Yale University Press, 1992), 155–206; Richard Marks, *Image and Devotion in Late Medieval England* (Stroud, Glos.: Sutton, 2004), 86–120.

[2] Ronald Finucane, *Miracles and Pilgrims: Popular Beliefs in Medieval England* (New York: St. Martin's Press, 1977), 18, 39ff. See also Jonathan Sumption, *Pilgrimage: An Image of Medieval Religion* (Totowa, N.J.: Rowman and Littlefield, 1975).

[3] See Patrick Geary, *Furta Sacra*, rev. edn. (Princeton: Princeton University Press, 1990).

and powerful ones) were omnipresent enough that they might hear prayer and answer it wherever they were called upon, and many pilgrimages to saints' shrines were not to request miracles but in thanks for them.[4] The guardians of a shrine, of course, assiduously collected accounts of these miracles, in order to prove their saint's power and to maintain the flow of pilgrim traffic, which could be quite lucrative. The shrine of the murdered twelfth-century archbishop St. Thomas Becket at Canterbury was perhaps the best-known in England, although there were many others, like St. Cuthbert at Durham or St. Thomas Cantelupe at Hereford.

Patronage operated in other ways too. It is perhaps only to be expected that over time, certain saints would become known for providing certain types of miracles to certain types of people. This patronage might be explained by details in the saint's hagiography: St. Lucy had had her eyes gouged out, so was a saint to pray to for eye troubles; St. Laurence was burned alive on a gridiron, securing his patronage of cooks; St. Matthew had been a tax collector, and so became a patron of tax collectors. In this way a Christian might acquire a panoply of protecting saints over the course of his life – one for the day he was born on and which may have bequeathed him his name, one or two for his locality, one or two for his profession, and several for personal preference. In his will of 1509, King Henry VII listed Saints Michael, John the Baptist, John the Evangelist, George, Anthony, Edward, Vincent, Anne, Mary Magdalene, and Barbara as his "accustomed Avouers."[5] And although saints were known for punishing people who dishonored them in various ways (by working on their feast days, for instance), it is clear that saints competed for earthly attention. One stark example of such competition occurred when a nine-month-old boy choked on a pilgrim badge of St. Thomas Becket. The family of the boy prayed, not to Becket, but to Henry VI, widely venerated as a saint after his death in 1471. Henry caused the boy to cough the badge out, and in thanks his parents made a pilgrimage to Henry's shrine at Windsor and deposited the badge there.[6] The former king had apparently eclipsed the former archbishop in terms of curative power.[7]

But just as a Christian could esteem several saints, so also could a saint mean several things simultaneously to different people, even to the same

---

4   Most of the miracles collected at the tomb of Henry VI at Windsor are of this type; see Ronald Knox and Shane Leslie, eds., *The Miracles of King Henry VI* (Cambridge: Cambridge University Press, 1923).

5   *The Will of King Henry VII*, ed. T. Astle (London: T. Payne and B. White, 1775), 3.

6   Knox and Leslie, eds., *Miracles*, 164–67.

7   For more on saints coming in and out of fashion, see Duffy, *Stripping*, 164–69.

people. Saint Anne was the (conjectured) mother of the Blessed Virgin Mary and grandmother to Jesus; as such, she could serve as a sanctifier of family dynasties, a help for women in childbirth, a model of female piety for cloistered nuns, and even, as the head of a family *tree*, a patron of woodworkers.[8] St. Katherine, a young Christian noblewoman from Alexandria who chose to be tortured and killed rather than marry a pagan prince, was of course a model of feminine sanctity, but also a patron of education and scholars (she had argued with and defeated fifty pagan philosophers by the force of her genius).[9] St. George also enjoyed a multifaceted patronage: he was variously an exemplary martyr, and a patron of soldiers, crusading, and chivalry, as well as of England. Such disparate meanings sometimes complemented each other, and sometimes they clashed; even a single valence of patronage could be the site of conflict as various groups tried to claim their space within it, or to use it to further some agenda. A biography of St. Anne, for instance, could be rewritten to bolster (or refute) the doctrine of the Immaculate Conception, a sermon on St. Katherine could contain a strong element of patriarchal social control for women, or John Lydgate's *Life of Saints Edmund and Fremund* could contain thinly veiled praise of King Henry VI, for whom it was written.[10] Clearly, saints were complex cultural signifiers, and St. George was no exception. His connection with chivalry certainly helped his adoption as a national patron; once established, people vied for status as members of that nation through venerating him, or used him to rebuke those who were not acting properly as members.

But what was this "nation" of England? The question is a highly problematic one, for the word remains notoriously difficult to describe, let alone define. Nations are generally held to be groups into which humanity is naturally divided, groups whose members share a certain set of cultural characteristics such as language, history, religion, law, and other customs, and whose members live in a delineated and usually contiguous physical space and who acknowledge each other as fellow-members, even if they are not personally acquainted. But what exact set

[8] Kathleen Ashley and Pamela Sheingorn, "Introduction," in *Interpreting Cultural Symbols: Saint Anne in Late Medieval Society*, eds. Kathleen Ashley and Pamela Sheingorn (Athens and London: University of Georgia Press, 1990), 1–68, at 2.
[9] Katherine Lewis, *The Cult of St Katherine in Late Medieval England* (Woodbridge, Suffolk: Boydell, 2000), 11–14.
[10] Ashley and Sheingorn, eds., *Interpreting*, 4–5; Lewis, *Cult of St Katherine*, 6; Karen Winstead, *John Capgrave's Fifteenth Century* (Philadelphia: University of Pennsylvania Press, 2007), 118–34.

of characteristics might constitute them, and how many of these characteristics may be shared with other nations, and how conscious (or proud) members must be of their own nations before they can be said to exist, are all matters of great contention. Further complicating the issue is the question of their origins. Most nationalists have viewed the existence of nations, especially their own, as being of great antiquity. The current dominant paradigm in their study, however, holds that they are much more recent creations, artifacts of modernity itself. Only such indisputably modern phenomena as, for example, the mass education systems required to train people to operate in an industrial economy, or the advent of standardized vernacular languages propagated by printed novels and newspapers (which give birth to "imagined" national communities), could have created the collectivities now known as nations.[11] In the Middle Ages, so the theory goes, for the vast majority of the population culture was a purely local phenomenon, with "nations" shading imperceptibly into each other across the vast expanse of Europe, all under the universalist imperative of the Roman Catholic Church. Nations only came into their own during the nineteenth- and twentieth-century "age of nationalism," when nationhood was conceived as the most important valence of human identity – and independent, unified statehood a nation's most important political goal.

Such a view, however, is not without critics. Medievalists have responded to it by demonstrating that the high Middle Ages are replete with examples of named human populations sharing ancestry myths, histories and cultures, possessing a sense of solidarity arising from common experiences, and living in a specific territory.[12] After about 900, the solidarity of these "peoples," as Susan Reynolds terms them, often coincided with the loyalties they owed to their king: due to changing inheritance laws, by which kingdoms were no longer divided among sons but inherited whole, "kingdoms and peoples came to seem identical –

11   Ernest Gellner, *Nations and Nationalism* (Ithaca: Cornell University Press, 1983), 35–38; Benedict Anderson, *Imagined Communities: Reflections on the Origin and Spread of Nationalism*, 2nd edn. (London: Verso, 1991), 22–36.

12   See, e.g., Anthony D. Smith, *The Ethnic Origins of Nations* (Oxford and New York: Basil Blackwell, 1986), 6–18, 32; Adrian Hastings, *The Construction of Nationhood: Ethnicity, Religion and Nationalism* (Cambridge: Cambridge University Press, 1996), 1–13; Susan Reynolds, *Kingdoms and Communities in Western Europe 900–1300*, 2nd edn. (Oxford: Clarendon Press, 1997), 250–331; Simon Forde, Lesley Johnson, and Alan V. Murray, eds., *Concepts of National Identity in the Middle Ages* (Leeds: Leeds University Press, 1995).

not invariably, but sufficiently often for the coincidence of the two to seem the norm to contemporaries."[13] With statehood, national solidarity was further strengthened among such peoples as the English, Danes, French, Hungarians, Poles, Scots, and Swedes. These groups may not have had all the characteristics that their modern descendants have, but there is historical continuity between the two, and modernists are wrong to ignore or diminish them, which they must if their theories are to be valid. For Anthony Smith, the biggest testament against the idea of constructed modern nations is the profound commitment that members often feel towards them. George Orwell observed, in 1941, that there was nothing to set beside national loyalty as a *positive* force in the modern world; "Christianity and international socialism are as weak as straw in comparison."[14] Ernest Gellner's focus on the mass culture taught in schools in order to sustain an industrial economy, for instance, does not explain why people should voluntarily choose to make sacrifices for national states. Two generations of Communist indoctrination in the Soviet Union and its satellites were not able to inspire the sort of loyalty and personal self-identification characteristic of nationalism; Stalin, indeed, felt it necessary to cast the repulsion of the Nazis in the Second World War as a liberation of the fatherland, a formulation by no means in accord with Marxist ideology. Similarly, Benedict Anderson's focus on the "imagined communities" engendered by "print-capitalism" does not explain how we get from imagining the nation to feeling and loving it, and sacrificing for it when called upon to do so. Could it be that the nation acts as insurance against our own mortality, uniting the dead, living, and the yet unborn in a single community of fate?[15] Modern nationalism may have an interest in developing and enforcing a "national" culture in addition to achieving or defending self-governance, but it is not free to invent such a culture out of nothing – people have to believe that their nations represent something about themselves. National identity is personal, familial, tribal identity writ large: the nation guarantees that there are other people "like us" with whom to share language, religion, culture, and who can help protect us from the predations of others. To be successful, nationalists must appeal to things that large numbers of people already possess in great degree. This fact has given modern nationalism its widespread and

13 Reynolds, *Kingdoms*, 260.
14 George Orwell, "England Your England," in *A Collection of Essays by George Orwell* (Garden City, N.Y.: Doubleday, 1954), 257.
15 Anthony D. Smith, *Nationalism and Modernism* (London: Routledge, 1998), 140.

lasting political potency, and suggests that as a human trait it is not entirely new.

This book, naturally, takes the second, revisionist position regarding the existence of medieval nations. National*ism*, the uncompromising demand that one's own nation possess its own unifed sovereign state, with the refusal to acknowledge other forms of political organization as even legitimate, may be a modern phenomenon, but *national*ism – a sense of belonging to a nation coupled with a feeling of partiality towards it – is not necessarily so, and is one reason why modern nationalism has been politically so strong.[16] Indeed, if the origin of any nation deserves to be located in the premodern era, that nation is England. For a variety of reasons, England has been termed the "prototype" nation, "God's firstborn,"[17] and its premodern genesis has been located in all eras from the age of Bede to the Puritan Revolution. This book is not prepared to argue that it was the advent of St. George as the patron saint of England that served as the magical catalyst for the formation of English nationhood. St. George, however, is an important (and hitherto largely unconsidered) aspect of it, since all collectivities need symbols through which they may affirm their existence. The English royal house had honored saints before, but England also had a strong tradition of sainted *opposition* to the crown. St. George, however, was a saint around which both rulers and ruled could unite to declare their common purpose. Before we discuss national saints, however, a short survey of why a medievalist would consider England a nation is in order.

The combination of the Venerable Bede (673–735) and King Alfred of Wessex (r. 871–99) provides a powerful argument that even Anglo-Saxon England was a national state, with Bede being the theorist of the English nation and Alfred putting the theories into practice. Bede's *Ecclesiastical History of the English Church and People* presupposes an essential unity to the "English people" that was far from obvious at the time, as those people were divided among several mutually antagonistic petty kingdoms and

---

[16] Some critics attempt to designate the second definition of "nationalism" as "patriotism." This is a legitimate word, but I do not believe that a useful distinction can be drawn between the two: since "patriotism" tends to have a more positive connotation than "nationalism," it usually serves to describe a nationalism to which a given writer is partial, bringing to mind the cliché, "I have principles, you have ideology."

[17] Hastings, *Construction of Nationhood*, 35; Liah Greenfeld, *Nationalism: Five Roads to Modernity* (Cambridge, Mass.: Harvard University Press, 1992), 27.

spoke mutually unintelligible dialects. Bede, however, imagines a threefold sense of national unity. First, there is unity in space and in time – the English are heirs to the Britons, the inhabitants of the entire island, who have lived there from before the time of the Romans. The Roman province of Britannia was united by loyalty to Rome and by its Christian faith, two characteristics that have reasserted themselves in Bede's time among the English. Second, there is ecclesiastical unity: after the council of Whitby the entire English church was subject to the archbishop of Canterbury, a unity that transcended the political divisions of the land. Bede's final chapter stresses that the current archbishop of Canterbury came from Mercia, showing that no particular part of England had a chokehold on this aspect of Englishness. Third, although three distinct Germanic peoples came to Britain in the initial migration in the fifth and sixth centuries, the Angles, Jutes and Saxons have merged into a distinct people, the English. Such Englishness, however, does at no time comprise the other inhabitants of the island, the Picts, Scots, or Welsh. Bede addresses the work to the king of Northumbria, Ceowulf, but emphasizes that it is a history of all England, not simply of Northumbria, which Bede has the effrontery to describe as a mere *provincia*. Bede, the biblical scholar, drew explicit parallels between his own English people and those of ancient Israel: both nations were under God, and would be punished severely if they deviated from the right path. The number of surviving manuscripts of the *Ecclesiastical History* attest to the popularity and influence of Bede's vision, as does King Alfred's decision to translate it into English in the tenth century.[18]

It is, indeed, during the century and a half between King Alfred and King Edward the Confessor (d. 1066) that the English nation was unified into a single state, with the concomitant strengthening of the nation that this entailed. Alfred of Wessex started to reconquer England from the Danes, but a deeper sense of national unity already existed, facilitating his efforts. Alfred's codified *Dooms* or laws, and the formalized participation of the nation in governing through the *Witan*, strengthened this political unification, and Alfred's translation of Bede and numerous other works into English, in order to create a vernacular literature, strengthened English national culture. The "triple impact" of economic life, political administration, and religion under Alfred and his successors clinched the development of an English national state. English coins were designed in London and minted at no fewer than forty-four places in the

---

[18]   Hastings, *Construction of Nationhood*, 36–39.

country, a fact that illustrates both bureaucratic centralization and economic vitality of the Anglo-Saxon state. The shire, the unit of local government, also had a role. Shires were neither feudal nor tribal in origin, but royal creations too small to have separatist pretensions but important enough to give their inhabitants a sense of participation in the governance of the realm, through the shire courts and the local *fyrd* (militia). Finally, the church became even more important in promoting a sense of national unity, since it was integrated with the state *and* the major producer of a vernacular literature unseen anywhere else in Europe, including parts of the Bible, St. Benedict's Rule, chronicles, sermons, and poetry.[19]

Thus, almost a millennium prior to the nineteenth century, we have a nation "imagined," and a state (in this case allied with a church) that proceeds to construct it further; one recent scholar has declared it a "certainty" that "Late Anglo-Saxon England was a nation state."[20] The conquest of this state by the Normans under Duke William the Conqueror in 1066 may have seemingly ended it, since a very sharp division was introduced into the kingdom between the French-speaking and continentally-inclined upper class of lay magnates and bishops, and the remaining lower-class English speakers, whose language almost entirely ceased to be written down. John Gillingham, however, has proposed that the distinction became meaningless in the 1120s and 1130s, i.e. two generations after the Conquest of 1066. The lords of England had come to perceive themselves as English, and if they continued to speak French it was not as a symbol of their retained "Norman" identity. French, throughout the twelfth century, was simply the international language of polite lay society and speaking it did not express affinity to France or any part of it, much as many Irish, Welsh, Scots, and Australians speak English today but may not be favorably disposed to the English themselves. Most of the upper classes lost their continental connections fairly quickly and

19   Hastings, *Construction of Nationhood*, 42; Patrick Wormald, "*Engla Lond*: the Making of an Allegiance," *Journal of Historical Sociology* 7 (1994): 1–24; Alfred P. Smyth, "The Emergence of English Identity, 700–1000," in *Medieval Europeans: Studies in Ethnic Identity and National Perspectives in Medieval Europe*, ed. A.P. Smyth (Houndmills, Hants.: Macmillan, and New York: St. Martin's Press, 1998), 24–52.

20   James Campbell, "The Late Anglo-Saxon State: A Maximum View," *Proceedings of the British Academy* 87 (1995): 47. For an opposing view, see Georges Tugene, *L'image de la nation anglaise dans l'"Histoire écclesiastique" de Bède le Vénérable* (Strasbourg: Presses Universitaires de Strasbourg, 2001).

took on the perception of being English, as revealed by such twelfth-century writers as William of Malmsbury, Henry of Huntingdon, Geoffrey of Monmouth, and Aelred of Rievaulx, in which one can find a sense that everyone has a place in the ongoing national story, that the Normans were now no different from earlier immigrants. The "Norman" invasion of Ireland in the mid-twelfth century is a misnomer: for the people on the receiving end this was a deed carried out by the English.[21]

Although a version of the French language continued to be spoken and written in England, it was only a matter of time before English came to be written too. Thorlac Turville-Petre has examined the widespread revival of English in the fifty-year period preceding the outbreak of the Hundred Years' War, 1290–1340.[22] This revival was not merely the result of the vicissitudes of fashion, but a statement of identity, underlined by the subject matter of the English works in question. In "The Simonie," the chronicles of Robert of Gloucester and of Robert Manning, the various works in the Auchinleck manuscript, the *South English Legendary*, *Cursor Mundi*, *Havelok the Dane*, and *Handlyng Synne*, writers defined England in terms of its land, its people and its language, and created a national history in which these three aspects of Englishness were combined. Turville-Petre also denies that regionalism impeded the development of national identity: although the division between north and south was apparent and quite old, and the English language itself was broken up into different dialects which were by no means mutually comprehensible, most texts that express some form of regional identity are concerned with ensuring that the regions they represent are not excluded from the nation as a whole. Turville-Petre has subsequently emphasized that the fifty-year period of 1290–1340 may have been exceptional, a product of war with Scotland, threats from France, and baronial discontent with Edward I and especially Edward II.[23] But if

---

[21] John Gillingham, *The English in the Twelfth Century: Imperialism, National Identity and Political Values* (Woodbridge, Suffolk: Boydell, 2000), 3–18. See also Michael Clanchy, *From Memory to Written Record: England 1066–1307* (Oxford and Cambridge, Mass.: Blackwell, 1993), 198, 213–14, who notes that, by the thirteenth century, most of the French spoken in England had to be learned from grammar books.

[22] Thorlac Turville-Petre, *England the Nation: Language, Literature, and National Identity, 1290–1340* (Oxford: Clarendon Press, 1996).

[23] Thorlac Turville-Petre, "Afterword," in *Imagining a Medieval English Nation*, ed. Kathy Lavezzo (Minneapolis and London: University of Minnesota Press, 2004), 340–46, at 340.

"the very act of writing English is a statement about belonging,"[24] people certainly continued to make that statement throughout the fourteenth and fifteenth centuries. John Langland, Geoffrey Chaucer, the *Gawain*-poet, and John Gower are some of the better-known later Middle English authors, and although their nationalism might not have been as overt as that discerned by Turville-Petre,[25] they too were not unconcerned with the idea of the nation. For instance, Peggy Knapp has shown how Chaucer's *Miller's Tale* exhibits the same sort of confidence in the "steady, anonymous simultaneous activity" of various members of a given community (the same sort of characteristic Benedict Anderson attributed to the modern novel), while Larry Scanlon has noted in the B-text of Langland's *Piers Plowman* an elevation of the commons, whereby the Crown is legitimated by the "kind wit" of the third estate, a radical reconception of sovereignty that was shared by the rebels of 1381.[26]

One might cavil that literary sources are not symptomatic of national feeling, but merely constitute wishful thinking on its behalf. More concrete, however, is the further development of the medieval English state. English constitutional and administrative history is an immense and longstanding field;[27] suffice it to say that William the Conqueror and his successors kept those Anglo-Saxon governmental institutions they found useful, while adding others that further buttressed their power, with the result that the English state soon became the most efficient in the medieval West. A central chancery still produced royal writs, although in Latin and not in English. The sheriffs, royal agents in charge of particular shires, were required to collect taxes for the king and present them twice a year at the court of the exchequer at Westminster, where the king's clerks would record the amount on pipe rolls and render tally-stick receipts for it. Sheriffs were deprived of some of their own power by the creation of *eyres*, circuits

24 Turville-Petre, *England the Nation*, 10.
25 See Derek Pearsall, "The idea of Englishness in the fifteenth century," in *Nation, Court and Culture: New Essays on Fifteenth-Century English Poetry*, ed. Helen Cooney (Dublin: Four Courts Press, 2001), 15–27, at 16.
26 Peggy Knapp, "Chaucer Imagines England (in English)," and Larry Scanlon, "King, Commons and Kind Wit: Langland's National Vision and the Rising of 1381," in *Imagining*, ed. Lavazzo, 131–60; 191–233.
27 See, *inter alia*, T.F. Tout, *Chapters in the Administrative History of Mediaeval England*, 6 vols. (Manchester: Manchester University Press, 1920–33); Bryce Lyon, *A Constitutional and Legal History of Medieval England* (New York: Harper and Row, 1960); R.C. Van Caenegem, *The Birth of the English Common Law* (Cambridge: Cambridge University Press, 1973).

traveled by itinerant justices who were employed consistently after 1166. As a result of these crown servants, who were based in Westminster, the county court was no longer a popular assembly, but a unit of the king's government, a cog in the administrative machinery. Local legal variations were replaced with a single, national system. Centralized courts were also strengthened under Henry II. The court of the King's Bench dealt with violations of the king's peace, and the court of Common Pleas dealt with civil disputes, both on a national level. While the itinerant justices made local administration uniform, the national courts humbled it, for the sake of central aggrandizement. All these agencies were staffed increasingly by men who may have been in minor orders but were not ecclesiastics as such, i.e. they were indisputably *royal* servants, often from humble backgrounds, and therefore of superior loyalty.[28]

All this state strengthening and centralization did not to lead to royal absolutism, however. For a number of reasons, baronial opposition parties, sometimes allied with the Church, were ultimately successful in forcing the king to recognize the "community of the realm" and to attain its assent to major decisions, chiefly those relating to taxes. William the Conqueror had parceled out lands piecemeal to his followers across the expanse of the kingdom, perhaps in order to avoid giving any one of them a large, geographically contiguous base that might facilitate rebellion against the crown, which had been a familiar event on the continent. William's policy had the effect of forcing the barons to work together if they ever wished to assert their rights vis-à-vis an over-mighty king, which made potential rebellions difficult to foment but particularly effective once they were organized. One such incident came in 1215, when King John was forced to ratify Magna Carta, a document that had the effect of requiring the king to respect the rights of all freeborn Englishmen and to govern by the rule of law. Another came in 1258, when Henry III issued the Provisions of Oxford which called, among other things, for great councils, or *parliaments*, to be held three times a year, at which lords, knights, and burghers from all parts of England would gather to negotiate with the king over royal policy. The provisions failed, but parliament has remained a distinguishing feature of English government to this day, and was regularly called throughout the late Middle Ages: 118 times, for instance, between 1307 and 1422.[29] Those kings who recognized the necessity of

---

[28] See Ralph Turner, *Men Raised from the Dust: Administrative Service and Upward Mobility in Angevin England* (Philadelphia: University of Pennsylvania Press, 1988).

[29] Hastings, *Construction of Nationhood*, 50–51.

working with parliament tend to be remembered as "wise" or "good," while those who did not tended to be deposed. Of course one must never indulge in the sort of "Whiggish" history that reads into English constitutional development a long narrative of "progress" (marred by the occasional "setback") as though the entire thing had been predetermined. By chance or design, however, England found itself, in the late Middle Ages, possessed of a strong and efficient government in which part of the nation had asserted, and successfully claimed, a stake.

Warfare was another activity in which the state and the nation intersected. Over the course of the fourteenth and fifteenth centuries the wars of the kings of England against Scotland and France were more or less constant and involved more and more people, often including plebian foot-soldiers and not only knights. Such people also increasingly served directly under the crown and were not mustered as part of anyone's feudal obligation. This meant that the wars cost more money, which in turn meant that the king needed to justify them to those who paid taxes.[30] All these facts combined to influence English national identity. The English army drew its membership from all estates of the kingdom and existed, as a body, to serve the king. Fighting against foreign enemies naturally intensified national sentiment among the forces doing the work: we are of one nation, our enemies are not. The propaganda required to justify the wars helped to universalize this sentiment among the rest of the nation. Negotiating with parliament required the king to justify his wars there, and the need to muster troops required that propaganda be disseminated throughout the kingdom. The chancery produced royal writs which were sent to various places to be read out; these appealed to the obligation to defend the king when called upon to do so, but also emphasized the dangerous threat posed by the Scots and French to the kingdom: both allegedly burned churches, and the French were interested in extirpating the English tongue.[31] Letters describing military exploits abroad were also circulated throughout the kingdom, and ordered to be read in churches at Mass.[32] Often these letters reported victories, which helped to justify the entire project. St. George became an aspect of English national identity in this context, as we shall see.

[30] Christopher Allmand, *The Hundred Years War: England and France at War, c. 1300–c. 1450* (Cambridge: Cambridge University Press, 1989), 102–11.

[31] Barnaby C. Keeney, "Military Service and the Development of Nationalism in England, 1272–1327," *Speculum* 22 (1947): 534–49, at 537, 544–45.

[32] Allmand, *Hundred Years War*, 139.

George was a saint, of course, and a question immediately poses itself: how could he become "English," when he was venerated in so many other nations within Christendom? How, indeed, could there be any national identity in the Middle Ages, when the Catholic Church was such a universal and powerful institution? There may be something to this question, but it is good to remember that the papacy's claims to universality were always checked by the reality of the princes' political and military power. This power grew ever stronger over the course of the late Middle Ages and often at the expense of the Church, whose prestige was greatly undermined by the "Babylonian captivity" at Avignon, the Black Death, and the Great Schism. Furthermore, the Church itself was divided into nations at certain levels, most notably in the College of Cardinals, whose members tended to vote as blocs to ensure the election of one of their co-nationals as pope. As we have seen, the English church could sometimes posture as the defender of the nation against the crown, as it did when ten senior ecclesiastics sided with the barons against King John at Runnymede, procuring the famous first clause of Magna Carta that "the English Church shall be free."

Thus, some of the possible characteristics of the premodern English state, and the nation it ruled. It needs to be stated, of course, that these characteristics cannot be lined up into some sort of teleological narrative of national progress from Anglo-Saxon England to the Reformation and beyond. Like saints' cults, nations are protean and ever-shifting, at all times meaning different things to different people. Derek Pearsall has proposed that national feeling came in and out of fashion over the course of the late Middle Ages, once during Turville-Petre's fifty-year period from 1290 to 1340, and perhaps again from 1410 to 1420, with other periods being rather indifferent to it.[33] But even if we take Pearsall seriously (other sources than literary ones give a different picture), it is clear that there was a "nation" to appeal to, a core idea of Englishness that resonated with English people. Robert Rouse noticed something similar in his investigation of the idea of Anglo-Saxon England in Middle English romance. Such an idea, at its various invocations, was "shaped not merely by the needs of the present, but also by the persistence of the past, in landscape, place-names, and folk memories"[34] – in other words, it existed

---

[33]   Pearsall, "Idea of Englishness," 15.
[34]   Robert Allen Rouse, *The Idea of Anglo-Saxon England in Middle English Romance* (Cambridge: D.S. Brewer, 2005), 10.

independently of the people employing it, and their audience. As Anthony Smith has noted, nations cannot be invented out of nothing.

A word may be interjected here, however, on attitudes towards the whole subject. It comes as no surprise that nationalists have tended to look on the existence of nations, particularly their own nations, in a favorable light, while modernist theorists of nationalism tend to be deeply skeptical of the phenomenon. The former might point to the pride, dignity, and sense of purpose that someone might have by virtue of his or her membership in a nation, while the latter point to the exclusion, violence and even genocide visited upon people who are deemed not to be members, or insufficiently enthusiastic members. If nations, as modernists contend, are recent, artificially constructed phenomena, then any evil that nationalism has caused becomes significantly less defensible, and alternate political arrangements to nation-states become more viable. Elie Kedourie, who located the birth of the concept of the nation in the German Enlightenment, claimed that national states "did not minister to political freedom, they did not increase prosperity, and their existence was not conducive to peace."[35] Whereas the Ottoman or Hapsburg empires could afford to treat their differing constituent nationalities with something approximating equality, a nation-state, being the expression of the will of the dominant nation within it, could not. Much of the misery suffered by Europe in the twentieth century was the result of nationalist conflict, from the Second World War (begun over the issue of Germans not living within Germany proper) to the ethnic cleansing resulting from the break-up of Yugoslavia in the 1990s. Patrick Geary's attitude toward the subject can be inferred from the title of his book *The Myth of Nations*, which was written explicitly against present-day ethnic nationalists like Slobodan Milosevic of Yugoslavia or Jean-Marie Le Pen of France, in order to expose the falsity of their claims.[36] Geary is a historian of the early Middle Ages, and asserts that the great migrations occasioned by the implosion of the Roman empire were a giant stew in which nothing resembling "nations" can be discerned;[37] Clovis, for example, was in no way a "French" king, contrary

---

[35] Elie Kedourie, *Nationalism*, 4th edn. (Oxford and Cambridge, Mass.: Blackwell, 1994), 134.

[36] Patrick Geary, *The Myth of Nations: The Medieval Origins of Europe* (Princeton: Princeton University Press, 2002).

[37] Of course, just because nations cannot be traced to the early Middle Ages does not mean that they cannot be traced to the high and late Middle Ages. (It is worth noting that England makes few appearances in *The Myth of Nations*, perhaps because it does not fit Geary's thesis.)

to the claims of the National Front party, which also wants to restrict and even reverse immigration into France today, not coincidentally. That sort of program, to Geary, is "poisoned," "dangerous," and "toxic," and should not be dignified with false history.[38]

One must keep in mind all ramifications of national consciousness, of course; St. George, in particular, helped to justify the English wars against Wales, Scotland, and France during the late Middle Ages, with all the misery that these wars produced. Recognition of the evils of nationalism, however, should not interfere with a historical investigation into the existence of nations. Neither should political opposition to such "nationalist" parties as the National Front: one could (falsely) believe that Clovis was the first king of "France," and *still* oppose the National Front's anti-immigrant platform. Susan Reynolds has written that "most medieval historians would deny that they are nationalists, but that is because, like many historians of the phenomenon of nationalism, they see it as something aggressive, xenophobic, and deplorable, but do not look hard at the ideas which underlie it."[39] St. George's patronage of the English is one such hard idea.

But how and why did he become England's patron? He was not the original Christian missionary to the English, as St. Patrick (d. 461) was to the Irish, or St. Denis (d. 250) was to the area around Paris, which subsequently became the seat of the kings of France. Nor was he a king who converted to Christianity and commanded his people to follow, as was St. Olaf of Norway (d. 1030) or St. Stephen of Hungary (d. 1038). Nor did St. George's principal shrine exist in England, as did St. Andrew's in Scotland, or St. James's in what became Spain. In England an efficient state ruled over a fairly homogeneous nation, but the saintly situation was different there. The pagan Germanic tribes that had invaded in the wake of the Roman withdrawal were divided into a number of petty kingdoms, so that when Pope Gregory the Great sent Augustine to the country in 597 only King Ethelbert of Kent (whose wife, Bertha, was already Christian) was received into the faith. Both Augustine and Ethelbert were eventually honored as saints, but their patronage was not extended to the entire English people, even as the various Anglo-Saxon kingdoms accepted Roman Christianity. Instead, each kingdom seemed to acquire its own saints, especially when they were killed by pagans and

---

[38] Geary, *Myth of Nations*, 15, 33, 35.
[39] Reynolds, *Kingdoms and Communities*, 251.

thus could be counted among the noble army of martyrs: Oswald, king of Northumbria, was martyred by the pagan King Penda of Mercia in 642; Ethelbert, king of the East Angles, was martyred in 794 by King Offa of Mercia; Edmund, king of the East Angles, was killed by the invading Vikings in 869; and Edward, boy-king of all England, was assassinated in 979.[40] Each of these had its own local cult, but even after Alfred's unification of the kingdom none of them took over as a national patron. Edward the Confessor, who died in 1066, was in many ways the culmination of the tradition of the Anglo-Saxon king saint and in his way well primed to become a national patron. Although not a martyr, in his own lifetime he enjoyed a reputation for holiness: he reputedly had a chaste marriage with his wife Edith, he was generous to the poor, and he richly endowed Westminster Abbey, allowing it to build a church with nave some 300 feet long. Miracles occurred at his tomb in Westminster Abbey, and although they may have been an expression of discontent against the invading Normans, England's new rulers had no wish to stamp out the cult, since the king had been half-Norman himself, had spent much of his childhood in Normandy, and had allegedly promised the throne of England to Duke William of Normandy, who proceeded to make good on his claim at the Battle of Hastings in October 1066. Although the miracles waned in the later eleventh century, they rose again in the 1130s, parallel with a drive for canonization by the monks of Westminster, who were very keen to be the guardians of a legitimate saint, and for their abbey church to be the permanent site for royal coronations and burials. Osbert of Clare, a twelfth-century prior of Westminster, wrote a Life of St. Edward in 1138 aimed at getting its subject canonized.[41] King Henry II was also interested in having Edward canonized: piety and personal veneration may have come into it, but Henry II was worldly and practical, and his later controversy with Thomas Becket illustrated quite clearly that he wanted to assert his authority over the English Church in the face of the

[40] See David Hugh Farmer, *The Oxford Dictionary of Saints*, 3rd edn. (Oxford and New York: Oxford University Press, 1992), 369–70, 163, 147–48, 151–52; also S.J. Ridyard, *The Royal Saints of Anglo-Saxon England* (Cambridge: Cambridge University Press, 1988).

[41] Bernhard W. Scholz, "The Canonization of Edward the Confessor," *Speculum* 36 (1961): 38–60, at 39, 48–49. See also Frank Barlow, *Edward the Confessor* (Berkeley and Los Angeles: University of California Press, 1970), 256–85; and Frank Barlow, ed., *The Life of King Edward who Rests at Westminster Attributed to a Monk of Saint-Bertin*, 2nd edn. (Oxford: Clarendon Press, 1992), 150–63.

Gregorian reformers.[42] Having a papally canonized saint-king (as opposed to just another popularly acclaimed saint-king) in his lineage would help endow him with the justification he needed. The combined efforts of the Westminster monks and Henry II bore fruit in 1161, when the brief papal schism worked in their favor and Alexander III canonized Edward in gratitude for Henry's support in the dispute with the anti-pope Victor IV. Edward was translated to an honored place in the Abbey two years later.

It is with Becket, however, that matters become more complicated, and force the relationship between royalty and sanctity in England to become different from that in France. There the monks of St-Denis, just north of Paris, had forged a powerful alliance with the Capetian kings that benefited both and served to propagate St. Denis as the patron and protector of the kingdom.[43] Thomas Becket, of course, had been Henry's loyal chancellor; Henry, therefore, had Becket promoted to the archbishopric of Canterbury in 1160, in the hope that Becket would in turn support Henry's actions as king, giving him the same prestige of holiness that he was looking for when he had Edward the Confessor canonized. To Henry's annoyance, Becket immediately became an obedient son of the Church and adopted the complete program of the Gregorian reformers, objecting to Henry's meddling, in any way, with the internal workings of the English church. In riposte to the canonization of Edward the Confessor, Becket attempted to procure the canonization of Anselm, the noted scholastic philosopher and the first Gregorian archbishop of Canterbury.[44] The tension between Henry and Becket became so acrimonious that Henry's ejaculation, "Will no one rid me of this meddlesome priest?" was taken seriously by four of the king's knights, who rode to Canterbury Cathedral and assassinated Becket there on 28 December 1170. This action shocked Christendom and Henry performed penance for instigating it. Miracles abounded at Becket's tomb, and Becket himself was canonized quickly in 1173. Canterbury subsequently became one of the most popular pilgrimage sites in England (it was the destination of the pilgrims "from every shire's end" in the *Canterbury Tales*) and in all of Europe.

Becket thereafter became a powerful check on the development of a national patron saint, insofar as a national saint was one that could

---

[42]   Scholz, "Canonization," 54.
[43]   Colette Beaune, *The Birth of an Ideology: Myths and Symbols of Nation in Late-Medieval France*, ed. Frederic L. Cheyette, trans. Susan Ross Huston (Berkeley, Los Angeles, and Oxford: University of California Press, 1991), 20–69.
[44]   Finucane, *Miracles and Pilgrims*, 36.

represent both rulers and ruled. Medieval English kings venerated Becket, but they did (or could) not *deploy* him in the same way that they did St. Edward the Confessor, to represent their right to rule. Becket even, according to Josiah Cox Russell, heralded a tradition of saintly *opposition* to the crown, in which baronial leaders, such as Simon de Montfort (d. 1265) and Thomas of Lancaster (d. 1322), who had been executed by unpopular regimes, were widely regarded as saints. Although neither of these figures was canonized, miracles were reported at their tombs, which became the objects of pilgrimage; venerating these saints became at least partially a way of critiquing the regimes that had executed them.[45] Meanwhile, the veneration of St. Edward the Confessor or St. Edmund the martyr extended little beyond court circles and the communities at Westminster and Bury St. Edmunds in Suffolk. In fairness, the crown may not have felt the need to invest any particular effort in promoting a national patron, since the strength of the state may have obviated the need for an English "supernatural focal point."[46] The fact remains, however, that a single national saint was not one of the ingredients of English nationhood prior to the fourteenth century, a saint that both rulers and ruled could venerate and thereby declare their status as members of that nation and participants in its affairs.

This situation began to change, starting in the late thirteenth century. Edward I used St. George to justify his wars against Wales and Scotland, and prescribed his protection for all levels of the army. Edward III resurrected this tradition, and his victories justified it. By the end of the century the protection that St. George exercised over the army had been extended to the entire English nation. Edward's longevity and the fact that warfare had become much more of a national endeavor during his reign were instrumental in this shift; the fact that Edward III deployed St. George to represent himself in peacetime and that he founded the prestigious Order of the Garter under the protection of St. George also helped. Richard II and Henry IV, both of whom had to face down significant rebellion during their reigns, found that St. George could be

---

[45] Josiah Cox Russell, "The Canonization of Opposition to the King in Angevin England," in *Anniversary Essays in Medieval History by Students of Charles Homer Haskins*, eds C.H. Taylor and J.L. La Monte (New York and Boston: Houghton Mifflin, 1929), 279–90; see also Simon Walker, "Political Saints in Later Medieval England," in *The Macfarlane Legacy*, eds R.H. Britnell and A.J. Pollard (New York: St. Martin's Press, 1995), 77–105.

[46] Wilson, "Introduction," 34.

invoked against them for allegedly not ruling well, but Henry V's spectacular victories restored a sense of common purpose between the king and his people. St. George thereafter became a means through which contenders for the throne justified their worthiness for it, and through which people declared their membership in an English nation. First, however, a look at the origins of St. George, and how his veneration arrived in England, is in order.

2

The Cult of St. George: Origins, Development, and Arrival in England

Over the course of its existence, the cult of St. George acquired an impressive number of aspects. Originally celebrated as an exemplary martyr, St. George was also celebrated as a patron of agriculture, a patron of warfare and crusading, and a patron of chivalry. Although official ecclesiastical opinion was not always enthusiastic about the saint, popular opinion was, setting the stage for him to become the national patron of England in the fourteenth and fifteenth centuries.

By tradition, St. George was a Christian army officer from Cappadocia in Asia Minor, who was martyred in the late third or early fourth century. Since no primary source account of his life or martyrdom exists, exactly where and when this event occurred, if it occurred at all, is anyone's guess. Such lack of documentation did not prevent the saint from becoming widely popular throughout the eastern Roman Empire from the sixth century on. Lydda (or Diospolis) in Palestine boasted St. George's tomb, whose existence and miracles were witnessed by late-antique pilgrims to the Holy Land, such as the early sixth-century Theodosius, the late sixth-century Antoninus, or the eighth-century Epiphanius the Monk.[1] Other sources from the Near East reveal other manifestations of the cult. The Life of St. John the Silentiary (454–558), for instance, refers to a monastery of St. George in Jerusalem, Procopius of Caesarea writes that the Emperor Justinian (527–65) built a church to St. George in Bizani, Armenia, and the *Patria* of the early sixth-century historian Heschius of Miletus records

---

[1] *Itinera Hierosolymitana Saeculi IIII–VIII*, ed. Paul Geyer (New York and London: Johnson Reprints, 1964), 139, 176; John Wilkinson, *Jerusalem Pilgrims before the Crusades* (Warminster: Aris and Phillips, 1977), 119.

several churches to St. George in Constantinople.[2] There is also sixth-century evidence for a monastery in Jericho, a church in Edessa, and a monastery at Dorylleon.[3] A Coptic church to St. George ("Mâri Girgis") was dedicated in 684 in Cairo, the first of some forty Egyptian churches and monasteries to the saint that came to exist by the thirteenth century.[4] St. George seems to have been especially popular in Arabia and Syria, since he is mentioned in several fifth- and sixth-century inscriptions there, such as one from a monastery at Ezra (a former pagan temple):

> The house of demons has become a house of God
> A saving light has shone where darkness covered
> Where sacrifices of idols, now choirs of angels
> Where God was angered, now God is propitiated
> A Christ-loving man, the noble John son of Diomedes
> From his own property has offered a gift to God, a building worth seeing
> Having placed in the same, the honorable relics
> Of the splendidly holy martyr George, who appeared to John himself.
> Not under sleep, but visibly. In the year nine, year 410.

or another from a church at Shakka:

> The house of the holy and victorious martyrs, George and the saints [who died] with him. As an offering of Bishop Tiberinus, the nave and the portico of the church were built from their foundations, in the 13th indiction of the year 263. [The work was performed] by the care of George and Sergius the greater, deacons.[5]

---

2   Eduard Schwartz, *Kyrillos von Skythopolis Texte und Untersuchungen zur Geschichte der altchristlichen Literatur* 49: 2 (Leipzig: J.C. Heinrichs Verlag, 1939), 204; Procopius of Caesarea, *Procopius VII Buildings,* trans. H.B. Dewing (London: William Heinemann and Cambridge, Mass.: Harvard University Press, 1921), 198; *Scriptores Originum Constantinopolitanarum,* ed. Theodore Preger (New York: Arno Press, 1975), 225, 228, 270, 280.

3   P.M. Abel, "Le tombeau de l'higoumène Cyriaque à Jericho," *Revue Biblique* 8 (1911): 286–89; Siméon Vailhé, "Une inscription byzantine de Jéricho," *Échos d'Orient* 14 (1911), 231–32; J.B. Segal, *Edessa, 'The Blessed City'* (Oxford: Clarendon Press, 1970), 190; Elizabeth Dawes and Norman H. Baynes, *Three Byzantine Saints: Contemporary Biographies translated from the Greek* (Oxford: Basil Blackwell, 1948), 174.

4   A.J. Butler, *Ancient Coptic Churches of Egypt* (Oxford: Oxford University Press, 1884), 1: 249; *The Churches and Monasteries of Egypt and some Neighbouring Countries attributed to Abu Salih, the Armenian,* trans. B.T.A. Evetts (Oxford: Clarendon Press, 1895), 46, n. 3, and 258–60.

5   William H. Waddington, *Inscriptions Grecques et Latines de la Syrie* (Rome:

Many more such pieces of evidence could surely be uncovered, most likely representing only a small fraction of those that once existed.[6] The Life of St. Theodore of Sykeon (d. 613), the bishop of Anastasiopolis in Galatia, provides a good, final example of St. George's popularity. George is a major actor throughout: he appears to Theodore's mother while her son is a child, and makes several interventions in Theodore's own life. A chapel of St. George serves as a place for Theodore to meditate and study the Holy Scriptures, and later as a hermitage for him. Later still Theodore constructs a church to the saint, for which he acquires a piece of the martyr's skull, a finger, and a tooth.[7] Such a prominent place given to St. George in the Life of another saint indicates, by the early seventh century, that George had become quite important indeed.

St. George's own legend is in the form of a Passion, not a Life – that is, it is mainly concerned with St. George's torture and death and not with anything else he may have done beforehand. The Passion is recorded in a great number of manuscripts and in numerous languages, not only Greek and Latin, but also Arabic, Armenian, Coptic, Ethiopian, Nubian, and Syriac.[8] All this literary activity is further testament to George's widespread

---

"L'Erma" di Bretschneider, 1968), nos. 2158, 2498. Other Syrian inscriptions to St. George recorded by Waddington include nos. 1981, 2092, 2126, and 2412m; for others in Syria and Arabia see Jean Lassus, *Sanctuaires Chrétiens de Syrie* (Paris: Paul Guenther, 1947), 171; Louis Jalabert and René Mouterde, *Inscriptions grecques et latines de la Syrie* (Paris: Paul Guenther, 1955) 5: 49; Hippolyte Delehaye, *Les Origines du culte des martyrs*, 2nd edn., (Brussels: Bollandists, 1933), 175; and F. Halkin, "Inscriptions grecques relatives à la hagiographie," *Analecta Bollandiana* 67 (1949): 98, 100, 105.

6   Wolfgang Haubrichs provides a list of some 86 manifestations of George's cult in the late antique East, although Christopher Walter suggests that "rigorous control" needs to be exercised over it. See Wolfgang Haubrichs, *Georgslied und Georgslegende im frühen Mittelalter: Text und Rekonstruktion* (Königstein: Scriptor, 1979), 225–32; Christopher Walter, "The Origins of the Cult of Saint George," *Revue des Études Byzantines* 53 (1995): 316.

7   Dawes and Baynes, *Three Byzantine Saints*, 89, 91, 93, 94, 99, 132; 91, 97; 127, 154.

8   See *Bibliotheca hagiographica Graeca*, ed. F. Halkin, 3rd edn. (Brussels: Bollandists, 1957), 1: 212–23; *Bibliotheca Hagiographica Latina Antiquae et Mediae Aetatis* (Brussels: Bollandists, 1898), 502–07, and *Supplementum* (1912), 143–46; E.A.W. Budge, *George of Lydda, the Patron Saint of England* (London: Luzac, 1930), v–vi, 63–66; Paul Peeters, "Une Passion arménienne de S. Georges," *Analecta Bollandiana* 28 (1909): 249–71; E.A.W. Budge, *The Martyrdom and Miracles of Saint George of Cappadocia* (London: D. Nutt, 1888), 1–37; Budge,

popularity. The Passion itself, however, is a hyperbolic martyrdom of the most elaborate sort, and therefore mostly useless for discovering anything about the historical St. George. Nevertheless, it is worth examining because it has implications for the development of St. George's cult. The earliest extant manuscript of the George Passion, the so-called Vienna Palimpsest, is in Greek and dates from the mid-fifth century;[9] fleshing it out with later but closely related sources[10] produces a story in which the Persian Emperor Datianus issues an edict calling together seventy-two subordinate kings and threatening the Christians in his realm with torture. George of Cappadocia, a captain in the military, gives all he has to the poor, arrives at court and confesses his faith in Christ. After refusing to sacrifice to idols, George is subjected to numerous inventive and prolonged tortures. For instance, he has iron boots filled with sharp nails put on his feet, has his head beaten with a large hammer, has molten lead and iron poured into his mouth, and sixty nails pounded into his head. Later, he is placed in a bronze bull, fitted out on the inside with sharp nails; the bull is revolved so that George might be ground to powder. Later still the emperor orders a red-hot helmet to be placed on George's head, iron hooks to rip his body apart, and torches applied to his sides. George feels no pain under all this torture, although he does die and is resurrected three times by the Archangel Michael. George also performs several miracles throughout his Passion: he converts the magician Athanasius and the emperor's wife Alexandra to Christianity, he turns fourteen wooden thrones into trees,

George of Lydda, 55–56, 66–68; W.H.C. Frend, "Fragments of a version of the *Acta S. Georgii* from Q'asr Ibrim," *Jahrbuch für Antike und Christentum* 32 (1989): 89–104; E.W. Brooks, "Acts of S. George," *Museon* 38 (1925): 67–115.

[9] D. Detlefsen, "Über einen greichischen Palimpsest der k.k. Hofbibiothek mit Bruchstücken einer Legende vom heil. Georg," *Sitzungsberichte der Kaiserlichen Akademie der Wissenschaften. Philosophish-Historische Class* 27 (1858): 383–404.

[10] Wilhelm Arndt, "Passio Sancti Georgi," *Berichte über die Verhandlungen der Königlich Sächsischen Gessellchaft der Wissenschaften zu Leipzig. Philologisch-Historische Class* 26 (1874): 43–70; Friedrich Zarncke, "Eine zweite Redaction der Georgslegende aus dem 9. Jahrhunderte," *Berichte über die Verhandlungen der Königlich Sächsischen Gessellchaft der Wissenschaften zu Leipzig, Philologisch-Historische Class* 27 (1875): 256–77. See also John Matzke, "Contributions to the History of the Legend of Saint George, with Special Reference to the Sources of the French, German and Anglo-Saxon Metrical Versions," *Proceedings of the Modern Language Association* 17 (1902): 478; Hippolyte Delehaye, *Les Légendes grecques des saints militaires* (Paris: Alphonse Picard, 1909), 51.

each bearing fruit according to its original type of wood, and resurrects a poor woman's ox. He raises several people who had been dead for 460 years and baptizes them, after stamping his foot on the ground to produce the needed stream of water. He causes the gable fork of a poor woman's house to grow some fifteen cubits high and to bear fruit, and heals her infant son of his blindness. He pretends that he is ready to sacrifice to idols, and is taken to the temple to do so. But instead he calls the god Apollo out of his statue, who admits that he is not the true God; George sends him to Hell, and breaks all the statues in the temple. The climax comes when Datianus passes the sentence of execution on George. As he is taken away George prays and fire comes down from heaven and consumes the emperor and the seventy-two kings. At the place of execution George prays, kneels down, and is beheaded. Water and milk flow from his body. An earthquake and a storm accompany this act, frightening those who witness it. The Passion ends with a coda attributing its authorship to Passecras, George's servant, who accompanied him through the seven years of torture, which finally ended on the eighth kalends of May (i.e., 23 April).

Although other versions of the Passion differ from this oldest one on many points of detail, they all tell, more or less, the same story of how George survived numerous inventive and prolonged tortures, and performed several miracles while doing so. As popular as this narrative may have been, however, it was not without detractors. One of them, allegedly, was the Pope himself. The *Decretum Gelasianum*, ascribed to Pope Gelasius (492–96) and supposedly promulgated by him at the Council of Rome in 494, proclaims:

> Who among Catholics doubts that martyrs suffered great things in their tortures, not by their own strength, but by the grace of God, and doubts them to have tolerated all things with the help of God? According to ancient custom and with singular wariness, however, certain legends are not read, because even the names of those who wrote them are not known, and other legends … are thought to have been written by unbelievers or idiots, such as those of a certain Cyricus and Julitta, and George, and others. Passions of this type that linger have been composed by heretics. On account of this, as it has been said, lest the opportunity arise even for gentle mockery, they are not read in the holy Roman Church. We therefore, with all devotion, and with the aforesaid Church, venerate all martyrs, and their glorious agonies, known to God more than to men.[11]

---

[11] *PL* 59, col. 160–61.

The final section of the decree designates a number of gospels, epistles, and patristic works as "apocryphal," such as the Acts of St. Peter or the Gospel of Matthias; the Passions of St. George and of Saints Cyricus and Julitta appear at the end of the list.[12] It should be noted that some manuscripts claim the "Gelasian decree" to be the work of Pope Damasus (366–84), and others of Pope Hormisdas (514–23), while some scholars hold that it is not of papal origin at all.[13] Whatever its provenance, the document does serve to illustrate ecclesiastical opposition to a certain type of saint's Passion. Various theories have been proposed why the legend of St. George was specifically included there,[14] but the simplest explanation, and one that applies both to George and to Cyricus and Julitta, relates to the hyperbole. (It does *not* relate to a dragon, the earliest textual example of which dates from the eleventh century, and which will be discussed below.)[15] That St. George survived, and did not even feel, numerous diabolical tortures over a period of seven years, that he died and rose from the dead three times, and that he performed miracles of conversion, healing, resurrection, and tree-growing are simply implausible. The other named legend is in the same vein: Julitta and her three-year-old son Cyricus suffered great torture, including being sawn in two and boiled alive, but they felt nothing. They also managed to convert 444 people to Christianity (who were subsequently executed, then resurrected), and turn the governor's leather shoes into a bull and a goat (which were slaughtered, providing food for 11,000 people).[16] Such fantastic and implausible detail may have been appealing to some people, but it is easy to surmise that some churchmen would find such legends embarrassing, or at least that their priorities were misplaced. The martyrdoms recorded in Eusebius of Caesarea's *Ecclesiastical History*, for instance, seem much more believable – each Christian gets one torture

12   *PL* 59, col. 162–64.
13   *Oxford Dictionary of the Christian Church*, 3rd edn., eds. F.L. Cross and E.A. Livingstone (Oxford: Oxford University Press, 1997), s.v. "Decretum Gelasianum."
14   See pages 131 and 142, n. 57.
15   This was a common error during the debates on the historicity of St. George in the sixteenth century; see John Milner, *An Historical and Critical Inquiry into the Existence and Character of Saint George, Patron of England* (London: J. Debrett, 1792), 23; Timothy Hugh Wilson, "Saint George in Tudor and Stuart England" (M.Phil. dissertation, Warburg Institute, 1976), 35.
16   *AASS*, Iun. IV, 24–28. The editor describes the miracles as "prorsus paradoxa et incredibilia."

only, and quite naturally dies after a day or two. Faced with this sort of contrast, one can see why certain ecclesiastics might not want wildly embellished martyrdoms given official sanction by being read in church, although people were presumably free to enjoy them outside such a context.

But the Gelasian decree, or at least the spirit behind it, did ultimately influence subsequent redactions of the legend of St. George, which tend to be shorn of some of the excesses of the original. Andrew, archbishop of Crete in the seventh and eighth centuries, composed an encomium to St. George which presents itself as more historically accurate: George is a tribune in the Roman army, the emperor is the Roman Diocletian (who actually existed and is much better known for his persecution of Christians than the Persian emperor ever was), and the martyrdom takes place at Nicomedia, the site of Diocletian's eastern palace. In addition, the tortures last seven days, not years, and are reduced in number, the miracles are also reduced in number, and George dies only once and permanently. This is the version accepted as authoritative by the Bollandists in their magisterial *Acta Sanctorum*;[17] others in this tradition include a life by Simeon Metaphrastes (fl. tenth century) and an encomium by Gregory of Cyprus (1241–90), the patriarch of Constantinople.[18] Versions of the legend with Diocletian as the persecutor may also have inspired people to read Eusebius's *Ecclesiastical History* in a particular way: Eusebius tells of an unnamed, wealthy young man from Nicomedia who tore up an imperial edict against the Christian church and was duly executed on the first day of the persecutions of Diocletian in 303.[19] It was perhaps only natural that, after the advent of the new legend, some people should identify this figure as St. George, as the Bollandists do in the *Acta Sanctorum*.[20] (This is not likely to be true, however, since the persecutions of Diocletian began on 24 February and St. George's Day has always been celebrated on 23 April.)[21] Still, the newer, simpler versions of the legend did not completely replace the older ones, which continued to influence new redactions of the legend throughout the Middle Ages, especially in the West. The

---

[17] *AASS*, Aprilis III, 101–03, 119–24.

[18] *AASS*, Aprilis III, 103–04, 124–33.

[19] Eusebius, *The History of the Church from Christ to Constantine*, trans. G.A. Williamson (Harmondsworth: Penguin, 1965), 284.

[20] *AASS*, Aprilis III, 108–10.

[21] More recent scholars have identified him as a certain Euethius. See Delehaye, *Origines*, 148; Eusebius, *History of the Church*, 332, n. 3.

thirteenth-century *Golden Legend*, for instance, while itself lighter on tortures than the earlier legends, still identifies the pagan persecutor as "Datian," not "Diocletian."[22]

Returning to late antiquity, however, we find that even if one pope condemned the legend of St. George, others supported the cult. Pope Gregory the Great (590–604) ordered a church of St. George repaired,[23] Pope Leo II (682–83) built a church to him and to St. Sebastian at Velabro in Rome,[24] and Pope Zacharius (741–52) discovered the saint's head (together with a note in Greek explaining what it was) in Rome, which he had translated to the church at Velabro.[25] Pope Leo III (795–816) at various times gave a gold cloth, a silver crown, and a silk cloth to this church,[26] and Pope Gregory IV (828–44) rebuilt it and endowed it with various gifts.[27] These were not the only acts of veneration offered to St. George in Italy. St. Agnellus (805–46) records that a monastery of St. George had earlier been built in Ravenna.[28] The Lombard Duke Cunibert (reigned as king 688–700) defeated his rival Duke Alachis in 680 and in thanks for the victory built a monastery to the saint at Costabissara.[29] The charters of King Louis II of Italy (r. 844–74) also reveal that by the ninth century there was a monastery to St. George at Reiti, a chapel to the saint at the village

---

[22] Matzke, "Contributions," 487, 492. The Passion of Saints Cyricus and Julitta had also been simplified by the time of the *Golden Legend*: in that text Cyricus is portrayed not as a wise and articulate far beyond his years but as a little boy whom the governor, out of apparent sentimentality, holds on his lap and utters endearments to while his mother is being tortured. The boy cries that he too is a Christian, scratches the governor's face and bites him on the shoulder, and the governor throws him to the floor, dashing his brains out. See Jacobus de Voragine, *Golden Legend: Readings on the Saints*, trans. William Granger Ryan (Princeton: Princeton University Press, 1993), 1: 323–24.

[23] Milner, *Historical Inquiry*, 11–12.

[24] *The Book of the Pontiffs*, ed. Raymond Davis, 2nd edn. (Liverpool: Liverpool University Press, 2000), 81.

[25] *The Lives of the Eighth-Century Popes*, ed. Raymond Davis (Liverpool: Liverpool University Press, 1992), 48.

[26] *Lives of the Eighth-Century Popes*, 200, 211, 227.

[27] *The Lives of the Ninth-Century Popes*, ed. Raymond Davis (Liverpool: Liverpool University Press, 1995), 55–56.

[28] *PL* 106, col. 526.

[29] Paul the Deacon, *History of the Langobards*, trans. William Dudley Foulke, ed. Edward Peeters (Philadelphia: University of Pennsylvania Press, 1974), 263.

of Wardistalla, and a castle named after the saint in Aprutino.[30]

Among the Franks, evidence for the cult also starts to appear in the sixth century. Venantius Fortunatus (c. 530–c. 610), bishop of Poitiers, wrote a dedicatory hymn for a church to St. George at Mainz, which had been built by Bishop Sidonius (d. 580):

> The mighty house of the famous martyr George,
> whose high honor is scattered about the world, shines forth:
> from prison, pain, hunger, chains, thirst, cold and flames,
> having confessed Christ, he turned his head to the stars;
> who, powerful in courage, buried in the east,
> behold! he offers riches in the west as well.
> Therefore, traveler, remember your prayers and fulfill your vows:
> loving faith obtains here what it seeks through merits.
> Bishop Sidonius built this temple becomingly,
> which things may profit the new temple of his soul.[31]

Gregory of Tours (539–94) included the saint in his martyrology, and claimed to know many miracle stories about him. One of these involved some couriers who were carrying relics of St. George and who stopped to pray with some monks in their newly-built oratory near Limoges; when it came time to leave, they found they were unable to lift their cargo until they had left some of it with the monks. Gregory also reports that some relics of St. George could be found in a village near Le Mans, in Maine, where they cure the blind, the lame, and those with chills and other sickness.[32] According to the Life of St. Bathild (written about ten years after its subject's death in 680), Queen Clothild (d. 544), the wife of King Clovis, had built a church to St. George at Chelles.[33] Both St. Germain of Paris (d. 576) and the late sixth-century Bishop Pabolus of Chartres consecrated churches to St. George.[34] Usuard, a ninth-century monk at

---

[30] Ludovicus II, *Diplomata*, in *MGH Diplomata Karolinorum* 4 (Munich: MGH, 1994), 119, 210, 236.

[31] Venantius Fortunatus, *De basilica S. Georgi*, in *MGH Auctorum Antiquissimorum* 4:1 (Berolini: Weidmann, 1881), 41. See also Hippolyte Delehaye, "Loca sanctorum," *Analecta Bollandiana* 48 (1930): 32–33.

[32] Gregory of Tours, *Glory of the Martyrs*, trans. Raymond van Dam (Liverpool: Liverpool University Press, 1988), 123–24.

[33] *Fredegarii et aliorum Chronica. Vitae Sanctorum*, ed. Bruno Krusch, in *MGH Scriptores rerum Merovingicarum* 2 (Hannover: Hahnsche Buchhandlung, 1888), 506.

[34] *Passiones vitaeque sanctorum aevi merovingici*, ed. Bruno Krusch, in *MGH Scriptores rerum Merovingicarum* 3 (Hannover: Hahnsche Buchhandlung, 1888), 542, 615.

the abbey of St. Germain-des-Prés near Paris, included George in his martyrology.[35] Finally, an intriguing story is recorded by the author of *The Deeds of the Abbots of Fontenelle*, written c. 830. One day, during the time of Abbot Austrulph (747–53), a container resembling a small lighthouse washed up on shore at Portbail, in the territory of Cherbourg. Inside it the locals found a beautiful manuscript of the four gospels and a reliquary containing a piece of St. George's jawbone. Count Rihwin of Cherbourg thought fit to sponsor the building of a basilica to St. George to house the relic, which worked many miracles. (The author surmises that a churchman from England or Germany must have been in Rome at the time Pope Zacharius discovered St. George's head, and received a piece of the jawbone from him as a favor. Returning by sea, his ship was probably wrecked and the relics washed ashore at Portbail.)[36]

If the ship was indeed headed to Britain, however, its being wrecked did not preclude the arrival of St. George there by other means. Adamnan, the seventh-century abbot of Iona, in *De Locis sanctis*, describes how the traveling bishop Arculf had told him about two miracles performed by St. George at Lydda: one, when an unbeliever had his lance and fingers stuck in a statue of St. George after striking it; and another, when a man, after trying to commute a vow of a horse to the saint for money, was forced to give up both the money and the horse.[37] Bede included George both in a short poetic martyrology:

> The executioners triumphed on the ninth Kalends of May,
> And George flew to heaven then, riding away.[38]

and in a longer martyrology that acknowledges the Gelasian decree:

> Eight days before the Kalends of May. The heavenly birth of St. George the martyr, who under Datianus, the most-powerful king of the Persians, who ruled over 70 kings, was notable for many miracles, and converted many to faith in Christ, and he comforted Alexandria the wife of Datianus himself up to her martyrdom; he himself, finally beheaded, accomplished his martyrdom, although the acts of his passion are numbered among the apocryphal scriptures.[39]

---

35 *PL* 123, col. 963–64.
36 *Gesta abbatum fontanellensium*, ed. S. Loewenfeld, in *MGH Scriptores rerum Germanicarum* 18 (Hannover: Hahnsche Buchhandlung, 1886), 40–42.
37 Adamnan, *De Locis Sanctis*, ed. Denis Meehan (Dublin: Dublin Institute for Advanced Studies, 1958), 111–17.
38 *PL* 94, col. 604.
39 *PL* 94, col. 886.

The early tenth-century Durham Ritual also commemorates St. George with a short prayer, which can be translated as

> God, you who gladden us by the merits and intercession of your blessed martyr George; grant favorably that we attain the benefits we ask of him, by the gift of your grace. Through the Lord.[40]

A short Passion of St. George by Bishop Leofric of Exeter, written in the early eleventh century, can be found in a manuscript in Corpus Christi College, Cambridge.[41] Perhaps the most literary attention bestowed on St. George in England was by Aelfric, abbot of Eynsham and later archbishop of York from 1023 until 1051, who included him in a set of sermons on saints' days,[42] and later wrote an Anglo-Saxon Passion of St. George.[43] In both of these texts, Aelfric acknowledges the Gelasian decree's disapproval of the St. George Passion, while still expressing enthusiasm for the saint. Both begin with lines that can be translated:

> Heretics have written falsehoods in their books
> about the holy man who is called George.
> Now will we tell you that which is true about him
> that error may not secretly harm anyone.[44]

Both texts also anglicize George somewhat, calling him a rich "ealdormann," from the "scire" (shire) of Cappadocia, with the emperor asking George what "byrig" (borough) he comes from.[45] Interestingly, both also have St. George praying before he was executed, not for God to consume Datianus with fire, but that

> God would give rain to the earth,
> because the heat was then wasting the land

---

[40] *Rituale Ecclesiæ Dunelmensis*, ed. J. Stephenson (London: J.B. Nichols, 1840), 52.

[41] It is partially transcribed in Aelfric, abbot of Eynsham, *An Anglo-Saxon Passion in the Cambridge University Library*, ed. and trans. C. Hardwick (London: The Percy Society, 1850), ii, n. 1.

[42] Aelfric, *Aelfric's Lives of the Saints: Being a Set of Sermons on Saints' Days formerly observed by the English Church, edited from Manuscript Julius E. VII in the Cottonian Collection, with Various Readings from other Manuscripts*, ed. W.W. Skeat (London: EETS, 1881) 1: 307–19.

[43] Aelfric, *Anglo-Saxon Passion*.

[44] Translation from Aelfric, *Aelfric's Lives of the Saints*, 1: 307, 309; cf. Aelfric, *Anglo-Saxon Passion*, 2. True to Aelfric's promise, the Passion records decidedly fewer tortures and miracles of St. George than do the earliest fifth-century legends.

[45] Aelfric, *Lives of the Saints*, 1: 308; Aelfric, *Anglo-Saxon Passion*, 2, 6.

Later

> the Lord sent rain-showers,
> and watered the earth, which before was burned up,
> even as George had prayed, before he bowed to the death.[46]

Datian is still killed by fire in both of Aelfric's versions, but it appears that a minor aspect of St. George patronage followed him to England. George may have been a soldier in life, but his name, from *geos* and *ergon*, means "earth-worker," or farmer, and his feast day of 23 April a day when crops are starting to grow in much of Europe. Such things may have prompted a connection between St. George and agriculture, and Sir James Frazer collected numerous examples of rituals that sought St. George's aid in crop growth in nineteenth-century Eastern Europe.[47] St. George's true status in England, however, is perhaps revealed by Aelfric's comment that he had already translated two volumes of saints' lives for the English people, but the present one, containing the legend of St. George, was for the edification of the monks – that is, St. George may have been celebrated more by ecclesiastics than by the populace at large.[48] St. George was, however, honored with the dedication of at least one Anglo-Saxon church, in Thetford, Norfolk.[49]

On the continent, however, a new meaning of the cult of St. George had filtered its way into the West by the eleventh century. Previously George had been celebrated as an exemplary martyr and, to a lesser extent, as a patron of agriculture. George, however, was also one of a number of saints that the Byzantines considered "military saints" – that is, saints who interceded directly in battle in order to influence the outcome. Although saints such as George, Mercurius, Demetrius, and Theodore (either in his aspect as Theodore the General or as Theodore the Recruit) may have been soldiers in life, previously their soldiery was specifically of the metaphorical kind; heroic resistance to torture for the sake of Christ. Once the Byzantines started fighting against the infidel Muslims and the pagan Slavs, however, they attached importance to the original profession of these saints, and imagined that it could aid their own military efforts, as

---

[46] Aelfric, *Lives of the Saints*, 1: 319; cf. Aelfric, *Anglo-Saxon Passion*, 29.

[47] J.G. Frazer, *The Golden Bough*, Part 1, *The Magic Art and the Evolution of Kings*, 3rd edn. (New York, 1935), 2: 75–79.

[48] Aelfric, *Anglo-Saxon Passion*, ii.

[49] F. Blomefield, *Essay Towards a Topographical History of the County of Norfolk* (London: William Miller, 1805), 2: 74.

indeed it did when such saints appeared in the sky during battles, encouraging the faithful.[50] That such a concept grew out of the Byzantine Empire is not surprising, given the intertwined nature of church and state there, when defending the one meant defending the other. Although church and state were more separated in the West than in the East, there is some evidence that military saints also made the occasional appearance when westerners found themselves fighting against non-Christians, and that George was an important participant. In 1004, for instance, George, Laurence, and Adrian gave assistance to Emperor Henry II in his war against the Slavs, in thanks for which Henry founded the cathedral at Bamberg dedicated to St. George, in which he was eventually buried.[51] Geoffrey Malaterra recorded, in the late eleventh century, that in a battle near Cerami in 1063 between Normans and Sicilian Muslims, St. George appeared in shining armor carrying a white banner decorated with a cross on his lance.[52] No such appearances are recorded in England, but military saints were not unknown there, particularly after the Norman conquest of 1066. The chronicler Orderic Vitalis, born in Shrewsbury in 1075 of a Norman father and an Anglo-Saxon mother, wrote his *Ecclesiastical History* while a monk at St-Evroul in Normandy. In it, he records that Hugh of Avranches, to whom William the Conqueror had granted the county of Chester, had a clerk named Gerold, who had come to England with him from Avranches, and

> to great lords, simple knights, and noble boys alike [Gerold] gave salutary counsel; and he made a great collection of tales of the combats of holy knights, drawn from the Old Testament and more recent records of Christian achievements, for them to imitate. He told them vivid stories of the conflicts of Demetrius and George, of Theodore and Sebastian, of the Theban legion and Maurice its leader, and of Eustache, supreme commander of the army and his companions, who won the crown of martyrdom in heaven.[53]

50 See Christopher Walter, *The Warrior Saints in Byzantine Art and Tradition* (Aldershot: Ashgate, 2003), 277–84. See also Delehaye, *Légendes grecques*, 1–9, and Carl Erdmann, *The Origin of the Idea of Crusade*, trans. Marshall W. Baldwin and Walter Goffart (Princeton: Princeton University Press, 1977), 6–7.
51 Adalbertus, *Vita Henrici II*, in *MGH Scriptores* 4 (Hannover: Hahnsche Buchhandlung, 1841), 793; Stephan Weinfurter, *Heinrich II. (1002–1024): Herrscher am Ende der Zeiten* (Regensburg: Friedrich Pustet, 1999), 250, 268.
52 Geoffrey Malaterra, *De Rebus Gestis Rogerii*, ed. E. Pontieri (Bologna: Zanichelli, 1926), 44.
53 Orderic Vitalis, *The Ecclesiastical History*, ed. Marjorie Chibnall (Oxford: Clarendon Press, 1972), 3: 217.

St. George's popularity with military men, following the Conquest, is perhaps revealed by Robert d'Oiley, a Norman knight, who built a castle in 1071 in the city of Oxford, to which he added a church dedicated to St. George in 1074. (This castle-church later gave rise to a college of St. George, of which the twelfth-century historian Geoffrey of Monmouth was a member.)[54]

It is the crusades, of course, that represent the Western apogee of the idea of the Christian warrior, and the crusaders' ultimate destination in the East, the home of the military saints, ensured that the Byzantine custom received even more currency in the West. Certainly George's presence everywhere in the East, where, unlike in England, he really was honored among the people, may have piqued the crusaders' interest in him. Crusaders would have encountered the sort of Eastern dedications to the saint mentioned above, and when they assembled at Constantinople they could hardly have failed to notice the church of St. George of Mangana there, which had been recently rebuilt by Emperor Constantine IX (1042–55) to rival Hagia Sophia. The Byzantine historian Michael Psellus (1018–96) describes the project as the "worst example" of the emperor's "foolish excesses," but has nothing but praise for the resulting building:

> It was not merely the exceptional beauty of the whole, composed as it was of most beautiful parts, but just as much the individual details that attracted the spectator's attention, and although he could enjoy to his heart's content all its charms, it was impossible to find one that palled. Every part of it took the eye, and, what is more wonderful, even when you gazed on the loveliest part of all, some small detail would delight you as a fresh discovery. To attempt to place its various merits in any order of preference was useless for, when all the parts were so lovely, even the least attractive could not fail to give pleasure inimitable. Its every detail excited the greatest admiration.[55]

The crusaders proceeded to cross the arm of St. George, as the Hellespont was also known, and then come upon St. George's gate and monastery at

---

[54] Royal Commission on Historical Monuments, *An Inventory of the historical monuments of the City of Oxford* (London: HMSO, 1939), 156. See also John Barron, "The Augustinian Canons and the University of Oxford: the Lost College of St George," in *The Church and Learning in Later Medieval Society: Essays in Honour of R.B. Dobson*, eds. Caroline Barron and Jenny Stratford (Donington: Shaun Tyas, 2002), 228–54.

[55] Michael Psellus, *Fourteen Byzantine Rulers*, trans. E.A.W. Sawyer (Harmondsworth: Penguin, 1966), 250, 252.

Antioch. It was at Antioch, indeed, that George's fame was assured, when the crusaders captured it in 1098. According to the *Gesta Francorum*, as the Christians were fighting the Turks there

> also appeared from the mountains a countless host of men on white horses, whose banners were all white. When our men saw this, they did not understand what was happening or who these men might be, until they realized that this was the succour sent by Christ, and that the leaders were St. George, St. Mercurius, and St. Demetrius. (This is quite true, for many of our men saw it).[56]

Again, George is not mounted in his original legend, nor does he carry a banner, a specific symbol of holy warfare.[57] Nevertheless, the patron of crusaders could not help but become like them. The whiteness of his horse and banner further underline the crusaders' good faith and purity of motive. The lasting impression that this appearance made (as well as the relative importance of George as a member of it) is recorded by Orderic Vitalis, who writes that

> when, during the siege of Antioch, the Christians had seen this saint [George] as their guide and forerunner and true champion in the battle against a people sunk in error, they had chosen to honour him always as their champion and defender.[58]

The story of the appearance at Antioch was included in most narrative accounts of the crusades, but another tradition of George's participation in them is found in the *Historia Hierosolymitana* of Raymond of Agiles. Raymond tells that once Antioch had been taken, a figure appeared to him and demanded that he take the bones of four saints, buried in the town, to Jerusalem. The four coffins were eventually found and carried off, but a fifth, which the crusaders failed to recognize, was left behind. That night a good-looking youth of about fifteen appeared to Raymond and asked him why he did not accept these relics along with the others? Raymond asks him who he is, and the youth replies, do you not know the name of flag-bearer of this army? Raymond answers that it is said to be St. George, and the youth replies, "You speak well, for I am he. Place my relics with the other ones." Armed with this treasure the army approaches Lydda and the Saracens flee before it, leaving a great many provisions,

---

[56] *Gesta Francorum et aliorum Hierosolimitanorum*, ed. R. Hill (London: Thomas Nelson, 1962), 69.

[57] Erdmann, *Origin*, 35ff.

[58] Orderic Vitalis, *Ecclesiastical History*, 5: 155, 157.

which are captured and offered in thanks to St. George. The crusaders also decide to institute a bishop at Lydda and Ramula, a town nearby, choosing the Norman Robert of Rouen. When the army finally reaches Jerusalem St. George appears again, this time dressed in white armor with a shining or snow-white ("nivea") cross on it. He leads them to victory as they storm the walls and slaughter the Saracens on 15 July 1099.[59]

Just as the crusades captured the imagination of all Europe, these new additions to the George legend found an audience in England, and George's popularity continued to grow there in the twelfth century. A church at Fordington, Dorset, has a bas-relief over the doorway depicting George appearing to the crusaders at Antioch (figure 3), while another tympanum at Damerham in Hampshire shows a mounted warrior subduing a human foe; this scene is commonly thought to represent St. George overcoming a Saracen. St. George also appears in tympana at Ruardean, Gloucestershire and at Brinsop, Herefordshire, where he is shown in both cases mounted and battling a dragon.[60] Twelfth-century wall paintings of the life of St. George exist in churches at Westmeston and Hardham, both in Sussex.[61] Simon de Freine, a canon at Hereford Cathedral in the late twelfth century, wrote a Life of St. George in Anglo-Norman verse,[62] perhaps commissioned as propaganda for the third crusade by William de Vere, who had been to the Holy Land.[63]

That crusading King Richard I has traditionally been credited with promoting St. George's cult to the status of a national one in England. This idea has been recently discredited: no evidence exists that Richard saw an apparition of the saint at the siege of Acre, placed his army under St. George's protection, ordered St. George's church at Lydda to be rebuilt, or promoted St. George's cross, a red cross on a white background, as an English national emblem.[64] These were all legends that grew up around

---

[59] *AASS*, Aprilis III, 155.
[60] Charles E. Keyser, *A List of Norman Tympana and Lintels*, 2nd edn. (London: Elliot Stock, 1927), lxxx–lxxxiv.
[61] Ethel Carleton Williams, "Mural Paintings of St. George in England," *Journal of the British Archaeological Association* 3rd series 12 (1949): 22–23, 32, 35, 37.
[62] Simon de Freine, "Vie de Saint Georges," in *Les Œuvres de Simund de Freine*, ed. John E. Matzke (Paris: Firmin-Didot, 1909), 61–117.
[63] Julia Barrow, "Athelstan to Aigublanche, 1056–1268," in *Hereford Cathedral: A History*, eds. Gerald Aylmer and John Tiller (London and Rio Grande: Hambledon Press, 2000), 40.
[64] Olivier de Laborderie, "Richard the Lionheart and the birth of a national cult of St George in England: origins and development of a legend," *Nottingham Medieval Studies* 39 (1995): 37–53.

Richard in Tudor times. Nonetheless, Richard did have some contact with the saint while on crusade: he married his queen Berengaria in St. George's chapel at Limassol, Cyprus,[65] and although he may not have rebuilt St. George's church at Lydda,[66] which had recently been destroyed by Saladin, he did spend six weeks encamped outside the town preparing his assault on Jerusalem.[67] According to the *Estoire de la Guerre saint* by the poet Ambroise, different members of his army called upon St. George for aid in battle.[68] Finally, Olivier de Laborderie is quite correct in showing that Richard had nothing to do with the famous St. George's cross. When the English King Henry II and the French King Philip Augustus met at Gisors in 1188 to plan the crusade, they decided that the English were to wear white crosses and the French to wear red ones.[69] Although it might be tempting to think that Richard was still declaring St. George the patron saint of the English crusaders (since, as we have seen, George appeared to the crusaders at Jerusalem wearing a "snow-white" cross), it is far more likely that the crosses of the participants in the third crusade, which are identified only by their colors, were simply an easy (and arbitrary) means of telling who belonged to which army.

In a similar way, the Council of Oxford in 1222 probably did *not* elevate the feast of St. George to being a minor holiday, thereby acknowledging George's patronage of England, contrary to almost everything written on

65 Stephen Runciman, *A History of the Crusades* (Harmondsworth: Pelican, 1971), 3: 45.
66 See Denys Pringle, *The Churches of the Crusader Kingdom of Jerusalem* (Cambridge: Cambridge University Press, 1998), 13.
67 Ambroise, *The Crusade of Richard the Lionheart*, trans. Merton Jerome Hubert (New York: Octagon Books, 1976), 293.
68 Ambroise, *Crusade of Richard the Lionheart*, 256–58.
69 Roger of Wendover, *The Flowers of History*, ed. Henry G. Hewlett (London: Rolls Series, 1886), 1: 144. Knowing that the red cross later became the English national emblem, some historians have assumed that the council at Gisors must have assigned red crosses to the English and white ones to the French, but other contemporary sources, such as Roger of Hoveden and Ralph de Diceto, agree with Roger of Wendover about the colors of the crosses: see *Chronica Majora Rogeri de Houendene*, ed. W. Stubbs (London: Rolls Series, 1869) 2: 335; *The Historical Works of Master Ralph de Diceto*, ed. W. Stubbs (London: Rolls Series, 1876), 2: 52. John Rous (1411–91), the Warwickshire antiquary, recognized the significance of the decision at Gisors: "Ex hoc conjectuari posset, quod Anglici tunc non habeant Sanctum Georgium pro patrono eorum, vel ad minus tunc non portabant crucem armis suis correspondum." *Historia Regum Angliae*, ed. Thomas Hearn (Oxford, 1745), 142. Rous is surely correct, even if St. George was not himself identified by a red cross in 1188.

the cult in England.[70] This point has been questioned by a number of people, including C.R. Cheney. There is a list of feast days allegedly promoted by the Council, but Cheney notes that of the seventy manuscripts of the canons published by the Council, not one contains the list of feast days. The list itself, moreover, commemorates St. Edmund Rich, who was not canonized until 1247, so it is probably spurious. Indeed, the first certain piece of legislation prescribing *festa ferianda* for the entire province of Canterbury, in 1362, does not mention St. George at all.[71]

Despite Richard I's non-support of the St. George cult and its non-elevation by the Council of Oxford, however, evidence exists that George's popularity did grow in English court circles during the thirteenth century. One of Henry III's household knights, for instance, the *miles literatus* Paulinus Piper, wrote a poem on the life of St. George that is now lost, and in 1245 ten marks were paid to Henry the Versifier for his service in composing the Lives of St. Edward and St. George.[72] In 1256, an image of St. George was placed over the king's entrance hall in Winchester.[73] In 1265–66, Henry III gave five pounds to decorate Robert d'Oiley's church of St. George at Oxford.[74] Henry III was, of course, dedicated primarily to the cult of St. Edward the Confessor; his rebuilding of Westminster Abbey and his naming of his son after the saint are the two outstanding indications of this devotion, in addition to the Life of St. Edward commissioned from Henry the Versifier. George, in fact, may have been more on the side of the barons in their disputes with the king: the continuator of the chronicle of Gervase of Canterbury records that at the battle of Lewes in 1264, when King Henry faced off against the rebel barons under Simon de Montfort, a soldier, bearing arms and an unknown banner, appeared alongside an archbishop in full pontificals who blessed the rebel army. After the battle the figures disappeared, and it was later adduced that they were St. George and St. Thomas Becket.[75]

---

[70] E.g. David Hugh Farmer, *The Oxford Dictionary of Saints*, 3rd edn. (Oxford and New York: Oxford University Press, 1992), 197.

[71] C.R. Cheney, "Rules for the Observance of Feast Days in Medieval England," *Bulletin of the Institute of Historical Research* 34 (1961): 123–24, 132–33.

[72] J.C. Russell, *Dictionary of Writers of Thirteenth-Century England*, rev. edn. (London: William Dawson and Sons, 1967), 94–95.

[73] *CLR 1250–61* (London: HMSO, 1959), 307–08.

[74] R. Allen Brown, H.M. Colvin and A.J. Taylor, *History of the King's Works*, Vols. 1 and 2: *The Middle Ages* (London: HMSO, 1963), 774.

[75] Gervase of Canterbury, *The Historical Works of Gervase of Canterbury*, ed. William Stubbs (London: Rolls Series, 1880), 2: 237–38.

Another development in the thirteenth century, although it took place outside of England, greatly influenced the perception of St. George in that country. The *Legenda* (eventually *Legenda Aurea*, or *Golden Legend*) of the Dominican Archbishop of Genoa Jacobus de Voragine, a collection of saints' Lives composed in the 1260s, was one of the most popular books in the medieval West, and its Life of St. George was highly influential. It begins, as do many of the saints' Lives in the *Golden Legend*, by contemplating the saint's name: "George," following different etymologies, means either tiller of earth, or holy sand, or holy wrestler, or pilgrim counselor.[76] Jacobus narrates a version of the story of George's martyrdom, and also notes two posthumous miracles of the saint: one, from Gregory of Tours, about the immovable casket of relics, and the other from the tradition of Raymond of Agiles, where George commands the crusaders to move his relics and appears to them before they take Jerusalem.[77] Between the etymology and the account of the martyrdom, however, is the story of St. George's encounter with a dragon, a story that deserves a full summary:

One day St. George, on a chance journey, comes from Palestine to Silene, a town in the province of Libya. In a deep lake nearby lives a terrible dragon, which terrorizes the populace by coming out and prowling the city walls, poisoning all who come near with its breath. To appease the dragon the townsfolk offer it two sheep a day, but eventually the number of sheep is so depleted that they have to offer it one sheep and one human being, chosen by lot from among the young people of the town. No family is exempt from the lottery, even that of the king, and eventually the lot falls upon the king's only daughter. The king tries to bribe the people with all his gold and silver, and up to half his kingdom, but they will have none of it: the princess is prepared for death and starts walking toward the dragon's lake. As chance would have it St. George is passing by and, seeing her tears, asks her the cause of her trouble. She tells him, and he offers to help, but the princess tells him to flee lest he also die. As they are talking the dragon rises from the lake, but George, mounting his horse and crossing himself, charges bravely at the dragon as it comes toward him, and with a prayer to God, levels his lance at it and hits it. He then instructs the princess to throw her girdle around the dragon's neck, which she does, and it meekly follows her like a dog on a leash. They bring it back into the city, and the townspeople flee, but St. George tells them to come back: Christ has delivered them from the dragon, and if

76 Jacobus, *Golden Legend*, 1: 238.
77 Jacobus, *Golden Legend*, 1: 242.

they agree to be baptized and become Christians, George will slay the dragon for them. Twenty thousand men and a number of women and children are baptized that day, and St. George beheads the dragon with his sword. The king builds a church in honor of the Blessed Virgin and St. George, from which flows a spring of great healing power. The king also offers George a large sum of money, which George distributes to the poor. George teaches the king to care for the church of God, to honor the priests, to assist with devotion at the divine office, and to have the poor always in mind. With that George returns to Palestine, in time for the prefect Dacian's persecution and his own martyrdom.[78]

Thus, Jacobus's addition to the legend of St. George, a story for which the saint very quickly became far more famous than for any of his heroic resistance to torture, or even for his appearance to the crusaders. The coupling of St. George with a dragon is not entirely original with Jacobus: the story is found in three twelfth-century Latin manuscripts,[79] as well as being depicted on the twelfth-century tympana at Ruardean and Brinsop mentioned above. It is fairly clear, however, that the Golden Legend itself is the major source for the dragon story in the West, and from the late thirteenth century St. George was almost invariably associated with a dragon in the Western imagination.[80] But how did St. George acquire this dragon in the first place? One influential theory draws a distinction between the legend and the iconography of the dragon story, proposing that artwork showing St. George and the dragon can be traced back to the sixth century, as part of a general Byzantine custom of showing saints overcoming dragons (or, occasionally, subdued human figures) as symbols of evil – certainly, no physical dragon appears among the many fantastic miracles in the early versions of the legend of St. George.[81] Such symbolic images, it is assumed, later gave rise to stories "explaining" them,[82] just

[78] Jacobus, Golden Legend, 1: 238–40.
[79] One in Johann B. Aufhauser, Das Drachenwunder der heiligen George in der greischen und lateinischen Überlieferung (Leipzig: B.G. Teubner, 1911), 182–87, and two in Johannes Monachus, Liber de Miraculis. Ein neuer Beitrag zu mittelalterlichen Mönchsliteratur, ed. P. Michael Huber (Heidelberg: Carl Winters Universitätsbuchhandlung, 1913), 124–32.
[80] Matzke, "Legend," 451; Wilson, "Saint George," 15; Jennifer Fellows, "St. George as Romance Hero," Reading Medieval Studies 19 (1993): 31–32.
[81] Even though the Emperor Datianus is called "the dragon of the abyss" in some of them: see Budge, George of Cappadocia, 223, 224.
[82] Milner, Historical Inquiry, 36 and n. ‡; Wilson, "Saint George," 15; Samantha Riches, St George: Hero, Martyr and Myth (Stroud, Glos: Sutton, 2000), 27.

as some people believed that St. Blaise was the inventor of the art of combing wool, based on a depiction of him holding the iron comb he was tortured with, or that the "true image" of Jesus's face impressed onto a cloth must have been procured by a St. Veronica. The *story* of St. George and the dragon may have much older precedents, most notably the ancient Greek legend of Perseus and Andromeda,[83] but its attachment to St. George's life is a product of the High, not the Early, Middle Ages, the result of a misunderstanding of a symbolic image.

This is a fetching and plausible theory, but not without its flaws. First of all, very few portraits that are indisputably of St. George, and that are indisputably datable, have come down to us. St. George was not the only saint to be shown killing a dragon, symbolizing the triumph of good over evil. St. Theodore was also shown mounted and killing a dragon, and legends attesting to such a deed were told of the saint from the ninth century.[84] Indeed, in the absence of some sort of label, it is often difficult to tell which saint a given dragon-killing picture refers to, and this fact complicates the theory that pictures of St. George killing a dragon gave rise to a story about him doing so.[85] Of those that are labeled one, in the form of a bronze die from Smyrna and in the possession of the Royal Berlin Museum in 1909, seems promising: it shows a rider mounted on a horse and spearing a snake with a lance, has a label "Ο ΓΕΟ" inscribed in

---

[83] Andromeda was the daughter of Cephus and Cassiopia, the king and queen of Philistia. When Cassiopia bragged that both she and her daughter were more beautiful than the Nereids, their protector Poseidon sent a sea-monster to devastate the land. An oracle informed Cephus that the only way to deliverance lay in sacrificing his daughter Andromeda to the monster, and his subjects thus forced him to chain her to a rock by the sea, so that the monster could be propitiated. Along came Perseus, who was fresh from his battle against Medusa and who had no trouble in dispatching the approaching beast, thus winning the hand of Andromeda in marriage. See Robert Graves, *The Greek Myths* (Harmondsworth: Penguin, 1960), 1: 240.

[84] Engelbert Kirschbaum, Günter Bandmann, and Wolfgang Braunfels, eds., *Lexikon der Christlichen Ikonographie* (Rome: Herder, 1976), 8: col. 450; Delehaye, *Légendes grecques*, 19–20, 27.

[85] Delehaye, *Légendes grecques*, 117; Kirschbaum, Bandmann, and Braunfels, eds., *Lexikon*, 6: col 369. For examples of such unlabeled dragon-killers see O.M. Dalton, *Catalogue of the Early Christian Antiquities and Objects from the Christian East in the Department of British and Mediaeval Antiquities and Ethnography of the British Museum* (London: British Museum, 1901), nos. 549, 556, 904, 914, 919, 990, 991.

it, and was dated by Oskar Wulff to the late sixth or early seventh century.[86] If this date is correct the die would certainly go a long way to proving the theory that pictures of St. George inspired stories about him, but according to Christopher Walter it is unclear why such a date has been assigned – certainly there is no date on the die itself.[87] One certain picture of St. George killing the dragon, in the church of St. Barbara, Soganh, Cappadocia, dates from the early eleventh century, and is claimed by Walter to be the first true depiction of the event.[88] Furthermore, not only might such pictures be more recent than previously supposed, the legend of St. George and the dragon may also be older than previously realized. Although most scholars have believed that a twelfth-century Latin manuscript at Munich represents the oldest account of St. George and the dragon, Walter draws attention to, and translates into English, an eleventh-century Georgian manuscript dealing with the same subject.[89] All this suggests that pictures and stories of St. George killing the dragon arose more or less at the same time, and are perhaps more closely related than previously supposed. That the earliest legend is in Georgian, and not Latin, suggests that the dragon story was native to the East and not the result of a misunderstanding by crusading Westerners, who supplied the story to explain the pictures that they did not understand. George may have acquired his dragon, in picture and story, simply by analogy to St. Theodore, who seems to have had one from an earlier date; Theodore may have acquired his dragon in the first place, and easily passed it on to George, because both were military saints. It is true that symbolic dragon-slaying precedes and extends beyond the category of military saint – Eusebius tells the story of a portrait that the Emperor Constantine had hung in the portico of the imperial palace, showing himself with a cross over his head and a dragon, stricken through with a dart, under his feet.[90] Unlike Constantine, however, both Theodore and George are usually mounted in Eastern depictions of their dragon-slaying, leading one to suspect that this detail is significant, referring both

---

[86]   Oskar Wulff, *Altchristliche und mittelalterliche byzantinische und italienische Bildwerke* (Berlin: Georg Reimer, 1909), no. 1128 (p. 231 and Tafel LVI).

[87]   Walter, "Origins," 318–19, n. 143.

[88]   Guillaume de Jerphanion, *Une Nouvelle province de l'art byzantine: Les églises rupestres de Cappadoce* (Paris: Paul Geuthner, 1936), 2: 322; Walter, *Warrior Saints*, 320.

[89]   Fellows, "St George as Romance Hero," 31; Walter, "Origins," 321–22.

[90]   Eusebius, *The Life of Constantine the Blessed Emperor* (London: Samuel Bagster and Sons, 1845), 116–17. Eusebius explicitly states the portrait to be an allegory of the triumph of Christ over Satan.

to their profession and to the dragon-stories that became attached to their legends. St. George's (and St. Theodore's) dragon-killing icon may therefore be connected much more closely to the dragon-killing story than previously thought.

The significance of St. George's dragon legend is also reflected in the *Golden Legend*. The book's entry for St. Theodore does not include the dragon story, but the work does contain a number of other dragons in a number of other legends. St. Margaret of Antioch, for instance, an early Christian virgin martyr, after being tortured, was thrown in jail and prayed to God to show her who her enemy was, and a hideous dragon appeared and came to Margaret to devour her. Margaret then either made the sign of the cross and it disappeared, or the beast swallowed her whole, and from inside she made the sign of the cross and it burst asunder, allowing her to escape.[91] Another example is found in the life of St. James: some surviving disciples, on their way to bury James, met a "fire-breathing dragon" with the sign of the cross, and split him up the middle.[92] Another disciple, St. Matthew, while preaching in Ethiopia, encountered two dragons "which belched forth sulfurous fire from mouth and nostrils and killed many people" at the command of two sorcerers. Matthew shielded himself with the sign of the cross and went out to meet the dragons; they fell asleep as soon as they saw him. Their sorcerer-commanders were not able to wake them, and Matthew ordered the dragons to go away, which they did, harming no one.[93] St. Donatus, a contemporary of the Emperor Julian the Apostate, rode an ass past a spring so polluted that anyone who drank from it died instantly. Donatus purified the water with his prayer, whereupon a dragon leapt from the spring, wound itself around the ass's legs, and reared up against the saint. Donatus killed the dragon either with a flick of his whip or by spitting on him.[94] St. Martha, who with her sister Mary had hosted Christ,[95] encountered perhaps the most distinctive dragon in the entire *Golden Legend*. After Christ's ascension she went to the Rhône valley in southern Gaul, where she converted the local populace to the Christian faith. At that time

> in the forest along the Rhone between Arles and Avignon, there was a dragon that was half animal and half fish, larger than an ox, longer than

---

[91] Jacobus, *Golden Legend*, 1: 369.
[92] Jacobus, *Golden Legend*, 2: 6.
[93] Jacobus, *Golden Legend*, 2: 184.
[94] Jacobus, *Golden Legend*, 2: 60.
[95] Luke 10: 38–42; John 11: 17–21; John 12: 2–3.

a horse, with teeth as sharp as horns and a pair of bucklers on either side of his body. The beast lurked in the river, killing all those who tried to sail by and sinking their vessels. The dragon had come from Galatia in Asia, begotten of Leviathan, an extremely ferocious water-serpent, and Onachus, an animal bred in the region of Galatia, which shoots its dung like darts at pursuers within the space of an acre: whatever this touches is burned up as by fire. The people asked Martha for help, and she went after the dragon. She found him in the forest in the act of devouring a man, sprinkled him with blessed water, and had a cross held up in front of him. The brute was subdued at once and stood still like a sheep while Martha tied him up with her girdle, and the people killed him then and there with stones and lances. The inhabitants called the dragon Tarsconus, and in memory of this event the place is still called Tarascon.[96]

Finally we have St. Michael the Archangel, who "drove the dragon, i.e. Lucifer, and all his followers out of heaven" when they rebelled against God, a battle that foreshadows Michael's battle with Antichrist in the Last Days.[97] In all these examples from the *Golden Legend*, it is clear that dragons symbolize evil: Margaret's and Michael's dragons are the devil in animal form, and Matthew's dragons are under the direct control of evil sorcerers. As manifestations of evil, the dragons of the *Golden Legend* have a certain spectral, ethereal quality that allows them to be killed or subdued by holy water (including holy spittle) or by the sign of the cross – physical force is not necessary for this task.

It is important to remember, however, that dragons were also real animals for medieval people, regularly included in bestiaries and encyclopedias alongside the camel or elephant, creatures perhaps no less exotic. The seventh-century Isidore of Seville, whose *Etymologia* influenced encyclopedists throughout the Middle Ages, describes the dragon as "the largest of the serpents" and, indeed of all land animals. It lives in caves, from which it emerges to fly through the air; it is crested, has a small mouth from which it thrusts out its tongue, and draws breath through "small pipes". Its power does not lie in its teeth, but in its tail, which it uses to club its victims to death.[98] Bartholomaeus Anglicus, a thirteenth-century English encyclopedist, adds that "oft four or five of them, fasten their tails together, and rear up their heads, and sail over sea and over

[96]   Jacobus, *Golden Legend*, 2: 23–24.
[97]   Jacobus, *Golden Legend*, 2: 201, 205, 206.
[98]   *PL* 82, col. 442.

rivers to get good meat."[99] Dragons, moreover, were occasionally seen at large. In England, the chronicler Matthew Paris recorded the appearance, in 1233, of two dragons fighting in the sky, at a time when relations between Henry III and his barons were worsening.[100] An anonymous chronicler of the late fourteenth and early fifteenth centuries tells that a huge dragon appeared in 1405 near Sudbury, killing sheep and shepherds; no arrow could pierce its scales, but it disappeared into a swamp.[101] These scientific and "real life" examples of dragons show that the creature was certainly thought to have existed, and although it may have portended bad things, in its natural form it was simply different in degree from other fierce and fearful wild animals – any damage it did was due as much to its great physical power as to any evil agency on its part. Indeed, in certain places medieval townspeople often paraded model dragons around on Rogation days and threw cakes and fruits into their jaws, suggesting that medieval people thought on some level that dragons could be negotiated with. The Roman custom of carrying dragon-standards into battle also survived into the Middle Ages, illustrating that the creatures were not so evil that Christians could not be represented by them.[102] The Bayeux Tapestry furnishes us with a famous example of this practice (figure 1).

To return to the legend of St. George, one notes that both the "symbolic" and the "natural" aspects of the dragon converge, in their way, in his legend, a combination that points to another aspect of the saint's patronage.[103] George's dragon is like the evil dragons of the *Golden Legend*: it is allowed to attack Silene, presumably, because of the paganism of the city's populace; George crosses himself before charging it; and like Martha's dragon, it is tamed by having the princess's girdle placed around

[99] Bartholomew Anglicus, *Medieval Lore: An Epitome of the Science, Geography, Animal and Plant Folk-Lore and Myth of the Middle Age*, ed. Robert Steel (London: Elliot Stock, 1893), 124.

[100] Matthew Paris, *Chronica Majora* (London: Rolls Series, 1876), 3: 243.

[101] John Trokelowe and Henry Blandeford, *Chronica et Annales Regnantibus Henrico Tertio, Edwardo Primo, Edwardo Secundo, Ricardo Secundo, et Henrico Quarto*, ed. H.T. Riley (London: Rolls Series, 1866), 3: 402.

[102] See Jacques Le Goff, "Ecclesiastical Culture and Folklore in the Middle Ages: Saint Marcellus of Paris and the Dragon," in *Time, Work and Culture in the Middle Ages*, trans. Arthur Goldhammer (Chicago and London: University of Chicago Press, 1980), 159–88, at 161, 178–82 for Rogation dragons, and 176 for dragon standards.

[103] Riches, *St George*, 149. Le Goff notes (at 162) a similar convergence of "ecclesiastical" and "folkloric" dragons in the Life of St. Macellus.

its neck. St. George's dragon, however, possesses a certain corporeal reality that the other dragons of the *Golden Legend* do not: the creature is first wounded by George's lance, and then killed by his sword. No other dragon in the *Golden Legend* is defeated as physically as this. What might this mean? For a saint to kill a dragon may be perfectly good hagiography, but for a solitary, mounted adventurer to rescue a princess by battling a fantastic monster may very well be a tale told of the chivalrous exploits of one of the knights of King Arthur, as recorded in the works of such romance poets as Chrétien de Troyes or Gottfried von Strassburg. Indeed, if in the eleventh century George became the preeminent patron of Christian knights liberating the Holy Land, it follows that George should eventually become the patron of the chivalric ethos that impelled and was impelled by the crusades, whether that ethos was exercised on crusade or not. Such a shift can be seen already in the twelfth century, when Simund de Freine's *Vie de Saint Georges*, although containing no dragon, describes the saint as:

> a knight, who had resolved
> To gain a reputation through knightly deeds
> With shield and lance he caused
> Much talk about God.[104]

A twelfth-century northern French Life of St. George also describes the saint as:

> A high-born man of noble lineage,
> Simple, pious, and giving no offence;
> Of good character, and holy life
> And well versed in the art of chivalry.[105]

Chivalry, of course, meant different things at different times and places, but from the twelfth century on romantic authors are fairly unanimous in regarding certain qualities as the badges of knighthood: *prouesse, loyauté, largesse* (generosity), *courtoisie* and *franchise* (that is, the self-confident comportment that comes naturally to those of good birth).[106] A knight is supposed to defend the Church, and women and children; a knight will also fight or go on elaborate quests in the service of a lady, with whom he might be deeply in love – but express that love far more through longing

---

[104] Simon de Freine, "Vie de Saint George," 64.

[105] *La Vie de la Vierge Marie de maître Wace: publiée d'après un manuscrit inconnu aux prémiers éditeurs, suivie de La vie de Saint George: poème inedit du même trouvère*, ed. V. Luzarche (Tours: J. Bouserez, 1859), 93.

[106] Maurice Keen, *Chivalry* (New Haven and London: Yale University Press, 1984), 2.

than by actually consummating it. That St. George became the patron of chivalry is further underscored by his acquisition of a lady, not the princess of Silene (whom he had in fact rejected) but the most sublime lady of all, the Virgin Mary herself. The king of Silene, in the *Golden Legend*, built a church to the Virgin Mary and St. George, and "Our lady's knight" is one of the most "hackneyed epithets" of St. George in late-medieval English poems and prayers addressed to him,[107] as in these lines from John Lydgate's rhyming Kalendar:

> O sacred Seynt George, oure lady knyght,
> To that lady thou pray now for me.[108]

or the chorus to the so-called Agincourt Carol, also from the fifteenth century:

> Enfors we us with all our myght
> To love Seynt Georg, Owr Lady knyght.[109]

There also grew up a legend that St. George had been armed by the Virgin herself and even, in England, that she had raised him from the dead.[110] Although these legends do not appear in any literary form, they are represented in art, such as the early fourteenth-century Taymouth Hours and Carew-Pointz Hours.[111] By the fifteenth century, visual cycles of the life of St. George that included his resurrection and arming by the Virgin Mary were installed as stained glass in the church of St. George in Stamford, Lincolnshire and in St. Neot's, Cornwall, and as alabaster carvings on retables of English construction in Borbjerg, Denmark and La Selle, Normandy.[112] This detail of the legend may indicate the lasting

---

[107] R.L. Greene, ed., *A Selection of English Carols* (Oxford: Clarendon Press, 1962), 227.

[108] John Lydgate, *The Minor Poems of John Lydgate*, ed. Henry Noble MacCracken, EETS ES 107 (London: EETS, 1911), 367.

[109] Greene, ed., *Selection*, 124.

[110] Peter Brieger, *English Art 1216–1307* (Oxford: Clarendon Press, 1957), 169; Francis Edgerton Bond, *Dedications and Patron Saints of English Churches: Ecclesiastical Symbolism, Saints and their Emblems* (London and New York: Humphrey Milford, Oxford University Press, 1914), 153.

[111] M.R. James, *A Descriptive Catalogue of the Second Series of Fifty Manuscripts (Nos. 51–100) in the Collection of Henry Yates Thompson* (Cambridge: Cambridge University Press, 1902), 70; M.R. James, *A Descriptive Catalogue of the Manuscripts in the Fitzwilliam Museum* (Cambridge: Cambridge University Press, 1895), 116.

[112] See Riches, *St George*, 72–88 on these four cycles.

influence of the earliest accounts of the martyrdom of St. George, where the saint was repeatedly raised from the dead, and it may also have come into the St. George legend in England from a legend about St. Mercurius, who according to the *Golden Legend* was raised from the dead by the Virgin for the specific purpose of killing the Emperor Julian the Apostate in 363.[113] One of the miracles of the Virgin appended to the mid-thirteenth-century *Lambeth Apocalypse* (also known as the *De Quincy Apocalypse*) shows the Virgin raising St. Mercurius to life and presenting him with a coat of mail, while two angels hover overhead, one proffering a helmet, the other a shield and spear (figure 2).[114] The shield is decorated with a red cross, and although the background is gold, not white, the cross itself is outlined in white and the device could be interpreted as the cross of St. George.[115] (We have already seen, of course, an association between George and Mercurius when they appeared together to the crusaders at Antioch.) This theory, if true, would represent the same sort of transference of the characteristics of one military saint to another as seen in George's acquisition of the dragon from Theodore.

As far as the cult of St. George is concerned, the shield device is exceedingly important, and further evidence that George had become the patron saint of chivalry, for no one claiming to adhere to the code of chivalry could possibly be without a coat of arms. St. George's arms, from the thirteenth century, consisted of a plain red cross on a white field, and throughout the West when the saint is shown carrying a banner, wearing a surcoat over his armor, or holding a shield, these things are almost invariably decorated with what can be described heraldically as *Argent, a cross Gules*. The general origin of this coat of arms seems obvious enough: it is a combination of, on the one hand, true heraldry, which arose in the twelfth century as a manifestation of a new sense of individual and chivalric identity, and on the other, the crusader's cross, sewn onto one's clothing as an outward and specific sign of crusading status, something practiced ever since Pope Urban II preached the first crusade at Clermont in 1095.[116] Exactly where and when St. George came specifically to bear

113   Jacobus, *Golden Legend*, 1: 130.
114   Lambeth Palace Library, MS 209, f. 45v [facsimile edition consulted].
115   Nigel Morgan, *The Lambeth Apocalypse: Manuscript 209 in the Lambeth Palace Library* (London: Harvey Miller, 1997), 57, 201.
116   On the origins of heraldry see, *inter alia*, Keen, *Chivalry*, 125–42 and Michel Pastoureau, *Traité d'héraldique*, 3rd edn. (Paris: Picard, 1997), 26–32, 37–58. For Urban's speech at Clermont, see Dana C. Munro, "Speech of Urban II at the Council of Clermont," *Translations and Reprints from the Original Sources of European History* 1: 2 (1895): 8

his coat of arms is somewhat difficult to surmise. A plausible explanation is that, just as the *Golden Legend* popularized the dragon myth in the West, so also was it responsible for the popularization of the so-called cross of St. George.[117] We have seen how Raymond of Agiles had St. George appearing to the crusaders outside Jerusalem dressed in white armor with a shining cross on it; when Jacobus recounts the episode, however, he states that when the crusaders

> had laid siege to the city, they did not dare mount the scaling ladders in the face of the Saracens' resistance; but Saint George appeared to them wearing white armor marked with a red cross, and made them understand that they could follow him up the walls in safety and the city would be theirs.[118]

Why did Jacobus transform the white cross into a red one? The answer might be found in the city he was writing in: Genoa. The church of San Giorgio was one of the oldest (seventh–eighth centuries) in the city, and over the course of the Middle Ages came to consider George as its patron, as the famous Genoese bank of San Giorgio (founded 1407) attests.[119] Genoa also came to employ a red cross on a white field as a civic coat of arms,[120] something prefigured as early as 1109, when Genoa declared itself an independent republic: a drawing in the margin of the Genoese municipal annals for that year shows the city's newly-constructed castle

---

[117] A manuscript map of Jerusalem (The Hague, Koninklijke Bibliotheek MS 76 F 5, f. 1), made in the late twelfth century, shows at its base St. George in full armor, riding a horse and spearing some enemies with a lance; both the saint's shield and a banner flying from his lance have red crosses on them. The arms of these crosses, however, are splayed and terminate before they reach the edges of the shield, and are thus not quite in the standard form that St. George's arms were to become (figure 4). Compare this, however, with a passage from the *Itinerarium Regis Ricardi*, stating that the Saracens, because they killed a Christian knight on a white horse with white armor and weapons in 1187, flattered themselves that they had killed St. George. See *Chronicles and Memorials of the Reign of Richard I*, ed. W. Stubbs (London: Rolls Series, 1864), 1: 7. St. George, we can therefore surmise, was not universally identified with the red cross in the late twelfth century.

[118] Jacobus, *Golden Legend*, 1: 242.

[119] Stephen Epstein, *Genoa and the Genoese, 958–1528* (Chapel Hill and London: University of North Carolina Press, 1996), 14; Farmer, *Oxford Dictionary of Saints*, 197.

[120] Jirí Louda, *European Civic Coats of Arms* (London: Paul Hamlyn, 1966), 136–37.

of Portus Veneris flying a banner with a cross on it.[121] This custom may, in fact, have been widespread in northern Italy: Carl Erdmann traces the evolution of the *carroccio*, or banner-wagon, of Milan, which by the mid-twelfth century consisted of a wheeled mast topped with an image of St. Ambrose, under which flew two white banners with red crosses on them. The *carroccio* would accompany the Milanese in times of war, and other Italian cities had their own versions of the wagon, which would also fly red-cross banners. Although for most of the twelfth century these banners were general Christian symbols (and were another example of how the West was becoming comfortable with the idea of Christian warfare), in the thirteenth century they started to take on a local significance: Milan's banners were known by the name of the city's patron St. Ambrose,[122] and the city's coat of arms showed a red cross on a white field. Padua and Bologna also have coats of arms consisting of red crosses on white fields,[123] and one can surmise that the design was bequeathed from a common practice – heraldry (and straightforward civic pride) usually demands that one's identifying symbol be unique. To return to Genoa, however, we can propose a progression: just as Milan's banners came to assume local significance, and to be known by the name of the city's patron saint, so also may Genoa's banners and thus coat of arms have come to be known by the name of St. George. Jacobus, therefore, when composing the *Golden Legend*, may have wanted to insert St. George's "proper" color combination in his Life of the saint. The immense popularity of the *Golden Legend* subsequently ensured that a formerly Genoese practice was picked up all over the West. Of course, other saints, and people, could be identified by a red cross on a white field,[124] and St. George is not always depicted bearing this coat of arms, but after the thirteenth century the vast majority of red crosses on white fields point ultimately to St. George. This is an important

---

[121] *Annali Genovesi di Caffaro e de' suoi Continuatori*, ed. Luigi Tommaso Belgrano (Genoa: Istituto Sordo-Muti, 1890), 15.

[122] Erdmann, *Origin*, 53–55.

[123] Louda, *Coats of Arms*, 104–05, 180–81, 196–97.

[124] *Argent, a cross Gules* is borne by Galahad in most Arthurian armorials, by the German diocese of Trier, and by the English family de Vere of Addingdon. See Michel Pastoureau, *Armorial des chevaliers de la table ronde* (Paris: Léopard d'Or, 1983), 67–68; Pastoureau, *Traité d'Héraldique*, pl. 1; Peter Coss, "Knighthood, Heraldry and Social Exclusion in Edwardian England," in *Heraldry, Pageantry and Social Display in Medieval England*, eds. Maurice Keen and Peter Coss (Woodbridge, Suffolk: Boydell, 2002), 51–52.

development, for while not as well-known as the dragon, this red-cross-on-white is perhaps just as important symbolically: St. George's dragon can be termed a negative attribute, the evil opposed to the saint's goodness, and while it may occasionally be displayed as a "trophy," St. George must usually be shown subduing it in order to complete the picture. A red cross on a white background, however, can be called a positive attribute, and can represent the saint independently of anything he opposes, and even independently of a figure of the saint himself (like such traditional saints' attributes as St. Catherine's wheel, St. Andrew's X-shaped cross, or St. Peter's keys). As such, *Argent, a cross Gules* could be displayed with all the flexibility that heraldry allows, further emphasizing George's chivalric nature and extending his presence by symbolic shorthand.

Thus, over the course of one thousand years, as the cult of St. George spread from its Near Eastern origins to embrace nearly all of Christendom, it acquired a number of different meanings. Initially celebrated as a heroic martyr, George subsequently became variously a patron of agricultural fecundity, of the military, of crusading, and of chivalry. These aspects are discernable in fourteenth- and fifteenth-century England, and had their part to play in the adoption of the saint as that country's patron.

3

Royal St. George, 1272–1509

St. George came to be associated with England through the initiative of the crown. This chapter uses court records, chronicle and literary sources, and artistic evidence to trace the story of how successive monarchs deployed him to consolidate their kingship. From the beginning, this deployment took place in a military context and was therefore something that the king shared with all ranks of his soldiers. Following the example of the crusading King Edward I, two other English kings widely regarded as "successful" (Edward III and Henry V) were especially devoted to St. George, while "unsuccessful" ones (such as Edward II, Richard II, and Henry VI) were not. St. George, therefore, became a figure that people could use to acknowledge someone as king, or to rebuke a king for not ruling well. Savvy kings came to realize that venerating St. George was expected of them if they wanted to be taken seriously.

In Chapter 2 we saw that Henry III gave money to St. George's church in Oxford, and had an image of St. George placed over his entrance hall in Winchester. These acts might be termed examples of the king's personal piety, taking place as they do either at court, or in the context of the almsgiving expected of all medieval Christian leaders. For the use of St. George in a more public and official capacity, however, we have to examine the reign of Henry's son and successor, Edward I (1272–1307). Edward had gone on crusade as a prince and had succeeded to the throne while abroad, returning to England in 1274. Although he frequently expressed a desire to lead another crusade, the only military campaigns he conducted were in Wales, France, and Scotland. Edward, however, was influenced enough by his crusading experience to employ the patron saint of crusading in his subsequent military engagements. In this way, St. George came to be a familiar companion to the English army, and a familiar patron of the English crown.

In 1277 Edward invaded Wales in order to force its prince, Llywelyn ap Gruffydd, to render homage to him for the principality, something that Llywelyn had repeatedly refused to do. The campaign was short and successful, extracting homage and a large indemnity from the prince. In 1282 Llywelyn rose again against Edward, who responded this time with a war of conquest that permanently annexed Wales to the English crown. Edward was able to achieve both victories through equipment and supplies that were vastly superior to those of the Welsh, but he also placed his faith in heavenly aid: for the 1277 campaign, Edward ordered 100 bracers (guards for left forearms of archers) and 340 pennoncels (triangular flags fixed to the heads of lances of footsoldiers) "of the arms of St. George" from Admetus, his tailor.[1] This practice was repeated in the campaign in the 1290s, when Edward again had his infantry wear armbands featuring the cross of St. George.[2]

These devices mark the first official "deployment" of St. George by a reigning English monarch. Michael Prestwich suggests that they functioned as a sort of uniform for the infantry, but any symbol could serve for a uniform – why did Edward specifically choose the "cross of St. George" (widely recognized, following the *Golden Legend*, as a red cross on a white field) for his troops in Wales? Apart from the fact that the cross was simple and easy to reproduce, two reasons suggest themselves. The first is that as the patron saint of the crusades, St. George was a natural choice for a king who had been on one himself, and whose subsequent wars could thereby take on the aura of crusading. The armbands and pennoncels were not exactly crusading badges or banners, but Edward was certainly hinting that his Welsh wars were comparable with the most prestigious and justifiable type of warfare that could then be waged. That Archbishop Pecham had been prevailed upon to excommunicate the Welsh gave Edward further justification for his use of the crusading saint.[3]

---

[1] PRO E 101 3/15.

[2] Michael Prestwich, *Edward I*, 2nd edn. (New Haven and London: Yale University Press, 1997), 199. Henry III's troops had worn red crosses on both arms at the battle of Evesham in 1265, but the device was not specifically associated with St. George, and may simply have acted as an answer to the Montfortian rebels who had worn white crosses at the battle of Lewes the previous year, when St. George appeared on their side. See Simon Lloyd, "'Political Crusades' in England, c. 1215–17 and c. 1263–5," in *Crusades and Settlement: Papers read at the First Conference of the Society for the Study of the Crusades and the Latin East and presented to R.C. Smail*, ed. Peter Edbury (Cardiff: University College of Cardiff Press, 1985), 116 and 119, n. 29.

[3] Lloyd, "Political Crusades," 199–200.

The second reason for Edward's use of St. George in Wales, albeit a more tenuous one, might have been the advent of the saint's dragon story. To this day one of the best-known symbols for Wales is a dragon: was Edward I, inspired by the recently-published *Golden Legend*, casting his army as St. George, riding out to slay the Welsh dragon? The eighth-century *Historia Brittonum*, traditionally ascribed to the monk Nennius, first records a sign witnessed by King Vortigern: two dragons, one red and one white, fought against each other; these foretold the struggle between the Britons, represented by the red dragon, and the Saxons, represented by the white. This vision is relayed in the twelfth-century *Mabinogion* and in the *History of the Kings of Britain* by Geoffrey of Monmouth, and is ultimately the reason why Owain Glyndwr in 1401 and Henry Tudor in 1485 carried red dragon standards. If the Welsh had taken the red dragon to heart as a national symbol in the late thirteenth century, it would have provided an extra incentive for Edward's use of the cross of St. George in their country. One must note, though, that Vortigern's vision also casts the Saxons as a dragon, and the Plantagenets themselves are known to have employed dragon standards in battle, like the one that Henry III commissioned in 1244, "in the fashion of a standard, of red silk sparkling over with gold, the tongue of which should be made to resemble burning fire, and to appear to be continually moving."[4] But the English never employed the dragon as a national symbol, and even if Edward himself flew a dragon standard in Wales, his deployment of the dragon-slaying St. George may indeed have been partly inspired by the national dragon of Wales.

For the future of St. George in England, however, the bracers, pennoncels, and armbands had a very important effect, and that was to ensure the democratization of the saint. St. George may have patronized crusading in the Levant, but by the late thirteenth century in Western Europe he had become the preeminent patron of chivalry, and thus had a strong following among its practitioners – the knights Robert d'Oiley and Paulinus Piper being two English examples. The St. George's cross as used in Wales, however, was more in the crusading tradition of all Christians being on the same side against the infidel, as the bracers and armbands were not for the chivalric elite but for the archers and infantry, i.e. the common soldiery. It is true that not every member of the lower ranks of the army would have received a cross of St. George, and the emblem may have served as a sort of livery badge to mark those soldiers mustered directly by the king, as opposed to those mustered by other barons as

---

[4] Ralph of Coggeshall, *Chronicon Anglicanum* (London: Rolls Series, 1875), 182.

part of their feudal obligations. By allowing commoners access to St. George, however, the emblems avoided a complete "chivalrization" of the saint, and helped to ensure that he did not become the predominant property of the English nobility, either against common people or against the king, as witnessed by the chronicler of the battle of Lewes in 1264, who had St. George fighting on the side of the barons against Henry III. St. George remained popular with the nobility, of course: the message of the armbands and pennoncels was not strong or sustained enough to undermine that. Their existence, however, clearly shows that Edward envisioned St. George as a protector of the entire army, and not simply of its knights.

Edward was pleased enough with the fortune that St. George brought him in his wars against the Welsh that he continued to honor the saint in his wars against Scotland. These wars began in 1296; both their immediate cause (a leader who owed feudal allegiance to Edward but was not rendering it to Edward's satisfaction) and intended result (annexation of the territory to the English crown) were the same as his earlier wars in Wales. A significant episode illustrating the king's esteem for St. George occurred at the siege of Carlaverock castle, Dumfrieshire, in 1300. The *Song of Carlaverock* records that, after the castle had been taken,

> the King caused [his men] to bring up his banner, and that of St. Edmond, St. George, and St. Edward, and with them, by established right those of Seagrave and Hereford, and that of the Lord of Clifford, to whom the castle was entrusted.[5]

Such banners, both sacred and secular, were integral to medieval warfare. For a prince to unfurl his banner was a legal declaration of war.[6] Any noble or knight who had joined Edward in his campaign would have had his own heraldic device and would have displayed it on a banner, and indeed the *Song of Carlaverock* contains abundant description of the arms of the earls, barons and knights who were present at the siege. A coat of arms was an emblem of individual and chivalric identity, and in banner form would have served as a rallying-point on the battlefield for any retainers who had accompanied its bearer to war. The saints' banners, of course, were different from those of the nobles – but the difference at Carlaverock was actually one of degree, not of kind. Carl Erdmann notes that banners of saints started to be carried into war in the West around

---

5 *The Siege of Carlaverock*, ed. N.H. Nicolas (London: J.B. Nichols, 1828), 87.

6 M.H. Keen, *The Laws of War in the Late Middle Ages* (Toronto: University of Toronto Press and London: Routledge and Kegan Paul, 1965), 106.

the year 1000, and are another indication that the Catholic Church was, at the time, becoming more comfortable with the idea of Christian warfare.[7] An example from England occurred in 1138, when the English carried the banners of St. Peter of York, St. John of Beverley, and St. Wilfrid of Ripon in the so-called Battle of the Standard against the Scots at Northallerton. All such banners, notes Erdmann, were normally kept by ecclesiastical institutions devoted to the saint in question and granted by them for use in war; they constituted the Church's blessing on a given military enterprise.[8] Such arrangements were still in operation in Edward's day: wardrobe accounts for the year 1299–1300 record payment of £1 to William de Gretham, monk of Durham, to bring the flag of St. Cuthbert on Edward's Scottish campaign, and £1 14s. 9d. to Gilbert de Grimsby, vicar of the collegiate church of St. John of Beverley, to bring the flag of St. John of Beverley on the same campaign.[9] These flags would have functioned in the same manner as the relics of the saints in question – they were holy objects, and would have bestowed supernatural aid on Edward and his army.

The flags of Saints Edmund, George, and Edward that were raised over Carlaverock castle, however, were themselves different from the flags of Cuthbert and John of Beverly. Although the Carlaverock flags would also have bestowed heavenly aid on the king, their *provenance* was different, a significant fact. The Carlaverock flags are mentioned in the wardrobe accounts: on 8 July, 10s. were paid

> to Lord William de Felton, for five lances bought for five of the king's flags to be carried in the war in Scotland in this present year, that is two flags of the arms of England, a third flag of the arms of St. George, a fourth of the arms of St. Edmund, and a fifth of the arms of St. Edward, for each lance, 2 s. – by the hand of William de Etchewiche his valet, at Tynewold.[10]

Even though the relics of St. Edward the Confessor and St. Edmund were possessed by major monastic foundations in England, the flags of these saints were not, apparently, in the possession of either Westminster or Bury, whose monks could lend them to the king for the duration of his

[7]   Carl Erdmann, *The Origin of the Idea of Crusade*, trans. Marshall W. Baldwin and Walter Goffart (Princeton: Princeton University Press, 1977), 45.

[8]   Erdmann, *Origin*, 51.

[9]   *Liber Quotidianus Contrarotulatoris Garderobae anno regni regis Edwardi primi vicesimo octavo* (London: Society of Antiquaries, 1787), 50, 51–52.

[10] *Liber Quotidianus*, 64.

campaign. Instead, the flags of these saints were treated, along with the arms of England, as being "the king's flags" – in this way they are different only in degree from the banners of the nobles. By 1300, the holiness of Edward and Edmund, it seems, inhered in the crown, and was no longer the exclusive property of the church to grant. What is even more surprising is that George should have shared this status – indeed, if the order of being mentioned in the wardrobe book is significant, George in fact outranked both Edward and Edmund. It is true that George had no major monastic foundation in England (there were six in 1216, none of them of much importance[11]), which may have allowed the king more freedom to claim George as royal property. Be that as it may, it is surely significant that St. George, by 1300, had been elevated in Edward's mind to having a status on par with that of two important, English, and royal saints, all of whom were unquestionably on Edward's side. (St. George, perhaps, filled a need that the others did not: all three saints were powerful, but St. George was the most explicitly warlike among them).

But Edward deployed St. George in peacetime too. A wardrobe book for 1306 records, on 23 July of that year, payment of one mark each to two brothers of a hospital of St. George of Flanders to carry an "image of the arms of St. George" before the king.[12] Even more significantly, in 1285 Edward gave gold figures of Saints George and Edward the Confessor to the shrine of St. Thomas of Canterbury. These figures had been made by William of Farndon, a London goldsmith, at a cost of £374, a considerable amount.[13] Although King Edward was not averse to honoring St. Thomas of Canterbury on other occasions,[14] in the context of the king's current dispute with Archbishop Pecham over the taxation of church property,[15] this donation (to Pecham's predecessor in office and martyr for ecclesiastical rights) is exceptional: its great richness was counteracted by the form it took, of two saints on Edward's "side," a deliberately double-edged statement on Edward's part. For our purposes, it is significant that as early as 1285, and well away from the field of battle, Edward was presenting St. George as his own.

---

11 See Alison Binns, *Dedications of Monastic Houses in England and Wales 1066–1216* (Woodbridge, Suffolk: Boydell, 1989), 18.
12 PRO E 101 369/11, f. 31. King Edward was not in Flanders at the time, and exactly which hospital the entry refers to remains elusive.
13 R. Allen Brown, H.M. Colvin, and A.J. Taylor, *History of the King's Works*, Vols. 1 and 2: *The Middle Ages* (London: HMSO, 1963), 481.
14 E.g., PRO E 101 364/13, f. 30; PRO C 47 4/2, f. 24v; E 101 368/6, f. 17v.
15 Prestwich, *Edward I*, 249–55.

Edward also honored St. George in his private devotions, not all of which were as overtly political as his gift to Canterbury. Wardrobe accounts reveal that the king regularly gave alms on 23 April "in honor of St. George,"[16] although he usually distributed alms three times a week and in honor of many other saints. More significant are the king's oblations. On St. George's Day in 1297, the king's agent William de Bruyn offered 7d. for a mass to be celebrated in a chapel of St. George in the church of St. Maurice in Plympton, Devon, and 7s. for the altar there; the next day John, one of the king's chandlers, gave 7d. for a mass to be celebrated at the church of St. George at Ashcombe, Devon, and 7s. for the altar there.[17] On 23 April 1300, the king's almoner gave an offering of one gold cloth and one candle of "the length of the king" to the church of St. George de Orcheston, Wiltshire; and on 23 April 1306, Edward gave 7s. to the altar of the chapel at the king's manor in Wolveseye "in honor of St. George."[18] Furthermore, on 1 March 1299, the king's almoner left an offering of 7s. before an image of St. George outside the saint's church in Southwark; on 17 December 1299, 7s. at the altar of the parish church of Brampton (near Guilsborough, Northants.) "in honor of St. George"; on 18 July 1300, 7s. at the altar of St. George's church at North Clifton, Nottinghamshire; and on 16 August 1306, 7s. at an altar showing an image of St. George, the location of which is unspecified.[19] Again, Edward honored a great many other saints' shrines with the standard 7s. donation throughout his reign – the king was by no means exclusively devoted to St. George. That Edward was willing to celebrate the saint independently of his feast day (as though he were one of the more important English saints, like Edward the Confessor, Thomas Becket, Dunstan, Cuthbert, or Richard of Chichester), however, indicates how much regard the king had come to have for him.

Edward I had much esteem for St. George, used the saint to represent himself both in war and in peace, and allowed people under his direct command to use the saint's symbolism, regardless of their own status.

---

16   See *Liber Quotidianus*, 20, PRO E 101 350/23; PRO E 101 351/15; PRO C 47 4/ 2, f. 26; Benjamin F. Byerly and Catherine Ridder Byerly, eds., *Records of the Wardrobe and Household 1286–89* (London: HMSO, 1986), 283; PRO C 47 4/4, f. 42; PRO E 101 353/16; BL Add. MS 7965, f. 3; PRO E 101 359/15; PRO E 101 361/21; PRO E 101 364/13, f. 30; BL Add. MS 8835, f. 2; PRO E 101 369 11, f. 25.
17   BL Add. MS 7965, f. 7v.
18   *Liber Quotidianus*, 34; PRO E 101 369/11, f. 32.
19   *Liber Quotidianus*, 30; BL Add. MS 7966a, f. 23, f. 28v; PRO E 101 369/11, f. 29v.

These terms of royal devotion survived Edward's reign, but not immediately. There is little evidence that Edward's son, Edward II, paid official homage to St. George; even his almsgiving makes no mention of the saint.[20] This situation may only be an apparent one, the result of a lack of evidence, but Edward II was so unlike his father that it is probable that he did abandon St. George, along with many other things from his father's reign. Rather than securing victories in Wales and Scotland, Edward II's lone military campaign ended in a colossal defeat at the battle of Bannockburn in 1314, and rather than working with Parliament, Edward ignored the great barons of the realm in favor, first of Piers Gaveston, and then the younger Hugh Despenser. (These and other blunders, coupled with an abrasive personality, eventually provoked a widespread rebellion against him that even his own queen Isabella joined, and he was deposed and murdered in 1327.) Two interesting and strangely parallel pieces of artistic evidence from the late 1320s suggest that Edward had not maintained royal identity with St. George, and that, as a result, the saint was becoming contested property between the king and his barons. Although these works are in the form of unique manuscript illuminations, and are not likely to have been viewed by a wide audience, they may be understood as acting, like political cartoons, as indicative of certain strains of popular opinion.

In 1327, Walter of Milemete, one of the king's clerks, presented the new king Edward III with a treatise (now at Christ Church College, Oxford) detailing the matters that pertained to "the nobility, wisdom, and prudence of kings," that is, advice such as "love God above all things" or "avoid unseemly amusements."[21] On folio 3a, immediately following a summary of the book's contents, is a portrait of St. George presenting a shield to a king of England (figure 5). Both figures are dressed as knights, with coats of mail, helmets, and swords, and surcoats of their arms proclaiming their identity: St. George wears his familiar *Argent, a cross Gules*, while Edward wears *Gules, three lions passant guardant in pale Or.*[22] These arms are also painted on the shield that George hands to Edward, and the message is clear: St. George is the patron and protector of the king of England, who

---

[20] E.g., PRO E 101 373/15, E 101 374/5, E 101 373/26, E 101 374/19, E 101 375/ 8, E 101 376/7.

[21] *The treatise of Walter De Milemete de nobilitatibus, sapientiis, et prudentiis regum, reproduced in facsimile from the unique manuscript preserved at Christ Church, Oxford*, ed. M.R. James (Oxford: Roxburghe Club, 1913), xvi, xvii.

[22] *Treatise of Walter De Milemete*, 5.

should therefore act in a manner befitting one of the saint's votaries. Such a message, of course, is most appropriate to a new king, but Milemete's treatise gives several indications that it was actually composed for Edward II, not Edward III. First, it was presented to Edward III almost immediately upon his accession – but Edward III's accession was sudden, and the treatise itself has 70 richly illustrated leaves, which would have taken some time to prepare. More important, throughout the treatise, the shields of England, England with a "label" of five points Azure (representing the heir apparent to the throne) and England "dimidiating" France (indicating the marriage of a king of England to a daughter of the king of France) appear repeatedly, suggesting that the treatise was indeed composed for Edward II.[23] That king had an heir apparent in the person of Edward III, and was himself married to Isabella of France (Edward III, of course, had produced no children at the time of his accession, and was married to Philippa of Hainault). In this context the appearance of St. George becomes urgent, calling Edward II to return to the royal values of his father, who had governed well and enjoyed military success, under the patronage of St. George.

The fact that Edward II was *not* exercising those values, however, is revealed by the other piece of evidence from the 1320s, a miniature from the *Douce Hours*, a book of hours composed in the diocese of Lincoln in the late 1320s and currently held by the Bodleian Library in Oxford (figure 6). This miniature shows two knights facing each other, and as in the Milemete treatise, both wear the full range of knightly equipment: coats of mail, helmets, surcoats, and spaulders, and both carry shields, swords, and spears with pennoncels on the ends.[24] One knight bears, on his shield, surcoat, and pennoncel, the arms of St. George; the other knight bears the arms of the earls of Lancaster (that is, the arms of the king of England, overlaid by a blue "label" of five points, each point charged with a gold fleur de lys). There had been three earls of Lancaster by the late 1320s: Edmund Crouchback (1245–96), the younger brother and close supporter of Edward I; Thomas (c. 1278–1322), Edmund's son and one of the leading opponents of Edward II; and Henry (c. 1281–1345), Thomas's younger brother and also an eventual rebel against Edward II. Most commentators consider the figure in the *Douce Hours* to be that of Thomas,[25] and if this

23 *Treatise of Walter De Milemete*, lxiv.
24 Oxford, Bodleian Library, MS Douce 231, f. 1v.
25 Otto Pächt and J.J.G. Alexander, *Illuminated Manuscripts in the Bodleian Library* 3 *British, Irish, and Icelandic Schools* (Oxford: Clarendon Press, 1973), 53 [no. 575]; Janet Backhouse, "Devotions and Delights," in *Age of Chivalry*, ed. Nigel

is the case it suggests that people were casting St. George in the role he played at the battle of Lewes in 1264, when he appeared on the side of the rebel barons against Henry III. In 1310, Thomas had become one of the leading Lords Ordainers (a clique of important lords set up to reform the royal household), was subsequently instrumental in the execution of the king's favorite Piers Gaveston in 1312, and was *de facto* ruler of England following the battle of Bannockburn in 1314. Although he alienated many through his rapacity, and was finally defeated at the battle of Boroughbridge in 1322 and executed shortly thereafter, his memory became only more popular as Edward's rule grew worse in the 1320s, a popularity that even expressed itself through a devotional cult that lasted down to the Reformation.[26] In the *Douce Hours*, therefore, we see that St. George, the patron saint of chivalry and just war, is granting his prestige to an opponent of the king. The question thus arises: is this miniature from the *Douce Hours* a witness to the general popularity of St. George among the knightly and baronial class,[27] or might it also be a specific rebuke to Edward II, whose father had had such an affinity for the saint and who by contrast was so unworthy of both Edward I and St. George? One cannot help but think it was a rebuke: although the *Douce Hours* were painted some twenty years after the death of Edward I, that king's use of the saint was strong and sustained, and was remembered, as the Milemete treatise shows. St. George might not yet have been the patron saint of the entire English nation, but this miniature, by illustrating him "switching

---

Saul (New York: St. Martin's Press, 1992), 81; Samantha Riches, *St George*, 105. Anthony Wagner, *Heraldry in England* (Harmondsworth: Penguin, 1946), 29 and pl. IV, and Prestwich, *Edward I*, pl. 17, hold that it is Edmund.

26 In 1327 the Commons supported his canonization, in the fifteenth century a hagiographical life of Thomas was written, and in Henry VIII's time Thomas's hat and belt were on display at Pontefract Castle, as remedies for headaches and difficulties in childbirth. See J.R. Maddicott, *Thomas of Lancaster 1307–1322: A Study in the Reign of Edward II* (Oxford: University Press, 1970), 329, and Arthur Reeves Echerd, Jr., "Canonization and Politics in Late Medieval England: The Cult of Thomas of Lancaster," (Ph.D. diss., University of North Carolina, 1983), iii, 21–24.

27 Edmund Crouchback's tomb in Westminster Abbey had a carving on one of the gables of St. George killing the dragon (see Joan Evans, *English Art 1307–1461* [Oxford: Clarendon Press, 1949], 140); Thomas of Lancaster himself had a bone of the saint which he gave to his godson Thomas of Warwick as a christening present (see *Testamenta Vetusta*, ed. N.H. Nicolas [London: Nichols and Son, 1826], 1: 80).

sides," serves to illustrate that the saint could represent baronial opposition to the king just as well as he could the king himself. It was up to Edward II's successors to unite these two strands of the veneration of St. George, to produce a genuine royal patron with a broad-based appeal.

Such a uniting is indeed what came to pass. Upon Edward II's deposition the crown passed to his fourteen-year-old son, who became Edward III. Real political power in England, however, lay in the hands of Queen Isabella and her lover Roger Mortimer, and it was not until 1330 that Edward became king in fact as well as theory, when he and some close friends managed to have Mortimer arrested and executed. From that point on Edward consciously sought to revive the military glories of his grandfather's reign, a project in which he enjoyed a considerable amount of success. Edward's forces defeated the Scots at Halidon Hill (1333) and Neville's Cross (1346), and the French at Sluys (1340), Crécy (1346), Calais (1347) and Poitiers (1356) in what later became known as the Hundred Years War. Edward not only revived the military success of his grandfather's reign but the symbolism as well, and it is at this time that St. George started to reappear among the ranks of the English armed forces. In 1338–39, for example, the constable of Bordeaux paid for fifteen standards; nine with the arms of St. George, six with the arms of Edward III, to set up in recently acquired places.[28] In 1345–46, Hugh de Bungeye, the king's armorer, commissioned three banners of the arms of St. George, and 800 pennoncels of the same for the lances of the soldiers.[29] Thomas of Snetesham, another royal agent, also ordered 95 pennoncels of the arms of St. George sometime between 1337 and 1347.[30] Flags bearing the arms of St. George were provided for the masts of the king's ships in the 1340s.[31]

This sort of propaganda was noticed. In the "Vow of the Heron," a poem written in the 1340s recounting the quarrel that is alleged to have started the Hundred Years War, Edward swears to Robert of Artois by Saints George and Denis (a patron saint of France) that he will fight for

[28] Malcolm Vale, *The Origins of the Hundred Years War: The Angevin Legacy 1250–1340* (Oxford: Clarendon Press, 1996), 262.
[29] PRO E 101 16/5, m. 3, 6.
[30] PRO E 101 20/9, m. 1.
[31] H.J. Hewitt, *The Organization of War under Edward III 1338–1362* (Manchester: Manchester University Press, 1966), 78–79.

the French throne.[32] The French King Philip VI had declared Robert of Artois guilty of treason; when Edward welcomed Robert at his court in England, Philip declared that Edward, who held the duchy of Aquitaine in fief from the French crown, was a rebellious vassal and had thus forfeited the territory. Edward responded to the confiscation with an aggressive counterclaim to nothing less than the throne of France itself: Charles IV, the last Capetian king of France, had died without an heir in 1328 and Edward III, through his mother Isabella, had a good claim to the throne. But the peers of the French realm, who held the ancient right to elect the king of France and who did not want the English Edward ruling them, passed him over in favor of Charles's cousin Philip of Valois by claiming that the Salic law, which forbade women from inheriting the French crown, forbade them from transmitting it also. In 1328, Edward was in no position to press his claim, and recognized Philip as the king of France and ultimately performed liege homage to him for Aquitaine. By 1340, however, he had renounced his homage and assumed the title "king of France and England," and quartered the arms of France with those of England. Proclaiming such "duality" was the cornerstone of the English propaganda effort throughout the Hundred Years War, and Edward's vow by Saints George and Denis in "The Vow of the Heron" is in this vein. The poem is in fact a clever anti-English satire, originating from the French court, and placing the blame for the outbreak of the war on Robert, who goads Edward into declaring war by serving him a heron, a symbol of cowardice. Nonetheless, the vow by the saints certainly indicates that Edward's use of St. George was having an effect.

More than any other event, however, the foundation of the Order of the Garter in the late 1340s institutionalized the place of St. George in English court, military, and even national life. The Garter was an early example of what Jonathan Boulton has called the monarchical orders of knighthood: "more or less formally constituted bodies whose principal class of members was restricted to laymen of noble birth and knightly profession," with a presidency attached to the crown of a particular domain, whose holder usually determined the membership of the order and its activities. Such orders may have been inspired by the older, religious orders of knighthood, and may themselves have arisen as a result of the dissolution of the Templars in 1312, but they existed for a distinctly

<hr>

[32] Thomas Wright, ed., *Political Poems and Songs relating to English History composed during the period from the accession of Edward III to that of Richard III* (London: Rolls Series, 1859), 1: 7.

different purpose than waging war against the heathen. Instead, monarchical orders were part of a general movement of state centralization in most kingdoms of the late medieval West, whereby the king reduced his formerly independent barons to a status of relatively docile subjectivity by a combination of military and legal intimidation, and liberal rewards for loyalty and service to his state.[33] Membership in an order was one of those rewards, and the Garter, from an early date, was recognized as one of the most prestigious.

The origins of this "brilliant creation," however, are not entirely clear. The original statutes are lost, and chroniclers recording the foundation do not agree with each other in many points of detail. Furthermore, there is no evidence that St. George was originally intended to be a part of it, and even in its final form there is nothing about a "garter" to suggest him. The chronicler Jean Froissart claimed that the Garter was founded in 1344,[34] but what actually seems to have happened then, according to the chronicler Adam of Murimuth, is that, after a weeklong tournament at Windsor, Edward made a solemn pronouncement that

> he would found a Round Table of the same manner and standing as that which the Lord Arthur, formerly King of England, had relinquished, to the number of three hundred knights, and to support and maintain it for men whose number was never to be increased. [Many] barons and knights whom prowess and fame have promoted by praise to be worthy, similarly swore to observe, sustain, and promote this project in all its details.[35]

Murimuth adds that Edward ordered "that a most noble house should be made there by a certain date, for the building of which masons, carpenters, and other builders were appointed, and both wood and stone began to be supplied, neither labour nor expense being spared."[36] Thomas of Walsingham reports further that this house "was to be called the Round Table. Its area had a distance of 100 feet from the centre to the

---

[33] D'A.J.D. Boulton, *The Knights of the Crown: The Monarchical Orders of Knighthood in Later Medieval Europe*, rev. edn. (Woodbridge, Suffolk: Boydell, 2000), xi, xv–xvi, 1.

[34] Jean Froissart, *Oeuvres de Froissart 4 Chroniques 1342–1346*, ed. Kervyn de Lettenhove (Brussels: Victor Devaux, 1868), 204.

[35] Adam of Murimuth, *Continuatio Chronicarum*, ed. Edward Maunde Thompson (London: Rolls Series, 1889), 232.

[36] Murimuth, *Continuatio*, 156.

circumference, and thus a diameter of 200 feet."[37] Finally, according to the anonymous continuator of the Brut chronicle, this Round Table was "to be holde ther at Wyndessore in the Whytson wyke evermore yerely."[38]

Legends of King Arthur and his knights of the Round Table were immensely popular in the courts of the later Middle Ages, a situation especially true in England, where Arthur had supposedly once reigned.[39] Edward I had gone so far as to stage a translation of the remains of Arthur and Guinevere at Glastonbury Abbey in 1278,[40] and both Edward I and Edward III had hosted tournaments with Arthurian themes.[41] It seems, however, that with the solemn declaration of the Round Table in 1344, Edward III had something different in mind, not simply a reference to but an actual "refounding" of the Order of the Round Table established by King Arthur so long ago. In doing so, and on the very spot that the original Round Table was alleged to have existed, it appeared that Edward was attempting to give himself the maximum possible prestige as Arthur's "heir" and to shore up support among his peers for his attempt to conquer France, something Arthur himself was reported to have done.[42]

Despite all the expenditure and solemn vows, Edward's Round Table was never fully realized. A few months later, funds were diverted to the campaigns in France, leaving a noble house only barely begun, and no record exists of any Round Table tournaments or other meetings being held at Windsor in the week of Pentecost, or at any other time, in any subsequent years. Instead, on St. George's Day, 1349, something called

---

[37] Thomas of Walsingham, *Chronicon Angliae, 1328–88, autore monacho quodam Sancti Albani*, ed. Edward Maunde Thompson (London: Rolls Series, 1874), 17

[38] *Chronicon Galfridi le Baker de Swynebroke*, ed. Edward Maunde Thompson (Oxford, 1889), 279.

[39] Even if we accept Christopher Dean's thesis that Arthur's medieval popularity has been greatly exaggerated (see Christopher Dean, *Arthur of England: English Attitudes to King Arthur and the Knights of the Round Table in the Middle Ages and the Renaissance* [Toronto, Buffalo, and London: University of Toronto Press, 1987]), Dean does admit (at 41) that "the mid-fourteenth century surge of interest in Arthurian chivalry represents the peak of the cult in England."

[40] The abbey claimed to have discovered the remains there in 1191. See Prestwich, *Edward I*, 120.

[41] Juliet Vale, *Edward III and Chivalry: Chivalric Society and its Context 1270–1350* (Woodbridge, Suffolk: Boydell, 1982), 16–19. See also R.S. Loomis, "Edward I: Arthurian Enthusiast," *Speculum* 28 (1953): 114–27.

[42] Boulton, *Knights of the Crown*, 108.

the Order of the Garter held its first meeting at Windsor. Several contemporary chroniclers make clear that they saw the Garter as the fulfillment of Edward's earlier vow (with Froissart even conflating the two), but numerous changes had been made to the project in the meantime. Rather than have 300 knights meet in a great hall, only the king, his son Edward Prince of Wales, and 24 knights met for mass in the chapel at Windsor castle. The Garter, indeed, took the form, not of a revived court of King Arthur, but of a lay devotional confraternity of the type then popular in European urban centers. The order was formally dedicated to the Holy Trinity, the Blessed Virgin Mary, St. Edward the Confessor and St. George. Members, dressed in the costume of the order, were to meet every year on St. George's Day at Windsor for mass and afterwards a feast. Members were to be "gentihomme[s] de sang, et chevalier[s] sans reproche," and were sworn to be loyal to the king and not to take up arms against one another. They were promised preferential treatment in any honorable enterprise the sovereign might undertake. Each member occupied his own stall in the chapel, over which he hung a sword, banner, and helmet.[43] Throughout the year a college of priests and 24 "poor knights," resident at Windsor, and supported by an endowment, offered prayers for the souls of the members. If the Round Table was a false start the Garter certainly was not: membership in it was, and remains, one of the highest honors an English sovereign can bestow.

Why the form of Edward's project should have changed so much between its initial proclamation and its eventual realization is somewhat of a mystery. The number of projected members of the Round Table (300) does seem rather unwieldy when compared to the Garter's 26, a number that would have allowed Edward a much better opportunity to ensure that only his most worthy companions-in-arms were rewarded with membership. A reduced membership, combined with confraternal model for the society, also allowed Edward to use the pre-existing chapel at Windsor castle, rather than to continue to build a great hall for the Round Table.[44] In this form Juliet Vale has famously argued that the Garter represented "two finely-balanced tournament teams" of twelve knights each, one led by the king, the other by the Prince of Wales, facing each other on opposite sides of the chapel.[45] One wonders if Edward might have become disenchanted with the original Arthurian theme: the strain

---

[43]   Boulton, *Knights of the Crown*, 129, 138–39.
[44]   Boulton, *Knights of the Crown*, 124.
[45]   Vale, *Edward III and Chivalry*, 91.

of Arthurian literature popular among the aristocracy of fourteenth-century England descended from the romances of Chrétien de Troyes and featured a respected, but passive and cuckolded King Arthur, presiding as the first among equals over a court of knights who engaged in their own illustrious, individual quests. Such a role may not have been one that Edward envisioned for himself and his magnates when he had such an important matter to attend to as the conquest of France: chivalric Arthurianism might have been suitable for tournaments, but it did not necessarily work in war, a fact recently proved at the battle of Crécy in 1346, when the English defeated the French by the rather unchivalric practice of archery.

The most important reason, however, that Edward chose a confraternal model for his society, and thereby ensured St. George a place in it, is that the French were planning to do the same thing. Duke John of Normandy, who succeeded to the throne of France in 1350 as John II, had received six letters from Pope Clement VI in 1344 granting him the right to establish a collegiate church at some place in France to the honor of the Blessed Virgin Mary and St. George. This church was to be staffed by twelve secular canons and twelve priests, and twice a year, on the feast days of St. George and of the Assumption of the Virgin (23 April and 15 August), 200 member knights were to gather, "not for jousts or tournaments or for any other act of arms, but for devotion."[46] This project may have been in response to the announcement of Edward's Round Table, and its confraternal structure may have been inspired by the Hungarian Society of St. George (founded in 1325 by Charles I, king of Hungary and a relation of the French royal house) or by the Order of St. Catherine, an order of knights founded within the previous twelve years in the Dauphiné of Viennois.[47] Edward perhaps heard of it during his campaigns in northern France in the 1340s, and elected to refashion his project along its lines. Edward may have been impressed by the fact that the pope had approved John's project, doubtlessly because it was explicitly formed for the purpose of devotion, not feats of arms, and Edward may have therefore changed the format of his society in the hopes of acquiring similar recognition. The issue that must have alarmed him the most, however, was John's attempt to claim St. George as a patron for his own society. The English king had made use of the saint for some time, but George was still a patron saint of international chivalry and by no means exclusively English. For the French

[46] Boulton, *Knights of the Crown*, 174–75.
[47] Boulton, *Knights of the Crown*, 177.

to start using him in such a public way while they were at war with the English, however, would have been a propaganda disaster for Edward, and something he would have been keen to avert. Edward, therefore, proceeded to make his society a confraternal one, if only so that he could incorporate St. George as one of its patrons. That only one side could have claimed the saint in this context is underscored by the fact that when John's society was finally realized in 1352 as the Order of the Star, it was dedicated to "Our Lady of the Noble House" alone – St. George was no longer listed as one of its patrons.[48]

And St. George certainly *was* the patron of the Order of the Garter. One would not know that from the name of the order and its insignia, a garter in the form of a small blue belt buckled to itself in a circle, nor from the order's motto, *Honi soit qui mal y pense* ("shame be to him who thinks ill of it"), usually written on the garter in gold lettering.[49] This device was

---

[48] Yves Renouard, "L'ordre de la Jarretière et l'ordre de l'Étoile: Étude sur la genese des ordres laïcs de chevalerie et sur le developpement progressif de leur charactère national," *Etudes d'histoire médievale* (Paris: SEVPEN, 1968), 104. Edward was able to found the Garter before John was able to found his own society because the English victory at Crécy in 1346 bestowed great prestige on Edward and gave him something to celebrate, while it left France in disarray, a situation compounded by the plague which ravaged France in the late 1340s. (It should also be noted that John's society almost immediately ran into difficulty when many of its members were killed in an English ambush in Brittany in 1352, and seemed to have effectively ceased operating with John's capture at the battle of Poitiers in 1356.)

[49] Why Edward should have chosen such a title and device for his society has been the subject of much debate. The most familiar story is recorded in Polydore Vergil's *Anglica Historia* (1555): at a ball, possibly held at Calais, a lady of the court dropped her garter and Edward, seeing her embarrassment, picked it up and tied it to his own leg, responding to the jeers of some of the knights present with the words "shame be to him who thinks ill of it," adding that soon many of them would be proud to wear garters. Although knights sometimes did wear articles of female clothing (usually sleeves) as signs of courtly devotion, it is difficult to imagine that Edward would want to name his prestigious society after a feminine undergarment, and the story may have originated as anti-English propaganda at the French court. Another theory is that the garter evolved from a knight's sword belt or strap to hold armor in place, but the device was known from the outset as a garter. Boulton has attempted to show instead that the garter was actually an object of male clothing, but obsolescent enough to be distinctive as a badge of membership, as today the bowler hat might be; Begent and Chesshyre, however, have

reproduced in two-dimensional form on banners, robes, and even bed sheets, and each member knight was required to wear an actual Garter on his left leg below the knee at all times. Furthermore, St. George was only one of four formal patrons of the society, the others being the Blessed Virgin Mary, St. Edward the Confessor and St. Edmund; the Windsor chapel and college of priests to staff it were also dedicated to the Blessed Virgin and St. Edward the Confessor, in addition to St. George.[50] No doubt exists, however, that St. George was the most important of all of them. The Order met every year on the saint's feast day of 23 April, and was even sometimes informally known as the Company of St. George (the chapel and its college of priests soon came to be known by similar designations). The breast badge on the formal habit of the member knights featured a garter encircling the arms of St. George, the well-known red

---

pointed out that garters were indeed worn by men throughout the fourteenth century, thereby discounting the theory of its obsolescence. Still, if men did wear garters in Edward's day, the device may have been chosen simply as an analogue to the insignia and title of the Order of the Band (or Sash), founded in 1330 by Edward III's cousin Alphonso XI of Castile and Leon, and may perhaps have been intended to symbolize the ties of loyalty that were to bind the members of the order together and to King Edward. The garter device, it seems, did predate the foundation of the society by some years: a wardrobe issue roll from c. 1346 records payment for two streamers of worsted powdered with blue garters, possibly for a ship involved in the Crécy campaign. In this context the attributes of the garter would have been far more important than the garter itself: blue and gold were the colors of the royal arms of France, and the motto was also in French, unlike all other mottoes ever used by the king, which were in English. "Shame be to him who thinks ill of it," therefore, most likely refers to Edward's claim to the throne of France. If, as Vale argues, the garter was merely the device of the Crécy campaign, the success of that campaign would have encouraged Edward to enshrine it as the preeminent symbol of his society, the members of which (most of whom had themselves been at Crécy) were sworn to uphold and to prosecute his interests across the channel. See Richard Barber, *Edward Prince of Wales and Aquitaine: A Biography of the Black Prince* (New York: Charles Scribner's Sons, 1978), 85, 87, 256 n. 10; Boulton, *Knights of the Crown*, 155, 157, 158; Peter J. Begent and Hubert Chesshyre, *The Most Noble Order of the Garter: 650 Years* (London: Spink, 1999), 16; Vale, *Edward III and Chivalry*, 79, 81–82.

50 The original chapel, built by Henry III in 1240, had been dedicated to Edward the Confessor; Edward III added Mary and George to the dedication in 1348. *CPR 1348–50* (London: HMSO, 1905), 144.

cross on a white shield.[51] In 1350/51, 4s. were paid to set up a figure of St. George in the chapel, which was later made the centerpiece of a great alabaster reredos.[52] The first seal of the college (figure 7), dating from 1352, featured a figure of Edward III kneeling before an armor-clad figure of St. George, who holds a shield and a lance, and stands under a triple Gothic canopy. The arms of St. Edward the Confessor and St. Edmund flank this tableau, but the full figure of St. George is clearly the most important pictorial element, and the legend around the exterior reads "Sigillum custodies et Capituli S. Georgii de Wyndesores."[53] Over the course of the fourteenth century the chapel acquired some relics of St. George: an inventory of 1384 reveals it possessed a silver gilt reliquary containing two fingers of St. George; an arm of silver plate, with a border of stones, containing part of the arm of St. George; and a chest containing one bone of St. George, part of the tomb of the Virgin Mary, and some of the blood of Thomas of Lancaster. Finally, a record of 1394 shows that 3s. were paid to a goldsmith to repair a table on which the story of St. George was painted.[54]

All this was of immense importance for the cult of St. George in England. The simple prestige of the Garter spread to all things associated with it, including its patron saint. Although very few people got to be members of the Garter, and some of those were foreign allies, admitted for diplomatic purposes, the order quickly became a sort of national institution, which people were aware of and to which all members of the knightly class could aspire (the founding members were not simply the top 24 peers of the realm but included some relatively low-ranking knights). The fact that people did know about the order is revealed by *Wynnere and Wastour*, a poem composed between 1350 and 1370 and celebrating the person of Edward III: the author of the poem feels confident about translating the Garter's motto into English as "Hethyng have the hathell that any harme thynkes," without fearing that its significance

51   Boulton, *Knights of the Crown*, 156 (figure 4.6), 161. Member knights came to encircle their own shields with representations of the garter, a practice that continues to this day, most familiar from the royal arms themselves. See Begent and Chesshyre, *Most Noble Order*, 193–96.

52   Brown, Colvin and Taylor, *History of the King's Works*, 873.

53   J.N. Dalton, *The Manuscripts of St. George's Chapel* (Windsor: Oxley and Son, 1957), xxxiv, pl. II.

54   Maurice F. Bond, *The Inventories of St. George's Chapel* (Windsor: Oxley and Son, 1947), 57, 59, 61, 93.

would be lost on the audience.[55] The poem also describes Edward's tent arrayed "With Ynglysse besantes full brighte, betyn of golde, / and ichone gayly umbygone with garters of inde, / and iche a gartere of golde gerede full riche," and later, Edward himself wearing "A grete gartere of ynde, gerede full riche."[56] Furthermore, *Sir Gawain and the Green Knight*, a fourteenth-century Arthurian poem written in the north-west Midlands dialect, has as its final line the Garter motto "Hony soyt q mal pence." Whether or not this line was added by later hand, by establishing a connection between the chivalry of the poem and that of the real-life Order, it illustrates the latter's widespread appeal.[57]

Such prestige was matched with money: St. George's Day became one of the most important days of the calendar in terms of expenditure celebrating it. Extant household records indicate that for most years following 1348, Edward celebrated St. George's feast day by spending approximately ten times the regular amounts on food, wine and service.[58] The regularity and longevity of the Garter celebrations were also important: the Garter met yearly for the remaining thirty or so years of Edward's life, and continued to do so after his death, since his successors had little reason to do away with his foundation, which was in any case well-endowed and did not impose onerous burdens on its members. This gave St. George a permanence in English court life. The situation of the Garter ceremony also worked to the advantage of its patron saint: George was a military saint, and most members of the Garter were military men, but the ceremonies of the Garter were fundamentally devotional, not military, and they took place both in times of war and in times of peace, and well away from any fighting that may have been going on. As such the Garter helped St. George to bridge the gap between military and civilian life. All of these factors combined to set George on the road to being the patron saint of the English nation: it is surely significant that

---

[55] *Wynnere and Wastoure*, ed. S. Trigg, EETS 297 (Oxford: EETS, 1990), 4 (line 68).

[56] *Wynnere and Wastoure*, 4 (lines 61–63), 5 (line 94).

[57] Israel Gollancz, ed., *Pearl, Cleanness, Patience and Sir Gawain: Reproduced in Facsimile from the Unique MS Cotton Nero A.x in the British Museum*, EETS 210 (London: EETS, 1923), 124v. See also W.M. Ormrod, "For Arthur and St George: Edward III, Windsor Castle and the Order of the Garter," in *St George's Chapel Windsor in the Fourteenth Century*, ed. Nigel Saul (Woodbridge, Suffolk: Boydell, 2005), 13–34, at 30.

[58] PRO E 36 204, f. 43v; E 101 393/11, f. 10; E 101 393/11, f. 47; E 101 396/2, f. 8v; E 101 397/5, f. 28v; E 101 398/9, f. 15v.

letters patent issued in 1351 refer to the chapel at Windsor as having been "erected by the king in the castle of Windsor in honour of the blessed George, the most invincible athlete of Christ, whose name and protection the English race invoke as that of their peculiar patron, especially in war."[59]

George did, of course, remain important to the English military effort. An account of naval expenses of 1360 reveals three ships named George, and an issue roll to the captains of ships, composed between 1370 and 1376, shows that banners of the arms of St. George, along with banners of the quartered arms of the king, had become standard issue to all ships under the king's command.[60] This connection between the king and St. George is further underscored in an account of John de Haytfeld, the king's armorer: in 1370, he ordered 134 worsted standards of the arms of St. George "with leopards in the chief."[61] These leopards came from the royal arms of England, and would have clearly proclaimed, "St. George is on the side of King Edward."

Other pieces of evidence from the reign of Edward III illustrate the importance of George to the English crown, in both official and personal capacities. An example of the former is a new design for the Great Seal of England that was cut in 1360, as a result of the treaty of Brétigny by which Edward (momentarily) renounced the title "King of France." The seal did not include this title in its legend, although it did depict Edward's shield as the quartered arms of France and England. On the obverse, flanking the enthroned Edward III, appeared the Virgin Mary, holding the Christ child, and St. George, dressed in armor and carrying his red-cross shield.[62] The seal, with modifications to its legend, remained in use until 1408. Another piece of evidence for the importance of St. George to Edward III, in this case on a more personal level, is a series of wall paintings on the east wall of St. Stephen's chapel in the royal palace of Westminster. They show Edward III and by his (by then) five sons kneeling in a row; at the head of the row, reaching back to encourage the king, is St. George. These paintings were destroyed c. 1800 but are known through several copies made of them, including one by Robert Smirke, kept by the Society of Antiquaries. They show each figure armed with a sword and a dagger and dressed in mail, with his legs and arms protected by plate armor and

[59] CPR 1350–54 (London: HMSO, 1907), 127.
[60] PRO E 101 27/24; E 101 30/13, m. 1–3.
[61] PRO E 101 30/16, m. 2.
[62] Alfred Wyon, The Great Seals of England from the Earliest Period to the Present Time (London: Elliot Stock, 1887), 37 and pl. X, no. 63.

his head by a helmet, and wearing a surcoat of arms for identification.[63] Finally, Edward possessed a relic of the blood of St. George,[64] and remembered St. George in his almsgiving. The king's almoner regularly distributed alms to 100 paupers to the value of 1.5d. each on St. George's Day "in honor of the saint,"[65] although of course many other saints were so honored. The Garter festivities, however, usually included devotional expenditure in addition to expenditure on feasting: in 1354, 1366, 1371 and 1377 Edward left alms to the value of 6s. 8d. at the great altar in the chapel of St. George at Windsor.[66]

Edward III, therefore, resurrected both his grandfather's military success and his use of St. George, the former of which further justified and popularized the latter. The Order of the Garter was Edward III's major innovation: just as Edward I had prescribed the cross of St. George to common soldiers, so now did the chivalric elite enjoy their own, shared use of St. George with the king. That the Garter ceremonies took place every year, and were supported by a college, gave St. George an institutional place in the kingdom independent of the tastes of the reigning monarch. This institutionalization became fully apparent in the reign of Edward's grandson and successor, Richard II, who ascended to the throne in 1377 at the age of ten. Over the next two decades the banner of St. George appeared repeatedly in connection with the authority of the monarch, who was for much of it a minor and not active in the daily governance of his kingdom, indicating how routine and "impersonal" the connection had become.

The Ordinances of War for the Scottish campaign of 1385, for instance, commanded that everyone in the English army, regardless of rank, was to wear a large sign of the arms of St. George on his front and back, and promised death to any enemy found so dressed.[67] The ordinances also proclaimed that anyone who led off a certain part of the army with a

---

63 E.W. Tristram, *English Wall Painting of the Fourteenth Century* (London: Routledge and Kegan Paul, 1955), pl. 5.

64 PRO E 101 385/19, f. 10.

65 BL Cotton Nero VIII, f. 203v; PRO E 101 388/5, m. 7; E 36 203, f. 88; E 36 204, f. 73v; E 101 393/11, f. 35, f. 61.

66 PRO E 101 393/11, f. 34; E 101 396/2, f. 30; E 101 397/5, f. 31; E 101 398/9, f. 23.

67 The Scots and French were ordered to wear the cross of St. Andrew, a white "X" on a blue field, for a counter-invasion. See J.H. Stevenson, *Heraldry in Scotland* (Glasgow: James Maclehose and Sons, 1914), 404 and n. 1.

banner or pennon of St. George, as though he were a captain, would be drawn and hanged, and anyone who followed would be beheaded and have his estate forfeited to the king.[68] Even though this expedition represented the last feudal summons in England,[69] Richard's agents still felt at liberty to prescribe a uniform for the entire army, with St. George in the lead. Ninety-two standards of the arms of St. George were in fact ordered for the Scottish campaign; that they were standards (not pennoncels), and that each one had a leopard in its chief, illustrate that they were indeed symbolic of royal command.[70]

This function of the banner of St. George was also seen, and explicitly acknowledged as such, in 1387. The Lords Appellant, a group of five lords parallel to the Ordainers of Edward II's reign, had put Richard under virtual house arrest, and Richard's close friend Robert de Vere, earl of Oxford and duke of Ireland, led a force to rescue him. The Appellants met De Vere at Radcot Bridge, near Oxford, where the earl "roused the fighting spirit of his troops and, raising the standard of St George, disposed his lines in battle order."[71] De Vere and his forces were defeated and he fled the kingdom; tried *in absentia*, he was condemned to death partly for "accroaching to himself royal power [by causing] the king's banner to be displayed in his company, contrary to the dignity of the King and his Crown."[72] Such dignity, in their view, was rightfully under their control. This event was even remembered in the 1399 articles of deposition against Richard, who was accused of inciting men "to rise up against the said lords and magnates of the kingdom and servants of the republic, [by raising] his standard against the peace which he had sworn publicly to keep."[73] It is clear, therefore, that by the late 1380s, the banner of St. George, "the king's banner," represented the crown as an institution, something that the "king's party" could not simply claim for itself.

[68] *Monumenta juridica: The Black Book of the Admiralty*, ed. Travers Twiss (London: Rolls Series, 1871), 1: 456.

[69] N.B. Lewis, "The Last Medieval Summons of the English Feudal Levy, 13 June 1385," *English Historical Review* 73 (1958): 1–26.

[70] John H. Harvey, "The Wilton Diptych: A Re-examination," *Archaeologia* 98 (1961): 21 and n. 8, quoting PRO E 364/30.

[71] *The Westminster Chronicle, 1381–1394*, eds. L.C. Hector and Barbara F. Harvey (Oxford: Clarendon Press, 1982), 220–23.

[72] *Chronicon Henrici Knighton*, ed. J.R. Lumby (London: Rolls Series, 1895), 2: 290; *Westminster Chronicle*, 268/69.

[73] *Rotuli Parliamentorum*, ed. J. Strachey (London, 1783), 3: 418 [item 20].

Such anxiety over the banner of St. George, both as far as the Appellants and even the ordinances of the 1385 invasion of Scotland were concerned, may partly be explained by one of the banner's most remarkable appearances in the entire reign. In the Great Revolt of 1381, according to the *Anonimalle Chronicle*, an army of commoners arrived at Blackheath, some three leagues from London, on 12 June and displayed two banners of St. George and sixty pennons.[74] A new poll tax, perceived as heavy-handed and unfair, coupled with simmering resentment over the Statute of Labourers of 1351, which had attempted to fix laborers' wages, motivated peasants in Kent and Essex to march on London. There they were joined by disaffected Londoners for three days of destruction, aimed mostly at the property of those deemed responsible for the tax, such as the king's uncle John of Gaunt. In the context of such an organized revolt, it is tempting to posit that the protestors of England saw St. George's cross as a truly national symbol, something that had been prescribed for them in war and that they were now free to use independently of the king's command, that could even symbolize the commons' collective identity *against* the king, implying that he had betrayed the real England. It is likely that some of them did feel this way. But while this may be how the banners and pennons of the *Anonimalle Chronicle* appear at face value, it is more likely that most participants in the Great Revolt held up the cross of St. George simply as the royal badge that by this time it had become. The rebels were not seeking to overturn the social order so much as to acquire greater respect within it, and to this end repeatedly expressed loyalty to King Richard, while disapproving of the conduct of his ministers.[75] Of course, such usage did not follow protocol: the commons did not want "war" as such, and they were certainly displaying the banners outside the king's direct command. The Great Revolt does, however, indicate that most of the civilian population, at least in the south-east, was aware that the banner of St. George was intimately connected to the authority of the king.

One final use of the banner of St. George during Richard's reign may be examined. The famous Wilton Diptych (figure 8), most likely painted during the late 1390s as a portable altarpiece for the king's personal use, shows on its left interior panel Richard kneeling, surrounded by figures representing Saints Edmund, Edward the Confessor, and John the Baptist. Each figure possesses familiar iconographical attributes. Edmund, dressed

---

74 R.B. Dobson, *The Peasants' Revolt of 1381* (London: Macmillan, 1970), 129.
75 Dobson, *Peasants' Revolt*, 127.

as a king, holds one of the arrows of his martyrdom. Edward the Confessor, also dressed as a king, holds a ring in reference to the legend of how he gave his ring to a beggar who turned out to be John the Evangelist.[76] John the Baptist is shown as an emaciated wild man, dressed in rough clothing and holding a lamb, referring to his words "Behold the Lamb of God," from John 1: 36. On the right panel, the Blessed Virgin Mary holds the infant Jesus. The two are surrounded by eleven angels, dressed in blue robes and each wearing, as is Richard himself, a breast badge of a white hart and a collar of broom cod. One of the angels holds a pole from which flies a white, forked banner with a plain red cross on it. The infant Jesus gestures toward this banner, while Richard's hands are open, perhaps in order to receive it. The Diptych is one of the finest pieces of late-medieval English art, and like most art, its meaning has been highly contested.[77] A possibility exists that its banner may not even that of St. George: *Argent, a cross Gules* did represent St. George in late medieval England, but normally such a device was depicted on a square standard or banner, or triangular pennoncel. The forked tail of the banner in the Diptych, however, implies very strongly that it is in fact the so-called banner of the redemption, commonly held by Christ in depictions of his resurrection, such as those by Piero della Francesca (c. 1460) or Ambrogio Bergnone (c. 1510). Nevertheless, several medieval illustrations of St. George holding a forked banner exist;[78] moreover, the pole of the banner of the redemption is usually surmounted by a small cross, while the pole of the Diptych banner is topped by a small orb.[79] A cleaning of the Diptych in the early 1990s has revealed that on this orb appears a miniature painting of a green

[76] The story makes its first appearance in the *Vita Sancti Aedwardi Confessoris* by Aelred of Rievaulx; see *PL* 195, cols. 769–70.

[77] See, *inter alia*, M.V. Clarke, "The Wilton Diptych," *Fourteenth Century Studies*, eds. L.S. Sutherland and M. McKisack (Oxford: Clarendon Press, 1937), 272–92; Francis Wormald, "The Wilton Diptych," *Journal of the Warburg and Courtauld Institutes* 17 (1954): 191–203; J.H. Harvey, "The Wilton Diptych"; Charles T. Wood, *Joan of Arc and Richard III: Sex, Saints, and Government in the Middle Ages* (New York and Oxford: Oxford University Press, 1984), 75–90; Sumner Ferris, "The Wilton Diptych and the Absolutism of Richard II," *Journal of the Rocky Mountain Medieval and Renaissance Association* 8 (1987): 33–66.

[78] E.g. on the rood screen at Hampstead Church, Norfolk, reproduced in J. Lewis André, "Saint George the Martyr, In Legend, Ceremonial, Art, Etc.," *Archaeological Journal* 57 (1900): second plate after 215.

[79] A point made in Harvey, "Wilton Diptych" at 21 and n. 6. One might also add, with Nigel Morgan, that "it would be very odd for the Christ as a Child

island, with a white castle and green trees against a blue sky, and a boat in the foreground sailing on a sea of now-tarnished silver leaf. Dillian Gordon has explained the significance of this detail by comparing it to an altarpiece formerly in the English College in Rome. The altarpiece showed Richard and his first wife Anne of Bohemia being presented by George and other saints to the Blessed Virgin Mary; Richard himself offered to the Virgin a "globe or patterne of England," and at the base of the altarpiece was the legend: "Dos tua, Virgo pia, Haec est, quare rege, Maria," that is, "This is your dowry, O holy Virgin, wherefore, O Mary, may you rule over it." The island in the orb of the Wilton Diptych may therefore, by analogy, be the island of Britain: Richard in one painting has offered Britain to the Virgin as her dowry, and in another waits to receive it back from her and her son so that he may rule it under their guidance. The idea that England was the Virgin's dowry was fairly widespread by the early fifteenth century: in 1400, Archbishop Arundel claimed that the English were "humble servants of her [the Virgin's] inheritance and the liegemen of her especial dower," and Thomas Elmham, in his metrical life of Henry V composed c. 1420, wrote that England was "Dos tua ... Mater pia, Virgo Maria, Henrico Rege, tu tua jura rege."[80] The banner of the Diptych, therefore, is most likely that of St. George, and acts in the painting as it then did on the field of battle, as a symbol of royal authority; even, according to Sumner Ferris, of Richard's ideas of royal absolutism.[81] The Wilton Diptych, however, does not depict a military scene, and the significance of the banner here is that it represents royal authority in an abstract, all-encompassing way, quite apart from the chain of military command in Scotland or at Radcot Bridge.

Richard himself, however, did not have much personal affection for St. George. About the only evidence for it is an ivory mirror he owned with a figure of St. George carved on the back, hardly a significant detail.[82] The

---

to bless a banner representing His own Resurrection in the context of the imagery of the Diptych." See Nigel Morgan, "The Signification of the Banner in the Wilton Diptych," in *The Regal Image of Richard II and the Wilton Diptych*, eds. Dillian Gordon, Lisa Monas and Caroline Elam (London: Harvey Miller, 1997), 179–88, at 180.

80 Dillian Gordon, "A new discovery in the Wilton Diptych," *Burlington Magazine* 134 (1992): 662–67.
81 Ferris, "Wilton Diptych," 43.
82 *The Antient Kalendars and Inventories of the Treasury of His Majesty's Exchequer*, ed. Francis Palgrave (London: Public Records Commissioners, 1836), 3: 332.

Wilton Diptych was most likely intended for Richard's personal use and can therefore be thought to closely reflect the king's devotional habits, and apart from the banner, St. George appears nowhere on it. Instead, we need to consider the central, dominating figure of the left interior panel: Edward the Confessor. The saint held a very strong appeal for Richard. The fact that Richard had not produced an heir, like St. Edward, may have come into it, although there is no evidence that Richard and his wife Anne of Bohemia had a chaste marriage, as Edward had reputedly had with his wife Edith.[83] Richard prayed at Edward's shrine at Westminster before meeting the rebels at Smithfield in 1381, a habit he continued in 1387 before the battle of Radcot Bridge, in 1392 at the reconciliation ceremony with the city of London, and in 1397 after the oath-swearing ceremony with Parliament.[84] Richard also lavished gifts on the Confessor's shrine and the abbey that housed it, such as a ring of gold with a "costly and valuable ruby" set in it and a rich set of vestments, and tried to ensure that the rebuilding of the church in the newly-fashionable Gothic style, begun by King Henry III and halted at his death, was completed.[85] Wardrobe books from Richard's reign show that the king treated the feast of the translation of St. Edward, 13 October, with a certain respect, hiring Dominican friars to preach and spending above-average amounts on food and wine.[86]

Perhaps the greatest evidence of Richard's esteem for St. Edward is heraldic. If we close the Wilton Diptych, we find the arms of the saint, which can be described as *Azure, a cross patonce between five martlets Or*, impaled with Richard's own on one of the exterior panels. Richard had employed these arms before: in 1389 the king made a grant to Nicholas Adams for having carried "our banner of St. Edward" in the Scottish campaign of 1385; the City of London was required to display the arms of St. Edward on London Bridge, along with statues of the king and queen, during the reconciliation ceremony of 1392; and for the Irish expedition of 1394–95, according to the chronicler Jean Froissart, Richard gave up

---

83   See Dyan Elliott, *Spiritual Marriage: Sexual Abstinence in Medieval Wedlock* (Princeton: Princeton University Press, 1993), 120–22, and Katherine Lewis, "Becoming a Virgin King: Richard II and Edward the Confessor," in *Gender and Holiness*, eds. S.J.E. Riches and Sarah Salih (London and New York: Routledge, 2002), 86–100.

84   *Westminster Chronicle*, 8–10, 206–09, 506–07; *Rotuli Parliamentorum*, 3: 355.

85   Nigel Saul, *Richard II* (New Haven and London: Yale University Press, 1997), 312–13, 315–16.

86   See, e.g., PRO E 101 402/10, f. 7, f. 33; PRO E 101 402/20, f. 8; PRO E 101 403/10, f. 35–35v; PRO E 101 402/5, f. 26.

the quartered arms of France and England and bore instead the arms of St. Edward.[87] But the adoption of the impaled arms, done publicly by the year 1397, was unlike anything that had gone before in royal heraldry, and it appeared in all manifestations of the royal arms: besides the Wilton Diptych, records exist that the impaled arms were etched on a number of Richard's silver vessels, engraved on his signet ring, and sewn on a red velvet mantel mentioned in his final wardrobe book.[88] Heraldic impalement normally expresses a close, personal connection, such as the one between husband and wife, or between an office and its holder, particularly that of a diocese and its bishop. The expression of such a "mystic union" between Richard II and his spiritual patron might have been heartfelt on Richard's part, but the usage struck some contemporaries as eccentric. The monastic author of the *Annales Ricardi Secundi* recorded that, on account of his "pride" and "vain thoughts," Richard changed his arms, "which his father and grandfather and uncles bore, and added to his shield the arms of St. Edward, so that arms of the saint took up the front part, and in the rest one could recognize the arms of his ancestors."[89] The king, the chronicler insinuates, has dishonored his ancestors by changing their arms according to a personal whim – one can almost detect the same tone that people had used to describe King Edward II when he lavished favors on the low-born Gascon knight Piers Gaveston earlier in the century.

According to Nigel Saul the "peacefulness" of Edward the Confessor was what appealed to Richard, as it had earlier to Henry III.[90] All medieval

---

[87] *CPR 1388–92*, 168; Caroline Barron, "The Quarrel of Richard II with London, 1392–97," in *The Reign of Richard II: Essays in Honour of May McKisack*, eds. F.R.H. DuBoulay and Caroline M. Barron (London: Athalone Press, 1971), 196, citing Guildhall Record Office, Bridge House Accounts Roll 12 m. 8, 9, 10; Jean Froissart, *Oeuvres de Froissart* 15 *Chroniques 1392–1396*, ed. Kervyn de Lettenhove (Brussels: Victor Devaux, 1871), 180–81. Froissart claims that Richard used the arms of St. Edward in Ireland because the Irish kings had sworn allegiance to Edward the Confessor in the eleventh century, and would do so for Richard if the king positioned himself as Edward's heir.

[88] Shelagh Mitchell, "Richard II: Kingship and the Cult of Saints," in *The Regal Image of Richard II and the Wilton Diptych*, eds Dillian Gordon, Lisa Monas, and Caroline Elam (London: Harvey Miller, 1997), 115–24, at 117.

[89] John Trokelowe and Henry Blandeford, *Chronica et Annales, Regnantibus Henrico Tertio, Edwardo Primo, Edwardo Secundo, Ricardo Secundo, et Henrico Quarto* (London: Rolls Series, 1866) 3: 223.

[90] Saul, *Richard II*, 312.

kings, of course, favored "peace," although most had no compunction against fighting to achieve it, and Edward the Confessor could help England at war, as we have seen when Edward I took his banner into Scotland. Richard, however, found in St. Edward, the peaceful king, a justification for not prosecuting the war in France. The war's expense and its lack of current victories may have made it unpopular by the 1390s, but certain professional warriors saw in the peace a loss of livelihood. Furthermore, the diplomatic terms that Richard was willing to accept – liege homage to the king of France in return for holding Aquitaine – in return for a truce were highly unpopular among the English gentry, who saw them as a betrayal of the whole point of the fifty-year-old war and an unconscionable surrendering of their king's liberties, from which depended their own.[91]

The problem, however, went deeper than a proposed truce with France. "Peace," to Richard, was something that he was meant to enforce in his own kingdom: on account of his belief in his own divine right to rule, it became synonymous with unquestioned obedience from his subjects.[92] This became fully apparent in 1397, when Richard started to demand forced loans from his subjects and arbitrarily arrested, and later executed, the three senior Lords Appellant. Edward the Confessor was deeply implicated in this absolutist project. Immediately following the announcement of the arrests in Parliament, the leading lords were taken to Westminster Abbey where they were made to swear their loyalty to the king at St. Edward's shrine.[93] It was during this time that Richard most likely had the Wilton Diptych painted (with its illustration of the return of the royal banner to himself) and publicly adopted his new arms. The latter action perfectly encapsulated the problem: it was arbitrary, based on a personal whim and an affront to the dignity of the kingdom – and St. Edward himself was at the center of the imbroglio. It would not have helped that Richard granted, to five dukes he created in 1397 (the so-called *duketti*), the right to impale their own arms with those of the Confessor:[94]

---

[91] Saul, *Richard II*, 219–21.

[92] In a letter to Byzantine Emperor Manuel Palaeologus in 1398, Richard declined to aid Manuel against the Turks, on account of his recent expenditure tramping down the "necks of the proud and mighty," and grinding them down "not to the bark only, but even to the root," and thereby restoring "to our subjects peace." See A.R. Myers, ed., *English Historical Documents* 4 *1327–1485* (London: Eyre and Spottiswoode, 1969), 174–75.

[93] *Rotuli Parliamentorum*, 3: 355.

[94] Clarke, "Wilton Diptych," 275.

1   Bayeux Tapestry, English, eleventh cent. (detail): King Harold beneath his dragon
    standard.

2 Lambeth Apocalypse, English, mid-thirteenth cent., f. 45v: The Virgin Mary raises and arms St. Mercurius.

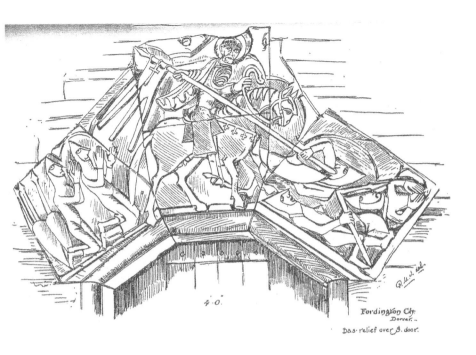

Fordington Ch.
Dorset.
Das relief over S. door.

3   Tympanum, Fordington, Dorset, twelfth cent.: St. George appears to the crusaders and slays Muslims.

4   Picture Bible, northern French, c. 1200, f. 1r (detail): St. George, bearing an early version of his arms, slays Muslims at Jerusalem.

5 Milemete Treatise, 1326–27, f. 3r.: St. George and ostensibly Edward III, in actuality Edward II. University of Oxford, Christ Church College Library, MS 92.

6   Douce Hours, c. 1325–30, f. 1r: St. George and St. Thomas of Lancaster. University of Oxford, Bodleian Library MS Douce 231.

7   (Opposite, top.) Seal of St. George's College, Windsor: St. George and Edward III. London, National Archives.

8   (Opposite, bottom.) The Wilton Diptych, English or French, c. 1397: Richard II, attended by Saints Edmund, Edward, and John the Baptist, receives the banner of St. George from the Blessed Virgin Mary.

9   Bedford Hours, French, c. 1425, f. 256v: The Duke of Bedford before St. George. London, British Library, Add. MS 18850.

10 Talbot Shrewsbury Book of Romances, French, c. 1445, f. 439: Henry VI and Garter knights venerate St. George. London, British Library, Royal MS 15 E VI.

11 Anon., *The Family of Henry VII with St. George and the Dragon*, 1505–09.

12 Reverse, English halfpenny, 1672: Britannia, after the Duchess of Richmond.

13 Reverse, English gold sovereign, 1817: the earliest version of Benedetto Pistrucci's classical St. George and the dragon.

14 Sir Edward Coley Burne-Jones, *Saint George*, 1877. Wadsworth Atheneum Museum of Art, Hartford, Conn.

15 Boy Scout Holy Card, twentieth cent.: Jesus instructs a group of boy scouts, while their patron kills a dragon behind them.

16   Recruiting Poster, British, 1915.

17 Pietermaritzburg, South Africa, 1920s: World War I memorial.

18 Wembley Stadium, London, 1 June 2007: An English football fan, dressed as St. George, cheers for his team as it plays against Brazil.

Richard was marking out his close supporters with the sign of St. Edward, at a time when he was politically alienating many other people in the kingdom. St. Edward, therefore, was directly associated with, and even justified, Richard's attempted absolutism, and for the time being represented the king at his worst; St. George, by contrast, now represented the memory of the king at his best: Edward III, who had worked with Parliament and who fought for his rights abroad, bringing honor and glory to the kingdom. It is surely significant that the Canterbury convocation petitioned, in 1399, the year of Richard's deposition, that "the feast of St. George the martyr, who is the spiritual patron of all English soldiers … ought to be instituted through all England and solemnly celebrated, just as other nations celebrate their patrons' feast days."[95] This petition may be seen as a rebuke to Richard, who had abandoned the arts of good kingship, like the rebuke delivered earlier to Edward II in the *Douce Hours*. The petition was effective: a list of feast-days for the province of Canterbury in 1400 included St. George for the first time.[96] St. Edward continued to be venerated by the kings of England, but his popular appeal, never great to begin with, was permanently damaged.

As bad a king as Richard II may have been, however, his successor, Henry of Lancaster, was himself a usurper. The founder of the Lancastrian dynasty was therefore compelled to deal with persistent challenges to his legitimacy, ranging from the recurring rumor that Richard II was still alive to the Percy rebellions of the years 1403, 1405, and 1408. The political position of St. George during Henry IV's reign, therefore, seems almost a continuation of that of Richard II. The saint was employed officially, including at Garter festivities, as the name of four royal ships, and on a new seal cut in 1408.[97] St. George was even one of six saints depicted on windows in the king's study in his palace at Eltham.[98] But Archbishop Richard Scrope of York, who elected to join the 1405 rebellion, issued a manifesto that referred to St. George as the "special protector and advocate of the kingdom of England."[99] Such an acknowledgement, and in such a

---

95 *Concilia Magnae Britanniae et Hiberniae*, ed. D. Wilkins (London: s.n., 1737), 2: 241.
96 Cheney, "Rules," 133.
97 PRO E 101 404/21, f. 23; PRO E 101 39/2, m. 2; Wyon, *Great Seals of England*, pl. XII, no. 73.
98 Brown, Colvin and Taylor, *History of the King's Works*, 935.
99 David A.L. Morgan, "The Cult of Saint George c. 1500: National and International Connotations," in *L'angleterre et les pays bourguignons: relations et comparisons XVe–XVIe siècles*, ed. Jean-Marie Cauchies (Neuchatel: Centre européen d'études bourguignonnes [XIVe–XVIe s.], 1995), 151–62, at 155, n. 20.

document, may be considered another rebuke to the reigning monarch, on the order of the 1399 petition to have St. George recognized as England's patron saint. According to Scrope, St. George was the patron of an England existing independently of the king, an England that could hold the king accountable for his misgovernance. In this case it failed (Scrope was executed and became himself the object of a religious cult), but the manifesto indicates how St. George, by the early fifteenth century, had started to become a truly national saint indeed.

But this disjunction between St. George as patron of the king and St. George as patron of the nation was to be healed in the reign of Henry's son and successor, Henry V, who came to the throne in 1413. Throughout his reign Henry made copious use of St. George, to whom the king was genuinely devoted in the manner of Edward I and Edward III. It was during this time, therefore, that the growing sense that George was the patron saint of the English nation, as revealed by the petition of 1399 and Scrope's manifesto of 1405, linked up with the proper, old-fashioned royal veneration of St. George. This veneration was matched with military success: Henry renewed the war in France and defeated the French soundly at Agincourt, subdued Normandy, and even had himself designated regent and heir of the kingdom of France with the Treaty of Troyes in 1420. These events justified Henry and they justified St. George, and the publicity surrounding them cemented the place of the saint in the English consciousness.

Both Henry's personal and public uses of the saint were manifold. The king owned tapestries of St. George and other military heroes, and offered devotions to the Trinity, the Holy Spirit, St. Edward, St. John the Baptist, St. George, and St. Mary on a daily basis, including at Westminster before leaving for France in 1415, and again at Canterbury on his way to France in 1416.[100] Echoing the statutes of Richard II's 1385 campaign in Scotland, he ordered every man in the army to wear a large red cross of St. George on the chest and back.[101] When he arrived at Harfleur he put up the flag of St. George there,[102] and famously invoked the aid of St. George at the battle of Agincourt in 1415, crying "in the name of Almyghti God and Saynt George, avaunt banarer! and Saynte George, this day thyn help!"[103]

---

[100] *Gesta Henrici Quinti: The Deeds of Henry the Fifth*, eds. Frank Taylor and John S. Roskell (Oxford: Clarendon Press, 1975), 153; Nicholas Harris Nicolas, *History of the Battle of Agincourt*, 2nd edn. (London: Johnson and Co., 1832), 24.
[101] *Black Book*, 1: 464.
[102] *Gesta Henrici Quinti*, 55.
[103] *The Brut, or the Chronicles of England*, ed. Friedrich W.D. Brie, EETS 136 (London: EETS, 1908), 2: 378.

Agincourt was of course a stunning victory for Henry, and the legend even grew up later that St. George was seen in the sky prior to the battle, as he had been seen at Antioch during the first crusade.[104] People then started "presenting" Henry's hero back to him: the triumphal reception into London following the victory featured a large statue of George in armor save for his head, holding in his right hand a sword and in his left a scroll bearing the motto: *Soli deo honor et Gloria*,[105] and in 1416, the Emperor Sigismund was inducted into the Order of the Garter, and gave Henry a gold statue of St. George and a relic of St. George's heart.[106] Henry even induced the Church to elevate the feast of St. George ("the special patron and protector of the nation") to the status of *magis duplex*, or greater double, which was done for the province of Canterbury in 1416 and for the province of York in 1421.[107] All this cemented St. George's place in English political life, and Henry's early death in 1422 helped cement it further by providing a "good" memory that could not be tarnished. The Bedford Hours (London, BL Add. MS 18850), commissioned by Henry's brother and regent for France, Duke John of Bedford, shows in a large illustration on one folio Duke John kneeling before St. George, who is dressed not only in a surcoat of *Argent, a cross Gules* but also the blue

---

104   R.T. Davies, ed., *Medieval English Lyrics: A Critical Anthology* (London: Faber, 1966), 155; Charles Augustus Cole, ed., *Memorials of Henry the Fifth of England* (London: Rolls Series, 1858), 123; John Capgrave, *Liber de Illustribus Henricis*, ed. Francis Charles Hingeston (London: Rolls Series, 1858), 117; Nicolas, *Agincourt*, appendix, 76. John Schwetman, in "The Appearance of Saint George above the English Troops at Agincourt: The Source of a Detail in the Historical Record," *Notes and Queries* 239 (Sept. 1994): 304–07, suggests that this legend grew up from a misunderstanding about the banner of St. George raised above the English troops.

105   *Gesta Henrici Quinti*, 105; see also 119 for a poem, formerly attributed to John Lydgate, a stanza of which describes the statue. See also Adam Usk, *Chronicon Adae de Usk AD 1377–1421*, ed. E.M. Thompson, 2nd edn. (London: Henry Froude, 1904), 128.

106   *The St. Albans Chronicle 1406–1420*, ed. V.H. Galbraith (Oxford: Clarendon Press, 1937), 100; James Hamilton Wylie and William Templeton Waugh, *The Reign of Henry the Fifth* (Cambridge: Cambridge University Press, 1929), 3: 13–14.

107   *The Register of Henry Chichele, Archbishop of Canterbury, 1414–1443*, ed. E.F. Jacob (Oxford: Oxford University Press, 1937–47), 3: 8–10 (quotation at 9); *Register of Thomas Langley, Bishop of Durham 1416–1437*, ed. R.L. Storey (Durham and London: Surtees Society 1959), 3: 5.

robes of the order of the Garter (figure 9). Benedicta Rowe has argued that the likeness of St. George is actually that of Henry V, whose legacy the English are to uphold.[108]

Henry V was survived by his infant son, who became Henry VI of England; on the death of Charles VI later in 1422, Henry also became king of France by the provisions of the Treaty of Troyes. Henry VI's career was not a very successful one: when he finally attained his majority, his general indifference to ruling well was punctuated only by periodic bouts of insanity, and Henry witnessed the English possessions on the continent dwindle away and England itself descend into civil war. It comes as no surprise, therefore, that most of the royal use of St. George during Henry's reign was not by the king himself but on his behalf, either as propaganda or out of hope that he would come to take his duties seriously. One soteltie (set piece pastry confection) served at Henry's English coronation banquet featured Saints George and Denis; the court poet John Lydgate wrote a rhyming commentary on it:

> O blessed Lady, Cristes moder dere,
> And thou seint George, that callid art his knight;
> Holy Seint Denyse, O martir moost entire,
> The sixt Henry here present in your sight,
> Sewith of grace on hym your hevenly light,
> His tender yougth with vertue doth avaunce,
> Bore by discent and title of right
> Iustly to reigne in England and in Fraunce.[109]

Shortly after his English coronation, Henry VI was sent to France to be crowned in right of that kingdom. One poem about this event, "Speed the King on His Journey" (from Lambeth MS 344), beseeches a number of saints to protect the king as he crosses the channel; St. George, unlike all the other saints mentioned in the poem, is mentioned in two stanzas:

> Seynt george, oure ladyes knight
> On whom all englond hath byleve,
> Shew vs thy helpe to god almyght,
> And kepe our kyng from all myscheve,

---

[108] B.J.H. Rowe, "The Clovis Miniature and the Bedford Portrait," *Journal of the British Archaeological Association* 25 (1962): 62–65.

[109] John Lydgate, *The Minor Poems of John Lydgate*, ed. Henry Noble MacCracken, EETS 192 (London: EETS, 1934), 624.

Thy art oure patronesse knyght y-poeve
To defene wyth fyght oure ladyes fe,
Seynt george, by oure helpe yn all oure greve,
        Saluum fac regem domine.

…

Swete seynt george, take to oure kyng heed,
To hys lynage and to other lordes all yn fere,
They mowe haue grace well to speed
And couere hem alle vnder thy banere.
To that gloryose gemme that shyneth so clere,
Gooddes moder and mayd of pyte,
Devoutly seyth all that bene here
        Saluum fac regem domine.[110]

Another poem about the event, "Mary, Take in your Hand this Dread Voyage" (in Arundel MS 249) is in a similar vein. The Virgin Mary, the Archangel Michael, and Saints Katherine, Alban, George and Mary Magdalene are asked to protect Henry on his voyage. The George stanza reads:

Blessed seynt Gorge, most in oure remembrance,
A-geynyst oure fone haue us alwey in mynde;
Pray for oure grace, oure spede, and oure gode chaunce,
As to englond thou hast be euer kynde.
And, thow fortune hath cast vs late be-hynde,
Yet fayle vs nat whan that we crye thi name,
ffor with thyn helpe we hope recure gode fame.[111]

(Unfortunately, although Henry did land in France on St. George's Day, and kissed an arm of St. George during his French coronation, the whole effort was a propaganda disaster for his regime.)[112]

Garter festivities and the concomitant celebration of St. George's Day did continue throughout Henry's reign.[113] One noteworthy occasion was

---

110   Carleton Brown, ed., *Religious Lyrics of the XVth Century* (Oxford: Clarendon Press, 1939), 198, 199–200.

111   Brown, ed., *Religious Lyrics*, 201.

112   Bertram Wolffe, *Henry VI* (London: Eyre Methuen, 1981), 51, 61; *A Parisian Journal 1405–1449*, trans. Janet Shirley (Oxford: Oxford University Press, 1968), 273.

113   An average of £142 was spent on it for each of the eight years for which there are records; see PRO E 101 408/24, f. 4v; E 101 409/19, f. 20v; E 101 409/11, f. 23; E 101 409/16, f. 16v; E 101 410/1, f. 11v; E 101 410/3, f. 16; E 101 410/6, f. 25v; E 101 410/9, f. 26.

in 1444, when Henry VI married Margaret of Anjou on the vigil of St. George's Day. A manuscript prepared as a wedding gift to Margaret by John Talbot, first earl of Shrewsbury (c. 1387–1453), contains a number of poems and romances and also a section on the order of the Garter; the folio introducing this section shows Henry VI and his garter knights grouped around an altar on which is a large image of St. George in armor, mounted, and spearing a dragon, while a princess and a sheep wait in the background (figure 10).[114] But this appears more as wishful thinking than as an accurate reflection of Henry's priorities, and the earlier efforts of propagandists to link Henry VI with St. George resurfaced in the 1458 poem "The Ship of State." Written during the first phase of the Wars of the Roses, it conceives of Henry VI as a warship, with different Lancastrian figures acting as different parts of that ship: Prince Edward is the mast, the duke of Exeter is the ship's light, the duke of Somerset is the rudder, the earl of Pembroke is the sail-yard, etc. The poem concludes:

Now help, saynt George, oure lady knyght,
And be oure lode-starre day & nyght,
To strength oure kynge and england ryght
And fell oure fomenus pryde.[115]

Alas for Henry, this did not come to pass. But if the king was not willing to acknowledge St. George himself, his rival was. When Edward, duke of York, defeated Henry VI at the battle of Towton Moor in 1461 he won the throne of England and was crowned Edward IV. One chronicler describes Edward as praying often to St. George, along with the Virgin and St. Anne.[116] Ten years later, before the Battle of Tewkesbury, when Edward won back the throne from a restored Henry VI, he "displayed his bannars; dyd blowe up the trumpets; commytted his caws and qwarell to Almyghty God, to owr most blessyd lady his mothar, Vyrgyn Mary, the glorious

114 BL Royal MS 15 E VI, discussed in G.F. Warner and J.P. Gibson, *Catalogue of Western Manuscripts in the Old Royal and King's Collections in the British Museum* (London: British Museum, 1921), 2: 177–79.
115 R.H. Robbins, ed., *Historical Poems of the XIVth and XVth Centuries* (New York: Columbia University Press, 1959), 191.
116 *Historie of the Arrivall of Edward IV. in England and the Finall Recouerye of his Kingdomes from Henry VI. A.D. M.CCCC.LXXI*, ed. John Bruce (London: Camden Society, 1838), 13. An image of St. George also appeared on a priedieu in a stained glass portrait Edward commissioned of himself in Canterbury Cathedral; see Madeline Harrison Caviness, *The Windows of Christ Church Cathedral Canterbury*, Corpus Vitrearum Medii Aevii, Great Britain 2 (London: British Academy, 1981), 262, illustration 446 (plate 184).

martyr Seint George, and all the saynts."[117] People also used St. George to acknowledge Edward's status as king. In 1461, a tableau of the saint, the dragon, the king, queen, and princess greeted him when he entered Bristol, "and atte the sleying of the dragon ther was a greet melody of aungellys."[118] Similarly, manuscript of John Lydgate's poem on the kings of England (BL MS Harley 2251, 4v.) has an extra stanza inserted for the new king:

> Comforthe al thristy and drynke with gladnes!
> Rejoyse withe myrthe thoughe ye have nate to spende!
> The tyme is come to avoyden yowre distres —
> Edwarde the fourthe the olde wornges to amende
> Is wele disposede in wille, and to defende
> His londe and peple in dede, withe kynne and myghte;
> Goode lyf and longe I pray to God hym sende,
> And that seynte George be withe hum in his righte.[119]

Most important of all was Edward IV's resurrection of the Order of the Garter from the factionalism it had fallen into during the latter years of Henry VI's reign. Edward used membership in the Garter as a diplomatic tool, ensuring that foreign princes whom he wanted as allies were elected, and bestowing it only on those Englishmen he personally favored, regardless of high birth or even kinship with himself. Edward rebuilt the chapel of St. George at Windsor Castle in beautiful Perpendicular Gothic style, richly endowed it with vestments, hangings, statues and service books, and had the College incorporated by Act of Parliament in 1483, whereby he increased the number of clerks and choristers serving it.[120] He even had himself buried in St. George's when he died in 1483. Of course, all of this may simply indicate Edward's recognition of, and willingness to use, political symbolism, rather than a specific affinity for St. George (especially since Edward's rival Henry VI had founded Eton College across the river Thames from Windsor Castle).[121] Nonetheless, in

---

117   *Historie of the Arrivall*, 29.
118   James Gairdner, ed., *Three Fifteenth-Century Chronicles*, Camden Society New Series 28 (London: Camden Society, 1880), 86.
119   *Warkworth's Chronicle of the First Thirteen Years of the Reign of King Edward the Fourth*, ed. James Orchard Halliwell (London: Camden Society, 1839), xxii.
120   Charles Ross, *Edward IV* (London and New Haven: Yale University Press, 1997), 274–76.
121   Edward even attempted to absorb Eton College into St. George's. See Ross, *Edward IV*, 269.

England, any attention paid to the Garter of necessity reflected on the figure of its patron saint. Edward did acquire the head of St. George for the College's collection (or, alternatively, embellished a reliquary containing a piece of St. George's skull),[122] and the king's third son was born at Windsor late in 1477 and named George in honor of the local patron, the first member of the English royal family to be so christened.[123] Edward's Garter activities, it must therefore be said, did indicate an appreciation of the saint.

St. George, therefore, handily survived the advent of the Yorkist dynasty. Edward's brother, Richard, duke of Gloucester, who usurped the throne from Edward's own son Edward V in 1483, had a short and troubled reign as Richard III. Not much evidence exists, therefore, as to Richard's affinity for or use of St. George, although one William Melbourne was paid 11s. 9d. "for sowing, gourlyng and frenging of baner of Saint George armes" for Richard's coronation on 6 July 1483.[124] Richard continued his brother's patronage of St. George's chapel, even moving the relics of Henry VI there from Chertsey Abbey, in recognition of their reputed sanctity and, perhaps, in order to make symbolic amends for his dynasty's ouster of the former king. At the battle of Bosworth Field in 1485 he raised St. George's banner; his opponent, Henry Tudor, earl of Richmond, also raised a cross of St. George as one of his three banners, by means of asserting his claim to the throne of England, and once again we see that veneration of St. George was one of the ways that different contenders for the throne of England laid claim to it. It was Henry who successfully prosecuted his claim at Bosworth by defeating Richard and thereby becoming King Henry VII; when he rode into London he deposited the banner in the cathedral church of St. Paul in thanks for his victory.[125]

---

[122] John Rous, *Historia Regum Angliae*, ed. Thomas Hearn (Oxford, 1745), 211; Bond, *Inventories*, 166.

[123] Edward's younger brother George, duke of Clarence, was born in 1449, i.e. before the family was royal. Edward's naming of his son George most likely did *not* reflect affection for his brother, who had a long history of treasonous behavior and who, earlier in 1477, had been imprisoned in the Tower for acting "as though he had used a king's power" in his judicial murder of Ankarette Twynho. Clarence was himself executed in the Tower in February 1478, traditionally by being drowned in a butt of Malmsey wine. See Ross, *Edward IV*, 241–43.

[124] Anne F. Sutton and P.W. Hammond, *The Coronation of Richard III: The Extant Documents* (Gloucester: Alan Sutton and New York: St. Martin's Press, 1983), 137. See also 158, 174.

[125] The others were "a Red ffyry dragon peyntid upon whyte & Grene Sarcenet,

Henry VII's use of St. George was certainly not his last. Henry became particularly enthusiastic about the saint, honoring him publicly and privately to show how good an English king he could be, even though his claim to the throne rested more on might than on right. Like Richard, Henry commissioned a large banner of St. George for his coronation on 30 October; Henry's used six yards of crimson velvet and cost 14s. Sixteen yards of white cloth of gold were also used to make horse trappings of St. George for the coronation.[126] The next year Henry's son Arthur was born at Winchester on 2 November, and baptized in the cathedral there soon afterwards. After the elaborate ceremony, which included an anthem to St. Swithun at his shrine, the prince was "borne to the King & Quene, and had the Blessinge of Almyghty God, our Lady and Seint George, and of his Fader and Moder."[127] And as they had for Edward IV, people acknowledged Henry VII as king through St. George. As Henry entered the city of Hereford in 1486, he was greeted by a figure of the saint, who addressed him:

> Moost Cristen Prince, and Frende unto the Feith,
> Supporter of Truth, Confounder of Wikkednesse,
> As People of your Realme holy reporteth and saith,
> Welcome to this Citie withoute eny Feintnesse;
> And thinke verely as ye see her in Likenesse,
> That this Worme is discomfited by Goddes Ayde and myn.
> So shall I be your Helpe, unto your Lives Fine,
> To withstounde your Enemyes with the Help of that blessed Virgin,
> The whiche loveth you right wele I dar playnly it say.
> Wherefor ye be right welcome, I pray God further you in your Way.[128]

Also like Edward IV, Henry VII realized the importance of the Order of the Garter. In 1487, he upbraided his treasurer Lord Dynham for not delivering enough money for the Garter ceremonies that year:

> we appointed a certain day for the fest of Saint George, to have been sollempnely holden at oure castel of Wyndsor, according to the good

---

and the third was a Baner of Tarterton bett with a dun Cowe." *The Great Chronicle of London*, eds. A.H. Thomas and I.D. Thornley (London: Corporation of the City of London, 1938), 238–39.

126 Leopold G. Wickham Legg, *English Coronation Records* (Westminster: Archibald Constable, 1901), 204, 201.

127 John Leland, *De rebus britannicus Collectanea* (London: Benjamin White, 1774), 4: 205.

128 Leland, *Collectanea*, 4: 197.

and auncient custome of this roy^me, at the whiche day there was no prouision in default of money that ye ought to have deliuered as it is said ... We therefore remembring that the fest of Saint George, the patron of this our royalme, hath yerely and contynuelly ben honnoured and obserued, and when it so hath been good grace and honnor hath beene to our said royme, pray you in our affectueux wise that vnto our servaunt John Saxby, oon of the clerks of our grenecloth, ye wol deliuer as moche money as may conveniently serue for the fest of St. George, to be kept on Sonday come sevenight.[129]

Henry was not only aware that St. George was the patron of the kingdom, but also that keeping his feast is essential to procuring "good grace and honor" for England. It cannot, therefore, be said that Henry was using the Garter for its political prestige alone. The next year matters had been set right and the feast was celebrated lavishly. It included the archbishops of Canterbury and York, the bishops of Lincoln and Exeter (as well as the bishop of Winchester, the prelate of the order), the Chief Justice of the King's Bench, and ambassadors from the Emperor, the king of Scotland, and the duke of Brittany. The queen and the king's mother, accompanied by a number of ladies-in-waiting, were also present. The chapter meeting was held "a great Tract of Tyme," and for the feast the "Hall was merveously ordered and servede."[130] At the feast, according to an antiquarian description, a song was sung in praise of the saint:

Here this Day Seint George, the Patron of this Place,
Honowred with the Garter, Chief of Chevalrye.
Chaplayns, Chapell singing, Procession keping Space,
With Archebishops and Bishops, besene noble;
Much People present to see Thee, King Henry.
Wherfor, now Seint George, all we pray to thee,
To kepe our Souveraigne in His Dygnitie.[131]

Another notable Garter feast was that of 1505, when Henry's new relic of the shinbone of St. George was borne in procession before him, which he had received earlier in the year from Louis XI of France.[132] It was a highly

---

[129] William Campbell, ed., *Materials for a History of the Reign of Henry VII* (London: Rolls Series, 1877) 2: 152–53.

[130] Leland, *Collectanea*, 4: 238–41.

[131] Leland, *Collectanea*, 4: 242.

[132] James Gairdner, ed., *Memorials of the Reign of King Henry VII* (London: Rolls Series, 1858), 82; *The Will of King Henry VII*, ed. Thomas Astle (London, 1775), 33–34. *The Great Chronicle of London* claims (at 329) that the relic came from "the kyng of Romayns."

valued possession, "of the kind never before given to any king of England" claimed the author of the *Annales Henrici Septimi*, and adds, tellingly, "*all England* is the witness to how much reverence and devotion our king accepted this rich jewel."[133]

St. George was also suitable for less formally religious occasions at King Henry's court. On Twelfth Night in 1494, Henry held a banquet in Whitehall, after which he knighted the Lord Mayor of London. Later they joined the French and Spanish ambassadors, and the Queen and her attendants, in Westminster Hall, and

> Anoon cam In the kyngs players and shewid a goodly Interlude before the kyng But or they hadd ffynysshid theyr play Cam In Ridyng oon of the kyngys Chapell namyed Cornysh apparaylid afftyr the ffygure of Seynt George, and aftir ffolowid a ffayer vyrgyn attyrid lyke unto a kyngys dowgthyr, and ledyng by a sylkyn lace a Terryble & huge Rede dragun, The which In Sundry placys of the halle as he passyd spytt ffyre at hys mowth And when the said Cornysh was cummyn before the kyng he uttyrd a certayn spech made In balad Royall, afftyr ffynysshyng whereof he began/ This antempn off Seynt George, O Georgi deo Care, wherunto the kyngys Chapell which stood ffast by answerid Salvatorem Deprecare, ut Gubernet Angliam, And soo sang owth alle the hool antempn wyth lusty Corage, In passe tyme whereof The said Cornysh avoydid wyth the dragon, and the vyrgyn was ladd unto Quenys standyng. [134]

After this play twelve lords, knights and esquires entered, along with twelve ladies, all in disguise, and danced for the entertainment of those present.[135]

A painting from the reign of Henry VII (figure 11), most likely commissioned for the chapel at the king's palace of Richmond, is especially noteworthy. Henry, kneeling at a prie-dieu, leads his three sons Arthur, Henry, and Edmund in prayer, and on the right Queen Elizabeth does the same with her four daughters Margaret, Mary, Elizabeth and Catherine. All wear crowns, furred robes, and chains with jewels. Each group kneels under a canopy with curtains hanging from it; between them an angel, with each hand, draws back the curtains to help reveal the people beneath them. This angel is not the painting's center of focus, however, for in the

---

[133] Gairdner, ed., *Memorials of Henry VII*, 82; emphasis added.

[134] *Great Chronicle of London*, 251.

[135] Robert Withington, *English Pageantry: An Historical Outline* (Cambridge, Mass.: Harvard University Press, 1918), 1: 112.

immediate background a large figure of St. George, in armor and wearing a surcoat of his arms, rides toward a dragon suspended in the air on the left side of the painting. St. George wields a sword with which he is about to strike the dragon; he has already used his lance, some pieces of which lie on the ground and one of which, with his banner attached, is stuck in the dragon. Further in the background the princess holds a sheep on a leash, and further still are the towers of Silene, although the king and queen are not visible in them. This painting, almost square and measuring over four feet on each side, is Flemish in origin and, from the number of children in the family, was painted sometime between 1503 and 1509, that is, after the birth of Catherine and before the death of Henry VII. It is a forceful statement of St. George's patronage of the royal family.[136]

Finally, when Henry died in 1509 he was buried in Westminster Abbey, in the Perpendicular Gothic chapel on the east end of the abbey church that the king had constructed, originally to house the relics of Henry VI, now widely regarded as a saint. (Henry VI was never canonized, however, and his body remained at Windsor.) St. George appears twice on Henry's tomb: once, in the guise of a Roman soldier, on a bronze medallion on the tomb itself, and another, slaying the dragon, on the grille surrounding the tomb.[137] Henry also bequeathed the relic of St. George he had acquired from Louis XI to be placed on the altar at his tomb on feast days, at the discretion of the chantry priests singing for him there.[138] Even at the end, St. George continued to watch over Henry.

Henry VII was not a warrior-king in the mould of Edward I, Edward III, Henry V or even Edward IV. Once on the throne he was content not to engage in any foreign military adventures. In no way, however, did this diminish royal support for St. George. Henry knew that kings of England were supposed to honor the saint, and he did so with a certain gusto. In this way he attempted to position himself as legitimate ruler of England in the eyes of his subjects. Despite the rebellions of Perkin Warbeck and Lambert Simnel, and the disquieting fear that Henry was practicing a form of renewed Ricardian absolutism,[139] he died in his bed and his dynasty

---

[136] George Scharf, "On a Votive Painting of St. George and the Dragon," *Archaeologia* 49 (1886): 243–300, at 243–46; and Oliver Millar, *Catalogue of the Tudor, Stuart and Early Georgian Pictures in the Collection of Her Majesty the Queen* (London: Phaidon, 1963), text vol., 52–53; plate vol., pl. 1.

[137] John Thomas Micklethwaite, "Notes on the Imagery of Henry the Seventh's Chapel, Westminster," *Archaeologia* 47 (1883): 377, 375; Scharf, "Votive Painting," 257.

[138] *Will of Henry VII*, 33–34.

[139] A.J. Pollard, *Late Medieval England, 1399–1509* (Harlow: Pearson, 2000), 376–78.

survived him. His attachment to St. George would not have impeded these achievements.

But why St. George? How did this foreign saint come to fill such a role in English political life? As this chapter has indicated, there was a certain amount of chance involved. Edward I, Edward III, and Henry V were not perfect as kings, but compared to Edward II, Richard II, or Henry VI, they were certainly remembered as "good," and their preference for St. George one of the things emblematic of this goodness – primarily embodied in military success and willingness to work with Parliament. But would a similar public (and publicly shared) devotion to St. Edward the Confessor on the part these kings have made that saint emblematic of good kingship? Could the English situation have grown up parallel to the French, with the monarchy and Westminster Abbey working hand in hand to produce a royal-national mythology based fundamentally around the figure of St. Edward the Confessor? Anything is possible, of course, but a number of factors suggest that such a scenario would have been unlikely. George was more warlike than Edward, and therefore justified an activity dear to the hearts of the nobility – although as a royal figure St. Edward could justify anything the king got up to, including war, viz. the banner of St. Edward raised above Carlaverock castle, or Edward III's cry of "A Edward! A George!" at the siege of Calais in 1351.[140] But Edward's royalty was a problem. Edward the Confessor had been a king, and as such fundamentally justified the king's right to rule, whether or not that rule was consensual or effective. St. George also justified the king's right to rule, but in origin George was noble, not royal, and thus enjoyed a certain amount of support among the English nobility independent of the king's use of the saint. It could be said, therefore, that Edward I's use of St. George, intentionally nor not, was a canny move, establishing a relationship of common purpose with his nobles (and also, as we have seen, with people lower on the social scale). In this way St. George came to be a reflection of the ideal English political situation, which was definitely monarchical, but in which the community of the realm enjoyed certain rights. Of course, kings often found this situation restrictive, and St. George could be turned against them, to imply that they were not ruling well. The solution, as the reigns of Henry VI and Henry VII showed, was to use the saint for cover.

St. George also enjoyed other attributes that recommended him for

---

140 William Worcestre, *Itineraries*, ed. John H. Harvey (Oxford: Clarendon Press, 1969), 349.

national patronage. One connection with England may have been through a third party: if England was "the Virgin's dowry," and St. George was "our lady's knight," then St. George was automatically the patron of England! Such a connection, however, is not explicitly made in any medieval source. What does seem clear is that George's foreignness was not a hindrance to his adoption as a national patron and may actually have helped it, since he would not have favored any one area of the country over any other, as would a native saint with his or her local cult. Moreover, as D.A.L. Morgan notes, the use of an international saint may have been an attempt, particularly by Edward III, to claim a space on the world stage; nationalism and internationalism going hand in hand.[141] As such, he would have reflected especially well on the English, buttressing their natural nobility.

St. George remained a saint, of course, who like all saints could inspire people to live good Christian lives, or intervene to help people in need. These qualities existed independent of his status as a national patron, although they could resonate with it. The extent of this resonation will be the subject of the next chapter.

[141] D.A.L. Morgan, "The Banner-bearer of Christ and Our Lady's Knight: How God became an Englishman revisited," in *St George's Chapel Windsor*, ed. Saul, 51–61, esp. 58.

4

Popular St. George in Late Medieval England

From the reign of Edward I, St. George was prescribed for all levels of the English army, both knights and foot-soldiers. By establishing the Order of the Garter, Edward III made the veneration of St. George an activity that he shared with the nobility and knighthood of England. In the reign of his successor Richard II, St. George came to represent the "good" memory of the "Edwardian settlement," which had been based on consultation with the nobility and joint prosecution of war in France, and was used as a rebuke to Richard's novel idea of "regality," expressed partly through his own veneration of St. Edward the Confessor.[1] Thereafter, what may be called the political community consistently recognized St. George as the patron saint of the kingdom. Kings would venerate St. George in order to prove their worthiness to rule England, while other people might invoke the saint in order to curry favor with the king, or to rebuke him for not ruling well.

A necessary question to ask, though, is how many people in the kingdom of England this situation actually describes. The army that Henry V mustered for the invasion of France in 1415 numbered some 10,000 men,[2] and the political community (king, bishops, nobility, substantial knights, and greater gentry) numbered perhaps 2% of the English population.[3] In

1   See G.L. Harriss, *Shaping the Nation: England 1360–1461* (Oxford and New York: Oxford University Press, 2005), 460–61 for some discussion about the conflict between "regality" and "good governance."
2   Harriss, *Shaping the Nation*, 542.
3   I.M.W. Harvey, "Was there Popular Politics in Fifteenth-Century England?" in *The Macfarlane Legacy: Studies in Late Medieval Politics and Society*, eds. R.H. Britnell and A.J. Pollard (New York: St. Martin's Press, 1995), 155–74, at 155.

other words, most English people were members neither of the military nor of the political community. Is it even possible, therefore, to speak of St. George as a "national patron"? It is true that the army was a sort of national institution – that is, English people might take pride in its successes even when they were not there to participate in them (they were certainly taxed to pay for them), and the political community by definition was influential beyond its numbers. However, can we truly speak of St. George as a national patron, when (potentially) so few people actually recognized him as such?

St. George certainly was popular throughout the kingdom of England. The traditional expressions of a saint's cult, such as church or guild dedications, artwork, or hagiography, all attest to this popularity. But the relationship between this popular cult and the royal-national one detailed in Chapter 3 is not necessarily clear. The terms of St. George's official veneration certainly set up the saint to be accepted by the broad mass of the people: the idea of the saint as the patron of England could have traveled both "downward" from the king and nobility, and "horizontally" from the army, colonizing the popular veneration of St. George by the English. An example of horizontal spreading may be seen in the Agincourt Carol, composed some time in the fifteenth century. Two stanzas of the carol link the English victory at Agincourt with the protection St. George will offer to his votaries in everyday situations:

> He kepyd the mad from dragons dred
> And fraid al Fraunce and put to fligh[t]
> At Agyncourt, the crownecle ye red:
> The French hym se formest in fyght.

> In hys vertu he wol us led
> Agaynys the fend, the ful wyght;
> And with hys banner us oversprede
> Yf we hym love with all our myght.[4]

These two aspects are particularly linked by the St. George banner overspreading "us," simultaneously the army at Agincourt and the average Christian in his fight against the "fend." As for downward influence, it is often asserted that royal veneration "resonated" or "united" with popular veneration, e.g. Jonathan Bengtson's suggestion that royal veneration of St. George "provided a way for the late medieval monarchy

---

[4]   R.L. Greene, *A Selection of English Carols* (Oxford: Clarendon Press, 1962), 124.

to establish a more intimate relationship with its subjects."[5] But did political veneration, in fact, ever really do this? Or were the national and popular cults like two ships passing in the night, with the politically engaged venerating the saint for his protection of the country, and everyone else venerating the saint for the same reasons they venerated other saints: protection on earth from disease, sudden death, and misfortune in general? James MacGregor has provided evidence that this situation may indeed have been the case. MacGregor shows that the vast majority of prayers to St. George in fourteenth- and fifteenth-century England called upon the saint as a martyr, knight, and dragon-slayer, to intercede for personal reasons, but not as a patron of England. Even those prayers that do acknowledge George's patronage of England do so only in passing – and only two specifically call on St. George to protect the king or realm of England.[6]

One can never, therefore, take evidence of the veneration of St. George as *ipso facto* evidence that a sense of national identity was "spreading" or "taking root" throughout fourteenth- and fifteenth-century England. St. George, like all saints, was a powerful intercessor against all manner of ill, and attracted votaries for that reason alone. And yet it is apparent that the royal veneration of St. George, which figured the saint as a protector of the king and realm of England, was indeed taken up by people beyond court or political circles as an expression of their English identity, or at least their desire for political engagement. This chapter will examine St. George's dedications, artwork, guilds and Lives in late-medieval England in order to determine the extent of that expression. "Royal" and "popular" veneration never entirely merged, but it is clear that there was a certain overlap, which produced a vision of an England that was simultaneously hierarchical and inclusive.

Charting the dedications of churches, chapels, monasteries, hospitals, and similar institutions is a well-established means of tracing the popularity of a given saint's cult. Such ecclesiastical institutions were usually named in honor of one or more saints, and reference has been made in previous chapters to things named after St. George, in England and elsewhere. Uncovering medieval dedications is not necessarily an easy task, however.

---

5   Jonathan Bengtson, "Saint George and the Formation of English Nationalism," *Journal of Medieval and Early Modern Studies* 27:2 (1997): 317–40, at 335.
6   James B. MacGregor, "Praying to Saint George in Fifteenth-Century England," paper presented at the 42nd International Congress on Medieval Studies, Western Michigan University, Kalamazoo, Michigan, 8 May 2007.

Medieval churches were certainly dedicated to particular saints, but often a church would be known colloquially simply by the name of the village it was in, and when saint cults fell out of favor after the Reformation it was very easy for parishioners to forget their church's dedication entirely. The current dedication of a medieval church building may not be the same as its pre-Reformation one(s), since the eighteenth- and nineteenth-century antiquaries who worked to reconstruct them often made mistakes.[7] A medieval source is the only guarantee of a church's medieval dedication.

With this caveat in mind, we can turn to Frances Arnold-Forster's *Studies in Church Dedications*, which recorded English church dedications as they were in 1899. Arnold-Forster lists 198 churches and chapels dedicated, in whole or in part, to St. George, of which 120 are designated as pre-Reformation (see Table 1). How accurate is this list? How many of these parishes actually were dedicated to St. George before the Reformation? Approximately 27 can be confirmed in documentary sources (see notes to table 1). Further investigation in local records would doubtlessly reveal the status of much of the remainder. But evidence exists that there were several more medieval dedications to St. George than Arnold-Forster knew about. Although Nicholas Orme lists the dedication of Ashcombe, Devon as unknown, we have seen that Edward I gave oblations to a church of St. George in Ashcombe "near Exeter" in 1297.[8] Alison Binns further notes that a church of St. George in Dunster, Somerset was granted to Bath Abbey and made a priory, c. 1090, and another Benedictine alien priory was founded in a church in Cogges, Oxfordshire, which if not dedicated to George at its founding in 1103 certainly was by the time of Edward III.[9] Orme, furthermore, gives evidence for Devonian churches to St. George in Beaford (by 1521), Broadclyst (1392), Cockington (1469), Harford (pre-Reformation), Manaton (1486), Seaton (1349), and Witheridge (pre-Reformation).[10] In his *Saints of Cornwall*, Orme lists one parish church at Treneglos dedicated to St. George (1281), and no fewer than nine medieval Cornish chapels to the saint, at Tealeburgh (1296), Bodmin (1405), Cotehele, East Looe (1530s), Trewan, Tolverne (1384), Woolston, Probus, and Truro

7   Nicholas Orme, *English Church Dedications, with a Survey of Cornwall and Devon* (Exeter: University of Exeter Press, 1996), 8–9.
8   BL Add. MS 7965, f. 7v.
9   Alison Binns, *Dedications of Monastic Houses in England and Wales 1066–1216* (Woodbridge, Suffolk: Boydell, 1989), 70, 96.
10 Orme, *English Church Dedications*, 131; Orme, personal communication, referencing Lambeth Palace Library, Reg. William Courtenay, part ii, f. 187; Orme, *English Church Dedications*, 147, 167, 180, 198, 218.

(1420).[11] In the diocese of Carlisle in the north-west of England, T.H.B. Graham and W.G. Collingwood found pre-Reformation chapels to St. George in the parish of Bromfield, Cumberland, and Kirkby Stephen, Westmorland.[12] Arnold-Forster claims that a church at Beckington, Somerset was dedicated to St. Gregory, when E.H. Bates shows it was named for St. George from 1484.[13] Finally, Arnold-Forster does acknowledge the church of St. George at Southwark, but mistakenly assigns its foundation to the eighteenth century, when the church was named with its dedication in a document of 1122.[14] This gives a total of 26 additional medieval churches and stand-alone chapels dedicated to St. George. It would seem, therefore, that if Arnold-Forster is inaccurate for St. George, we do not need to understand her total number of dedications as somehow inflated; if anything, it is too modest. All of her attributions in Devon, for instance, are confirmed by Orme, who provides several more.

A number of hospitals were also dedicated to St. George. "Hospital" encompassed a variety of institutions, including houses for the poor, aged or pilgrims as well as those for the sick, blind, and leprous. The college of Windsor, because it maintained poor knights, qualifies as a hospital, and the Cornish chapel of Bodmin, established in 1405, was hosting poor people by 1492.[15] Other foundations included a poorhouse in Shrewsbury, founded in 1162, an almshouse for men in Wybunbury, Cheshire founded in 1464 and sharing a dedication with the Holy Cross, and an almshouse in Yeovil, Somerset, founded in 1477 and sharing a dedication with St. Christopher.[16]

These dedications can help us map the popular veneration of St. George in time and space, and also reveal his relative popularity. Arnold-Forster

11   Nicholas Orme, *The Saints of Cornwall* (Oxford and London: Oxford University Press, 2000), 125–26.
12   T.H.B. Graham and W.G. Collingwood, "Patron Saints of the Diocese of Carlisle," *Transactions of the Cumberland and Westmorland Antiquarian and Archaeological Society* N.S. 25 (1925): 18, 23.
13   E.H. Bates, "Dedications of the Churches of Somersetshire," *Proceedings of the Somersetshire Archaeological and Natural History Society* 51 (1905): 116.
14   Martha Carlin, *Medieval Southwark* (London and Rio Grande: Hambledon Press, 1996), 94.
15   David Knowles and R. Neville Hadcock, *Medieval Religious Houses: England and Wales* (New York: Longman, 1971), 337, 314; Nicholas Orme and Margaret Webster, *The English Hospital, 1070–1570* (New Haven and London: Yale University Press, 1995), 187.
16   Knowles and Hadcock, *Medieval Religious Houses*, 332, 337, 338.

establishes no more precise dates of foundation than "pre-Reformation," but by comparing what dates we do know we can get an idea about the saint's chronological popularity over the course of the high and late Middle Ages. Table 2 lists 41 pre-Reformation dedications, whose dates of first mentioning are spread fairly evenly from the twelfth through the sixteenth centuries, illustrating a sustained popularity for St. George from the Norman Conquest through the Reformation. Even more important than when churches were founded was the question of where they were located. Table 3 lists all known dedications to St. George, both from Arnold-Forster and other sources. It is clear that St. George was most popular as a dedication in East Anglia and in the south-west, and less popular in the north and parts of the Midlands, but what is most striking is the wide distribution of dedications over the entire country: almost 80% of counties had at least one, and almost 70% had at least two, indicating that St. George was not the preserve of a particular area of England but of the country as a whole.

But this picture of a sustained, widespread cult of St. George needs to be tempered somewhat, for St. George was by no means the most popular saint in medieval England. Studies of *all* dedications in a discrete area give a sense of his relative popularity, and although Arnold-Forster's collection of pre-Reformation church dedications may be misleading, any errors in it are likely to be systemic and would not affect the relative standing of a particular spiritual patron. Table 4 illustrates Arnold-Forster's top twenty pre-Reformation dedications; George stands in nineteenth place in terms of overall popularity. Many saints, it seems, were more popular than George. The Virgin Mary, the mother of Christ and the only saint worthy of *hyperdulia*, has by far the most dedications. Disciples of Christ, such as Peter, James, John the Evangelist, and Andrew; other biblical saints such as John the Baptist, Mary Magdalene, Paul, and Michael; and the more abstract cults of the Trinity and of All Saints outranked George nationally. Of the non-biblical, early saints, of whom St. George is one, Arnold-Forster lists Nicholas, Laurence, Leonard, Martin, and Giles as more popular than George. But George *is* in the top twenty of all church dedications nationally, out of approximately 300 in Arnold-Forster. He was more popular than other saints in the categories delineated above, such as the disciples Matthew or Thomas, or Luke or Paul (as a single dedication), or the Holy Cross. Other popular early saints, such as Barbara, Katherine of Alexandria or Christopher were not as popular as St. George for dedicatory purposes, and other military saints like Demetrius, Mercurius, and Theodore came nowhere near his popularity. He even had more dedications than most native English saints, such as Cuthbert or

Alban. Thus, it may be safely said that while George may not have been the most popular saint in England, in the late Middle Ages he was certainly more popular than average.

George's widespread popularity is also revealed in the proliferation of images to the saint. Reference has been made to some twelfth-century sculpted tympana of St. George in England and to various works of art commissioned on behalf of the English king. Churches throughout England were also decorated with stained glass, paintings, and sculptures of saints. Difficulty arises in trying to study such medieval images, of course, since many of them were damaged or destroyed during the Reformation and the Commonwealth, and of those many were later restored, perhaps not entirely accurately.[17] So many of them do remain, however, that a comprehensive survey of medieval images is quite out of the question. We therefore cannot form an idea of the relative popularity of St. George's cult based on his share of a total number of medieval images. Nonetheless the Courtauld Institute of Art in London has records of surviving medieval stained glass, and one survey has been done of medieval mural paintings of St. George in England. Many more wall paintings and stained glass images of St. George must have existed prior to the iconoclasm of the sixteenth and seventeenth centuries, of course, but these surveys may also be used to indicate St. George's geographical popularity. Tables 5 and 6 indicate that 74% of counties had a mural, 51% a window, and 79% both. More significant is that the vast majority of churches with stained glass or mural paintings of St. George were not actually dedicated to the saint. Only churches at Brinsop, Kelmscott, and Stamford are recorded as having stained glass images of the saint and were also dedicated to St. George, while a mural painting of St. George is shared with a dedication to the saint only at Trotton. That parishioners did not need to have their church dedicated to St. George in order to commission art in his honor further underscores the saint's popularity.

Artwork reveals not only that the saint was popular, but also why. How St. George was depicted indicates what people admired or valued about him. In almost all depictions, the saint is armed with sword or lance and dressed in armor or mail, and his red-cross arms could be shown in the usual places: on a surcoat, shield, banner of some kind. George's aspect as a dragon-slayer is similarly popular: most of the windows and mural

---

17   See Richard Marks, *Image and Devotion in Late Medieval England* (Stroud, Glos.: Sutton, 2004), 2–3.

paintings show him in this activity. The saint could be mounted or standing, using a lance or a sword, and/or striking the creature in the mouth or on the breast, but his action was dramatic and edifying to anyone seeing it. The influence of the *Golden Legend* is noticeable from the thirteenth century, when the details of the St. George story in that work, such as the princess, the lamb, the king and queen, and the walls of Silene, start to appear in mural paintings. The earlier story of St. George's martyrdom was not entirely eclipsed, although it was usually shown as part of a life cycle of the saint such as at Hardham, Westmeston, St. Neot, or Stamford, and rarely shown on its own. Whether or not dragon-slaying was supposed to be a model for their own behavior, people quite clearly enjoyed the story, and wanted to see it depicted.

The saints that are associated with St. George in a given church also reveal how he was perceived. St. Michael was sometimes portrayed next to St. George, as he was on the walls of Bovey Tracey and Slapton, and in windows at Besthorpe, Haddon Hall, Peterborough, Trull, or West Hallam. St. Michael appeared with St. George on the great seal of England, and St. Michael made an appearance in the original Passion of St. George, when he twice reanimated the saint. People, however, most likely enjoyed Michael's dragon-slaying almost as much as they did George's. Michael can be shown with a set of scales for the weighing of souls, but he was most often shown killing a dragon, in reference to Revelation 12: 7–9: "And there was war in heaven: Michael and his angels fought against the dragon; and the dragon fought and his angels, And prevailed not; neither was their place found any more in heaven." George and Michael made a great dragon-slaying duo, and sometimes the only way to tell George and Michael apart is that the latter has wings: Michael is often armored and sometimes even bears a cross on his armor or shield. The window at Trull, in fact, shows the dragon-slaying trio of Saints George, Michael, and Margaret, all engaged in their favorite activity.

Overall, and perhaps surprisingly, St. Christopher is the saint most associated with George, especially in fourteenth- and fifteenth-century mural paintings. "Christopher," as the *Golden Legend* tells us, means "Christ-bearer," and from this fact came a story concerning the saint that, if it did not make its first appearance in that work, certainly became widely popular on account of it.[18] Christopher, formerly named Reprobus, was of immense size and fearsome countenance. A hermit who instructed

18   David Farmer, *The Oxford Dictionary of Saints*, 3rd edn. (Oxford and New York: Oxford University Press, 1992), 97.

Christopher in the tenets of Christian faith assigned him to dwell beside a mighty river and help ferry people across it, as a service to the Lord. One day a little child Christopher was carrying on his shoulders grew heavier and heavier, such that Christopher feared that he would founder and drown. He made it across, however, and the child turned out to be Jesus, who informed him that he was carrying not only the weight of the whole world, but also of its creator.[19] The saint therefore came to be considered the patron of travelers, and was invoked against water, tempest, plague, and sudden death. Paintings of him carrying the child Jesus on his shoulders through water appeared often in medieval churches; usually they were painted on the north wall opposite the porch, so that they could be seen by all who entered, since it was widely believed that anyone who saw an image of St. Christopher would not die that day.[20] George appears with Christopher on the same wall of thirteen churches, and reflects him on the opposite wall of two more, while a third church shows them both painted over the chancel arch;[21] Aldwincle church showed the two together in stained glass.

The pairing of George with Christopher prompted E.W. Tristram to posit that in these contexts George represented the second, knightly estate, while Christopher represented the third estate of peasants and laborers, whom he sustained under the weariness of their burdens.[22] Something like that may have been at work, especially since sermons were sometimes used to expound on the obligations of different types of people, and church decoration could be used to illustrate sermons. One would think, however, that if estates theory was so common a sermon topic that it justified permanent and prominent mural paintings, a saint representing the first estate, the Church (e.g. Thomas Becket or Hugh of Lincoln), should also have been on display, especially since it would have been a churchman who gave the sermon, and in a church building. One wonders, instead, that if St. Christopher was painted in churches for the miraculous properties his image possessed, similar properties may have inhered in

[19] Jacobus de Voragine, *The Golden Legend: Readings on the Saints*, trans. William Granger Ryan (Princeton: Princeton University Press, 1993), 2: 10–14.

[20] Farmer, *Dictionary of Saints*, 98; see also Desiderius Erasmus, *The Praise of Folly*, trans. Clarence H. Miller (New Haven and London: Yale University Press, 1979), 63.

[21] J. Lewis André, "Saint George the Martyr, in Legend, Ceremonial, Art, Etc.," *Archaeological Journal* 57 (1900): 204–23, at 218.

[22] E.W. Tristram, *English Wall Painting of the Fourteenth Century* (London: Routledge and Kegan Paul, 1955), 26, 118. See also Marks, *Image and Devotion*, 100–02 .

the image of St. George. This would especially make sense in terms of the late-medieval phenomenon of images replacing relics as the focus of Christian devotion.[23] In German-speaking lands, George and Christopher were both members of a group of saints known as the fourteen holy helpers, whose intercession was especially valued against disease and sudden death, and whose veneration grew in strength once recurring plague put healing power in especial demand.[24] It is true that the "fourteen holy helpers" as such received little attention in England, but it has been proposed that the nine "auxiliary saints" of Giles, Christopher, Blaise, Denis, George, Margaret, Barbara, Katherine, and Martha functioned as the English equivalent of the continental cult. These nine frequently appeared together on rood screens, and verse devotions to these nine appear in an East Anglian Book of Hours of c. 1480:

> Giles, Christopher, Blaise, light from heaven,
> Dionysus, George, healing leaven,
> Margaret, Barbara, Martha, Katherine,
> Save us from all calamity of sin.[25]

These saints also appear in a collection of ten verse prayers by John Lydgate, with the preface that "These holy seyntys folwyng ar pryvyledged of our lord Ihesu that what man or woman praieth to them rightfully shal have his bone [good]."[26] George's patronage of physical regeneration may have been stronger in Germany, where he was a common dedication for leprosaria, than in England, where he had all of five hospitals named in his honor.[27] Nevertheless it appears that in England, too, George may have shared some of Christopher's efficacy against disease and sudden death. In this context the dragon he slays becomes symbolic of all the hardship available to medieval people on a daily basis, and helps further to account for his popularity.

---

[23] Eamon Duffy, *The Stripping of the Altars: Traditional Religion in England, 1400–1580* (New Haven and London: Yale University Press, 1992), 167.

[24] Farmer, *Dictionary of Saints*, 185. The other saints included Acacius, Barbara, Blaise, Catherine of Alexandria, Cyricus, Denys, Erasmus, Eustace, Giles, Margaret, Panaleon, and Vitus; for one or other of these were sometimes substituted Anthony, Leonard, Nicholas, Sebastian, or Roch.

[25] M.R. James, *A Descriptive Catalogue of the Manuscripts in the Fitzwilliam Museum, Cambridge University* (Cambridge: University Press, 1895), 139.

[26] John Lydgate, *The Minor Poems of John Lydgate*, ed. Henry Noble MacCracken (London: EETS, 1911), 120. See also Duffy, *Stripping*, 178.

[27] See Marie-Luise Windemuth, *Das Hospital als Träger der Armenfürsorge im Mittelalter* (Stuttgart: Franz Steiner Verlag, 1995), 124.

Medieval murals and stained glass do not overtly suggest that St. George was popular on account of his status as a national patron, however. Less than a third of the images of the saint in stained glass show him bearing the same coat of arms used by the English on the field of battle. Only one image, the late fourteenth-century window at Heydour, can be said to be explicitly "national." It shows George flanked by St. Edward the Confessor and St. Edmund the Martyr, the two main royal patrons after George himself. Edward and Edmund are also dressed as armed knights, contrary to traditional iconography (such as on the Wilton Diptych) showing them as robed kings: at Heydour, at least, the model of George as the English royal patron was even influencing the image of the older king-saints. But on the whole this brief survey of mural paintings and stained glass seems to confirm James MacGregor's study of prayer to St. George: in liturgical or devotional contexts, the saint was valued as an intercessor and a model of chivalric behavior, but not necessarily as a patron of England.

The guilds of St. George in England, however, tell a somewhat different story, for it is with them that we discover a certain uniting of political and popular piety. Guilds were associations of laypeople brought together for some common purpose, the most familiar being the craft and merchant guilds of major cities. Far more common, however, were the religious guilds of smaller towns and rural villages. The members of such guilds, or fraternities, usually came from the same parish and would join together for mutual aid and friendship, and to perform works of charity. These could include sponsoring improvements to the fabric of the parish church, dispensing aid to indigent members or to the poor at large, holding feasts and processions on holidays, and perhaps most importantly, providing funerals for deceased members and masses to expedite their souls through purgatory. One should not generalize too broadly about such guilds, for different guilds emphasized different activities, and any one might exhibit substantial change in character over time. Furthermore, the distinctions between merchant, craft and religious guilds were not always sharp, for the former two usually had a significant religious aspect to them, while the latter could develop practical functions or a social character that were quite ancillary to their originally religious purpose.

Whatever their function, it has been estimated that there were some three guilds for every parish in England, giving a total of approximately 30,000 guilds in the country by the fifteenth century, an immense number.[28]

---

[28] Gervase Rosser, "Going to the Fraternity Feast: Commensality and Social Relations in Late Medieval England," *Journal of British Studies* 33 (1994): 430–46, at 430–31 and n. 3.

No national survey of guilds exists, although Nicholas Orme's study of Cornwall revealed seven guilds to St. George in that county (see Table 7), and Richard II's 1388 inquest into the nature and function of guilds produced 500 returns to the chancery (mostly from Cambridgeshire, Lincolnshire, and Norfolk) revealing ten St. George guilds (see Table 8). Other St. George guilds may be found in other sources (Table 9); many more await discovery in record sources. An analysis of these may illuminate aspects of the veneration of the saint in late-medieval England, including a substantial overlap between popular and political veneration.

It is certainly clear that when a guild was dedicated to St. George, it really was *dedicated* to St. George. Guilds were associations of laypeople that were voluntary in a way that parishes were not, and although the primary purpose of most guilds may have been to speed members' souls through purgatory, their names were not simply arbitrary, but reflected genuine devotion to their referents on the part of guild members. Of all the information in the returns of 1388 (which was concerned with sedition and with the possibility of loss of revenue to the king), religious practice may be seen as the most accurate, since it did not entail anything the guilds wished to hide from the government.[29] The summaries that Herbert Westlake provides allow us to see that the St. George guild of St. Margaret's parish at Lynn, for example, hired a priest to sing at St. George's altar "in the worship of God and the holy martyr, and for all the brothers and sisters," who would sponsor five candles on festivals and four torches on St. George's Day and at funerals.[30] The guild at Norwich was formed "in honour of St. George and to maintain a light at the daily mass," and on St. George's feast day all guild members would hear both evensong and mass and would pray for departed members. The fraternity also provided benefits of 8d. a week for members in poverty, towards which each member contributed 1/4d. a week; the balance went towards the making of an image of St. George.[31] The guild at Great Yarmouth's charnel house existed "to the honor of god and the glorious martyr," paid for a candle before the image of St. George during divine service, and heard solemn mass at St. Michael's on the feast of St. George.[32] Warwick's guild provided

[29] Barbara A. Hanawalt, "Keepers of the Lights: Late Medieval English Parish Gilds," *Journal of Medieval and Renaissance Studies* 14 no. 1 (Spring, 1984): 21–38, at 22.
[30] Herbert F. Westlake, *The Parish Gilds of Medieval England* (London: Society for Promoting Christian Knowledge, 1918), 194.
[31] Westlake, *Parish Guilds*, 203.
[32] Westlake, *Parish Guilds*, 218.

four tapers and four torches to be carried to the church of Our Lady for a solemn mass on St. George's Day; Littleport's members all assembled for mass on behalf of the dead on 23 April; and Lincoln's guild sponsored a candle before St. George's image in his church.[33] People may have had mixed motives for joining a guild of St. George, but once members they could hardly fail to become votaries of the saint.

This devotion was often expressed publicly through the annual processions or "ridings" of St. George that many guilds performed on his feast day. The best-known and best studied of these occurred at Norwich, where the procession was an annual event by the 1420s. Details varied from year to year, but in most years all members of the St. George guild assembled in a certain place on the morning of 23 April, or on some other predetermined day if St. George's Day conflicted with Holy Week. They dressed in the brightly colored livery of the guild, and processed through the city. The march was led by someone carrying a gilded ceremonial sword with a dragon's head carved on the handle, and included people carrying torches and banners of St. George. At the center of attention were actors playing St. George and the dragon. St. George was elaborately dressed, sometimes in coat armor, sometimes in a gown of bright and expensive material, and often with jewels and a chain; his horse too had gilded armor and was adorned with ribbons and laces. The man playing the part was paid a small fee, and enjoyed the services of gaily dressed attendants as he rode throughout the city, but he did have work to do: at the end of the parade outside Norwich Cathedral he battled with a man walking inside a model dragon.[34] At least once the dragon was equipped with gunpowder in order to produce the effect of fire breathing. St. George always triumphed, and after the battle he entered the cathedral to make an offering at the altar, followed by the guild members, who heard mass for the souls of their deceased brothers and sisters.[35]

In York something similar must have occurred, since on 11 March 1502, Sir William Todd, a former mayor of the city, bequeathed to the guild of

---

[33] Westlake, *Parish Guilds*, 144, 170, 232.

[34] Several eighteenth- and nineteenth-century dragon costumes used in the annual procession are on exhibit in the castle museum in Norwich.

[35] Mary Grace, ed., *The Records of the Gild of Saint George in Norwich, 1389–1547: A Transcript with an Introduction* (Norwich: Norfolk Record Society, 1937), 16–18; Benjamin R. McRee, "Unity or Division? The Social Meaning of Guild Ceremony in Urban Communities," in *City and Spectacle in Medieval Europe*, eds. Barbara A. Hanawalt and Kathryn L. Reyerson (Minneapolis and London: University of Minnesota Press, 1994), 189–207, at 195–98.

St. Christopher and St. George his "fyne Salett [helmet]" which he wished to "be vsed euere at the Ridyng of Saynt George with in the said Citie."[36] The guild of St. George at Leicester sponsored an annual riding ceremony including St. George and the dragon,[37] as did the Lostwithiel guild in Cornwall, whose St. George was dressed in plate armor (which one year cost 13d. to clean and 4d. to put on) and was accompanied by a piper.[38] Riding the George was one of the principal solemnities of the guild at Salisbury: in 1420 the guild members carried a "Jorge harnyssed [armored]" in procession on St. George's Day, and in 1510 the members were to provide men who were "well and cleanly harnyssed to waite on the George yearely to Church and from Church."[39] The guild of St. George at Little Walsingham united with the guild of the Annunciation in 1540; for the next five years the records of the Annunciation guild show payments for the bearing and the mending of the dragon, presumably the one killed by St. George.[40] The guild at Dublin put on a procession involving St. George, a maiden, a dragon, the king and queen of "Dele," and various attendants, and even people playing the Emperor Datianus and his wife.[41] Although the guild at Chichester apparently did not sponsor a riding of St. George as such, the members purchased a quarter cask of wine that they partly consumed on St. George's Day and, after hearing a service in the chapel of St. George in the cathedral, distributed the rest to the populace at large.[42] They also sponsored jugglers and minstrels who performed on the day.[43] All these displays were by no means the only

---

36   Eileen White, *The Saint Christopher and Saint George Guild of York* (York: Borthwick Institute, 1987), 16.

37   William Kelly, *Notices Illustrative of the Drama, and other Popular Amusements ... of the Borough of Leicester* (London: John Russel Smith, 1865), 38, 46–50; Robert Withington, *English Pageantry* (Cambridge, Mass.: Harvard University Press, 1918), 1: 30.

38   Sally L. Joyce and Evelyn S. Newlyn, eds., *REED: Cornwall* (Toronto and Buffalo: University of Toronto Press, 1999), 412, 428–29, 499–500.

39   Charles Haskins, *The Ancient Trade Guilds and Companies of Salisbury* (Salisbury: Bennet Brothers, 1912), 40.

40   David Galloway and John Wasson, eds., *Records of Plays and Players in Norfolk and Suffolk, 1330–1642* (Oxford: Malone Society, 1980), 76–77.

41   T.F. Thiselton-Dyer, *British Calendar Customs, Past and Present* (London: George Bell and Sons, 1876), 198; Withington, *English Pageantry*, 1: 31–32.

42   A.R. Wright, *British Calendar Customs*, ed. T.E. Lones (London: Folk-Lore Society, 1938), 2: 180.

43   Cameron Louis, ed., *REED: Sussex* (Toronto and Buffalo: University of Toronto Press, 2000), 14–18.

guild-sponsored public celebrations in late-medieval England, but they would certainly have been noticed, and due to the perennial appeal of the saint's combat with the dragon, quite popular as well.

So far, this is all fairly conventional late-medieval piety. But many guilds of St. George recognized the saint's connection to the kingdom of England. Some guilds, for instance, were directly connected to royal authority. The most prominent example of this phenomenon is the fraternity of arms of St. George, established in Dublin in 1473 or 1474. At that time Sir Gilbert Debenham, James Norris, David Ketting, and Sir Robert Bold were sent by Edward IV to Ireland to deal with the myriad complaints of the men of the Irish Pale about the chronic raiding they were suffering at the hands of the native Irish. In the Irish Parliament of that year, Debenham welcomed the creation of a military order, the fraternity of St. George, to be administered by a guild consisting of the chief men of the Pale, headed by the earl of Kildare, and financed by a new poundage to be introduced on imports and exports. Although Parliament dropped its support for the fraternity in 1476, and Kildare died in 1478, his son and successor Garrett Mor Fitzgerald, eighth earl of Kildare, managed to curry favor with Edward IV and to receive regular subsidies from him for the maintenance of the fraternity. St. George was a perfect patron for this society, dedicated as it was to the military defense of the king's interests overseas.[44] Another example of connection between St. George and royal authority is seen at Warwick, where Richard II had granted a charter to the guild of St. George there to allow the formation of a guild of burgesses and other brothers and sisters, who would support a chantry of two chaplains, singing in a chapel on the gate called "Hongyngyate" of Warwick. The grant may have been arbitrary, but the guild's dedication would have done it no harm. Such a dynamic was also at play when Henry V granted a royal charter to the St. George guild of Norwich in 1417 – and even at its foundation in 1385, the Norwich guild enjoined its members to pray for all brothers and sisters of the fraternity, and "all trewe men yat trauaillen in ye kynges viage [business]."[45]

In a similar vein, other guilds dedicated to St. George acknowledged that they considered the saint to be the patron and protector of the English

---

44 Art Cosgrove, ed., *Medieval Ireland, 1169–1534* (Oxford: Clarendon Press, 1993), 2: 603–08.

45 [Joshua] Toulmin Smith and Lucy Toulmin Smith, eds., *English Gilds: The Original Ordinances of More than One Hundred Early English Gilds* (London: EETS, 1870), 2.

king and people. This happened as early as 1368, when Chichester's guild was founded "to the honor of the Holy Trinity and St. George the martyr, the patron and protector of the English."[46] At Totnes, Devonshire, the parish church of St. Mary there instituted a celebration, in 1415, for the souls of all those who had in life contributed towards the fabric of the church, to be said on St. George's Day, consisting of three masses, one "in honour of the Blessed Virgin Mary mother of the omnipotent Deity, a second requiem mass for the souls of all included in the said anniversary and for the souls of all the faithful dead, the third in honour of St. George the Martyr patron of all England."[47] These latter words seem to be the only reason why St. George was attached to the anniversary celebration at all, the point of which, as stated, was to commemorate those who had improved the fabric of the local church of St. Mary. St. George was indeed "our lady's knight," but in the guild charter he was specifically acknowledged as the patron of all England, not the protector of the Virgin Mary.

The most telling intersection of royal and popular devotion is seen in the surprisingly large number of guilds dedicated to St. George that were also guilds of local governments. Again, the most well-known example of this phenomenon occurred at Norwich, whose St. George guild attracted some of more substantial citizens of the city after it received its charter in 1417. After a period of turmoil in the 1430s and 1440s, when the guild became identified with particular faction in city politics, it was decided through the mediation of royal justice William Yelverton that the guild should remain open to all but that its chief officer should be the outgoing mayor of the city and that all aldermen and common councilors of the city should be allowed to join. This arrangement effectively made the guild into the guild of the Norwich Corporation, freeing it from becoming the tool of a particular political party, and indeed allowing it to survive the tumult of the Reformation, one of the few such guilds so to do.[48] In Exeter, the city chamber ruled in 1533 that each of its 24 members should also be a brother of the fraternity of St. George, located in the chapel in the Guildhall, and pay 4d. a year for membership dues to it.[49] At Salisbury

[46]   L. F. Salzman, ed., *The Victoria History of the County of Sussex* (London: Institute for Historical Research, 1935), 3: 92.

[47]   Hugh R. Watkin, *The History of Totnes Priory and Medieval Town, Devonshire* (Torquay: by the author, 1917), 2: 332.

[48]   Ben R. McRee, "Religious Guilds and Civic Order: The Case of Norwich in the Late Middle Ages," *Speculum* 67 (1992): 69–97, at 78, 83, 89–91.

[49]   Orme, personal communication, referencing Devon Record Office, Exeter City Archives, Chamber Act, Book II, f. 32v.

the city corporation of 24 alderman and their 48 assistants merged with the guild of St. George in that city some time in the fourteenth century; the guild maintained a chaplain whose salary came from the city corporation.[50] The Chichester guild of St. George was reorganized in 1446 such that the mayor of Chichester was always the guild's master.[51] At Leicester, the members of the city corporation, while not under the compulsion to join the guild of St. George there, did pass a resolution in 1498 that all who had been chamberlains should contribute 6d. a year to the guild, while those who had not been chamberlains should contribute 4d. a year to it.[52] The fact that William Todd, who bequeathed a helmet to the St. Christopher and St. George guild of York, was the former mayor of that city is suggestive. Although the guild of St. George at Dublin was not the guild of the city corporation as such, the current mayor was responsible for acquiring a horse for St. George for the annual procession, and the former year's mayor was charged with finding people to play the parts of the emperor and empress.[53] Although no guild of St. George existed at Bristol, a chapel of St. George, adjacent to the Guildhall, served as the official chapel of the corporation in the fifteenth century, and the city also occasionally contributed to a celebration of St. George's Day.[54] It is also worthwhile noting that the guild at Totnes was to say its three masses "in the presence of the Mayor and his colleagues or others in their place."[55]

Other corporate guilds claimed the patronage of other saints, of course, such as Holy Trinity at Coventry, or St. Anne at Lincoln. That so many corporations, however, should organize themselves under the patronage of one of the saints of the English royal house is not likely to have been by chance. The cities were aping the royal practice of venerating St. George, but on no account was any city claiming to be an equal of the king, or attempting to challenge his authority. Nor, on the other hand, was the

---

50   Haskins, *Ancient Trade Guilds*, 26, 27.
51   Salzman, ed., *Sussex*, 3: 96–97.
52   Kelly, *Notices*, 46.
53   Thiselton-Dyer, *English Calendar Customs*, 198; Withington, *English Pageantry*, 1: 31–32.
54   Mark C. Pilkinton, *REED: Bristol* (Toronto, Buffalo and London: University of Toronto Press, 1997), xxviii, 6–7, 9–10. See also Betty R. Masters and Elizabeth Ralph, eds., *The Church Book of St. Ewen's, Bristol, 1454–1584* (Bristol: Bristol and Gloucestershire Archaeological Society, 1967), 46, 49, 51, 69, which record payments from the churchwardens of the parish for carrying a cross on St. George's Day in the 1460s.
55   Watkin, *Totnes*, 2: 332.

king simply commanding cities to act in a certain way on pain of some punishment. Rather, in voluntarily organizing civic religion around the veneration of St. George, these corporations were partaking in an authority that devolved from the king but which they themselves exercised at the local level – in this way the use of St. George was like the city charter itself, granted by the king but enacted by locals. It is true that the guilds of city corporations were mostly for local elites, but these elites were less likely to have been among the top 2% of population that comprised the national political community, than the "middling sort" of prosperous artisans and traders, who also served as jurors, bailiffs, constables, or churchwardens, and who shouldered much of the burden of petty administration in the kingdom.[56] These local elites were not choosing other saints through which to express their corporate identity; their use of St. George indicates that they were conscious of their status as participants in the kingdom. Moreover, their processions were for the consumption of everyone in the city. Certainly, other corporations, while not associated with *guilds* of St. George, did sponsor St. George's Day processions in their cities. For instance, the chamberlains' account books of Newcastle-upon-Tyne record payment, on 18 and 19 April 1510, for the raw materials, construction and parading of a dragon, presumably to be used on the upcoming St. George's Day.[57] Although no guild of St. George existed at Canterbury as far as we know, John Tofer, the parson of the church of St. George there, attested in 1541 that a statue of the saint had been borne in procession on his day "in the honor of God and the King, with Mr. Mayor, the aldermen, their wives, with all the commons of the same going in procession."[58] St. George's Day processions at Stratford[59] and Coventry[60] were likely to have had official support as well. These mayors and aldermen were willing to sponsor St. George's Day processions for the same reason that other mayors and aldermen organized themselves into

[56] See A.J. Pollard, *Late Medieval England, 1399–1509* (Harlow: Longman, 2000), 255.
[57] J.J. Anderson, *REED: Newcastle upon Tyne* (Toronto and Buffalo: University of Toronto Press, 1982), 13–14.
[58] James Gairdner and R.H. Brodie, eds., *Letters and Papers, Foreign and Domestic of the Reign of Henry VIII* (Vaduz: Kraus Reprint, 1965), 2: 309.
[59] Kelly, *Notices*, 42–43.
[60] R.W. Ingram, *REED: Coventry* (Toronto: University of Toronto Press, 1981), 88, 113, 151. See also Thomas Sharp, *A Dissertation on the Pageants or Dramatic Mysteries anciently performed at Coventry* (Totowa, N.J.: Rowman and Littlefield, 1973), 161.

guilds of St. George: by the mid-fifteenth century it was something that English towns were expected to do, much as present-day local governments in the United States provide fireworks to celebrate Independence Day. They, and the residents of their towns, saw themselves as part of an English nation.

A similar nationalization of St. George can also be seen in his late-medieval English Lives. As mentioned in Chapter 2, Aelfric and Simund de Freine, both residing in England, had composed legends of St. George in Anglo-Saxon and Anglo-Norman respectively, while the *Golden Legend*, although written in Latin, an import from Italy, and a collection of readings on some 182 saints' days and other Christian festivals, was popular and influential in England. The first legend of St. George written in Middle English can be found in the early fourteenth-century *South English Legendary*, a collection of saints' Lives similar to the *Golden Legend*, and was followed by two more such collections, the *Festial* of John Mirk (an early fifteenth-century collection of homilies) and the *Speculum Sacerdotale* (also fifteenth-century).[61] John Lydgate (c. 1370-c. 1451) wrote a Life of St. George in the early fifteenth century, and William Caxton (c. 1415–91) translated the *Golden Legend* into English, which was printed by Wynkyn de Worde in 1512. Finally, Alexander Barclay (c. 1475–1552) freely translated and embellished the *Georgius* of Baptista Spagnuoli "the Mantuan" into English in 1515. The dragon story does not appear in the St. George legend of most extant manuscripts of the *South English Legendary*, but it does appear in at least one,[62] as it does in all other late-medieval English versions of the St. George legend. All accounts of St. George's martyrdom in these legends feature far fewer tortures, and miracles, than do the earliest Passions of St. George, although the details vary. In their place, as Jennifer Fellows notes, a steady "chivalrization" of the St. George legend occurred as newer versions were composed. While the *Golden Legend* and the *South English Legendary* emphasize that George's killing of a dragon was a means to the end of converting the populace of Silene, *Mirk's Festial* emphasizes

---

61   *The Early South English Legendary or Lives of Saints*, ed. Carl Horstmann, EETS 87 (Millwood, N.Y.: Kraus Reprint, 1987), 294–96; John Mirk, *Mirk's Festial: A Collection of Homilies*, ed. Theodore Erbe, EETS Extra Series 96 (Millwood, N.Y.: Kraus Reprint, 1987), 132–35; *Speculum Sacerdotale*, ed. Edward H. Weatherly, EETS 200 (London: EETS, 1936), 129–33.

62   Minneapolis, University of Minnesota MS Z 822 N 81, edited by R.E. Parker in "A northern fragment of *The Life of St. George*," *Modern Language Notes* 38 (1923): 97–101.

the dragon-fight more for its own sake, having the creature "spyttyng out fure, and profer[yng] batayll to George." The *Speculum Sacerdotale* and John Lydgate pay more attention to George's fight with the dragon than to his martyrdom – the *Speculum Sacerdotale* even has the dragon-fight happening, paradoxically, after the martyrdom, while Lydgate has it that

> This name George by Interpetacioun
> Is sayde of tweyne, the first of hoolynesse,
> And the secound of knighthood and renoun,
> As that myn Auctour lykethe for to expresse,
> The feond venqwysshing of manhhode and prowesse,
> The worlde, the flesshe, as Crystes owen knight,
> Wher-euer he roode in steel armed bright.

Note that the second, chivalric meaning of "George" receives far more explanation than the first, "holy" one. Finally, Mantuan, and thus Barclay, have a prolonged and detailed dragon-fight with specific parallels drawn to secular sources, with the princess standing "as Andromeda" to the monster, for example, and with the dragon being killed in combat, like the dragon-fights of romance and unlike previous accounts of the legend of St. George, in which the beast is only wounded at first and then dispatched after the populace agrees to accept Christianity.[63]

Parallel to St. George's chivalrization is his nationalization, starting with John Mirk and culminating in Alexander Barclay. At the end of his homily on St. George, Mirk enjoins his listeners to

> pray we to Saynt George that he wyll be our helpe at oure need, and *saue thys reem* to the worschyp of God and his modyr Mary and all the company of Heuen.[64]

John Lydgate begins his rhyming Life of St. George with two stanzas:

> O ye folkes that here present be
> Which of this story shal haue inspeccion
> Of seint George ye may be holde & see
> His marterdom and his passion
> And how he is protector and patron
> This holy martir of knyghthode lode sterre
> To englisshemen both in pes and warre

---

[63] Jennifer Fellows, "St. George as Romance Hero," *Reading Medieval Studies* 19 (1993): 27–54, at 33–36.
[64] *Mirk's Festial*, 135, emphasis added.

In whos honoure sithen gon ful yore
The thridde Edwarde of knyghthode most entier
In his tyme by assent of Wyndesore
ffounded the order first of the gartere
Of worthi knyghtys and ay fro yere to yere
xxiiijti cladde in oo lyveree
Vpon his day kept the solempnyte.[65]

William Caxton's life of St. George ends with a coda, which is by no means found in any other version of the *Golden Legend*:

This blessyd and holy martyr saynt Georg is the patrone of this royame of Englonde / and the crye of men of warre. In the worshyp of whome is founded the noble ordre of the garter / and also a noble college in the castell of Wyndesore by kynges of Englonde / in whiche college is the herte of saynt George whiche Sygysmonde the emperour of almayne brought and gaue it for a grete and precyous relyque to kynge Harry the fyfte. And also the sayd sygysmonde was a broder of the sayd garter / and also there is a pyece of his hede whiche college is nobly endowed to the honour and worshyp of almyghty god and his blessed martyr saynt George. Thenne lete vs praye vnto hym that he be the specyall protector and defensor of this royame.[66]

Mantuan, as could be expected, does not acknowledge George's connection to England, but Alexander Barclay does. The title page itself advises that St. George is the "patron of the royalme of England," and in the dedicatory preface to the duke of Norfolk, Barclay announces that it is his purpose "to laude saynt George: our glorious patron / And moue his seruauntes vnto deuocyon," since

the wryters / of euery nacyon
Commende theyr patrons / praysynge theyr lyfe & name
Than to our patron / ought we to do the same.[67]

Another introduction, offered in Latin to Nicholas West, bishop-elect of Ely, speaks of "Georgium Militum principem nostrum Regnique nostri Patronum," and in the first chapter Barclay announces that he will tell "the life of our patron, St. George the worthy knight."[68] Other such

---

[65] E.P. Hammond, "Two Tapestry Poems by Lydgate," *Englische Studien* 43 (1910): 13.

[66] In Alexander Barclay, *The Life of St. George*, ed. William Nelson, EETS 230 (London: EETS, 1955), 118.

[67] Barclay, *Life of St. George*, 1, 5.

[68] Barclay, *Life of St. George*, 7, 15.

references to George being "our patron" are scattered throughout, including in an "apostrophe ad anglos" which appears after George's conversion to Christianity during adolescence:

> O English youth, it is both sin and shame
> to see in thy patron such manly doughtiness
> And thou to spend thy time in thriftless game
> The ground of vice and rot of wretchedness
> flee from such folly use noble besynes
> And things that at ende may help a common wealth
> or else that may be unto thy soules health.[69]

All of these works attest that, by the early sixteenth century, the idea of St. George as a national patron had become a literary trope. Of course, the extent to which they reflected, or inspired, any popular notions of St. George's status is impossible to ascertain, although the fact that the *Festial* was a collection of homilies, meant to be preached in church, suggests that the idea was certainly a fit one for public consumption. John Lydgate, for his part, was a monk at Bury St. Edmunds in Suffolk. He was well connected and wrote poems for powerful patrons, including King Henry VI, for whom he acted as a court poet. Such things may have inspired Lydgate to designate St. George the patron saint of the kingdom, in order to flatter his employers; however, it should be noted that he composed his Life of St. George for the Armorers Guild of London,[70] for whom he would have been under no obligation to designate George the patron of "Englishmen" (not just of the king or of a more abstract "England") "both in peace and war." Caxton also enjoyed occasional royal patronage at the courts of Edward IV and Richard III;[71] this fact may explain his willingness to acknowledge George as the patron, special protector, and defender of the kingdom of England, and the cry of its men of war, as well as the patron of the order of the Garter. Barclay, who was a monk at Ely cathedral, did not have connections at the royal court like Lydgate or Caxton, although the duke of Norfolk was a member of the order of the Garter and the victor of the battle of Flodden Field in 1513, and Bishop West had been dean of Windsor.[72] Nonetheless, all this literature would have found an audience beyond its commissioners or dedicatees, particularly after

[69]   Barclay, *Life of St. George*, 22.
[70]   Derek Pearsall, *John Lydgate (1371–1449): A Bio-bibliography* (Victoria, B.C.: University of Victoria Press, 1997), 31.
[71]   *Dictionary of National Biography*, s.v. "Caxton, William."
[72]   Barclay, *Life of St. George*, xv–xvi.

the advent of commercial printing in the late fifteenth century; Caxton's and Barclay's works would certainly not have hurt the propagation of the idea that St. George was the national patron. Mirk's and Caxton's Lives, indeed, were contained in collections of saints' lives, and as such read primarily for devotion, and even ask the reader to *pray* that St. George would defend the kingdom, another instance of the overlap between the political and devotional cults of the saint.

Of course, these two aspects never overlapped completely. It is clear that St. George was popular independent of his political symbolism. A saint from the early days of Christianity, he had a long record of miraculous intervention at important times, especially during the first crusade. His auxiliary power continued into the fifteenth century, and was acknowledged by Lydgate and others. In an age of rudimentary medicine and uncertain social welfare, people always welcomed supernatural aid. The dragon story, clearly one that people enjoyed, provided a graphic illustration of the potentialities of George's help – whatever evil the dragon represented, George was there to kill it.

It is likely too that the specific *chivalric* form of this legend was appealing to people, even those who were not knights. As an ideal, chivalry had an appeal far beyond the knightly class,[73] and St. George's slaying of a dragon, and rescuing of a princess, would have been exciting and compelling to anyone who heard it (St. George, indeed, was a pure knight, far more chivalric than any of chivalry's real-life exemplars). Furthermore, the princess's role was more than merely passive: rather than trying to escape her fate in a cowardly manner, she calmly accepted it and walked towards the dragon on her own, she spoke out and warned St. George of the danger they both faced, and used the magic power of her girdle to subdue the dragon and bring it into the city of Silene. (The Sarum rite prayer specifically acknowledges Sabra's role when it claims that the dragon was "overcome by a girl in honor of [God's] blessed and most glorious martyr,

---

73   Maurice Keen, *Chivalry* (New Haven and London: Yale University Press, 1984), 128. And as M.I. Finley notes, "the evidence of what has been called the peasant type of heroic poetry, oral epics composed and recited among peasants rather than in the halls of barons – a very widespread type in many regions of Europe and Asia – tends to argue that they told the same kinds of stories, about the same kinds of heroes, with the identical values and virtues, as the aristocratic epic of the Homeric type." See *The World of Odysseus*, rev. edn. (New York: Viking Press, 1965), 120.

George.")[74] Many ridings of St. George featured a princess, often with several female attendants. So although St. George was male and engaged in manly activity, a female had an essential part to play in the unfolding drama, which would have increased its appeal. And if Sabra was not enough, there was always the Virgin Mary, whose knight St. George was. Art occasionally showed St. George being resurrected and armed by the Virgin, and literary sources such as Lydgate's rhyming Kalendar, the Agincourt Carol, another fifteenth-century carol "And by a chapell as I came," and a a charm against the Night Mare (a creature that would enter stables at night and disturb the horses, tire them out by riding them, and tangle their manes) all mention St. George as "our lady's knight."[75] The immense popularity of the mother of Christ was also reflected onto St. George, thereby buttressing his own popularity.

But it is equally clear that this popular cult coincided to some extent with the political one. The Agincourt Carol's linking of the fight of the English army against the French, with the fight of the average Christian against the devil, both under the banner of St. George, is one concrete example. The acknowledgement of Mirk, Lydgate, Caxton, and Barclay that St. George was the patron of the realm of England – and especially Mirk's and Caxton's requests, in devotional texts, that the reader pray to St. George to protect the realm – is another. But the guilds of England are perhaps the clearest example of the willingness of English commoners to value St. George as the patron of their kingdom. Not only is St. George acknowledged as such in many guild charters, guilds of St. George acted as the guilds of a number of civic corporations (and even when they did not, civic corporations were willing to sponsor ridings of St. George). By the mid-fifteenth century, a royal and military practice had spread to the provinces.

Did it stop there? Guilds often contained strong elements of social control, either of their own members, or of those guilds considered beneath them. In this way the local ridings of St. George have been read as a means

74 *Horae Eboracensis: The Prymer or Hours of the Blessed Virgin Mary According to the use of the Illustrious Church of York*, ed. Canon Wordsworth (Durham and London: Surtees Society, 1920), 131–32.

75 John Lydgate, *The Minor Poems of John Lydgate*, ed. Henry Noble MacCracken (London: EETS, 1911), 367; Greene, ed., *Selection*, 124; R.L. Greene, *The Early English Carols* (Oxford: Clarendon Press, 1935), 223; Rossell Hope Robbins, ed., *Secular Lyrics of the Fifteenth Century*, 2nd edn. (Oxford: Clarendon Press, 1955), 61.

by which local elites cemented their place against their inferiors. Samantha Riches contrasts the pageant of the St. George guild of Norwich with that of the Corpus Christi processions at Coventry and Stratford: whereas the former was performed by guild members only, the latter included all guilds in the city. The connection between St. George guilds and local government, where it existed, also represents a form of social control: the local elites used St. George, the patron of chivalry, to impress upon the local commoners their obligation to obey their betters.[76] This dynamic, however, does not explain everything. On a general level, it would be just as true to say that the corporations were claiming the right to be taken seriously as members of the political nation – that the audience were their superiors as much as their inferiors (just as the cities presented tableaux of St. George to the king, when he came to visit). More importantly, although the processions on the feast of Corpus Christi may have involved all the guilds of Coventry and Stratford, hierarchy was an integral part of these processions too, and determining that hierarchy could involve a great deal of rancor, as Miri Rubin reminds us.[77] All medieval conceptions of community involved some form of hierarchy, but such hierarchy did not diminish the community itself, even when it broke into open rebellion: the peasants of 1381 repeatedly expressed their allegiance to the king, for instance, in part through St. George's banner. Riches notes that all inhabitants of Leicester were compelled to come and watch the St. George's Day processions in that city, a case of "having fun because you were told to."[78] In other cities, however, it is quite likely, on account of the perennial appeal of the dragon-fight, that the inhabitants would *want* to come to see the colorful and exciting pageantry (and just because one was not marching in a procession does not mean that one was not participating in it). At Chichester, as we have seen, St. George's Day featured jugglers, minstrels, and free wine, for the consumption of everyone.

This participatory aspect of St. George's English patronage is on display in Barclay's *Life of St. George*. When the inhabitants of Silene need to appease the dragon, they pass a motion "by Act of Parlyament" that a lottery should be held to determine which of their children is to be fed to it. The king subsequently has to "alay the malyce of the comons" by sacrificing his own daughter when her lot is chosen. St. George, therefore,

---

[76]   Riches, *St George*, 137–38.
[77]   Miri Rubin, *Corpus Christi: The Eucharist in Late Medieval Culture* (Cambridge: Cambridge University Press, 1991), 260ff.
[78]   Riches, *St George*, 138.

after he rescues the princess becomes the "Champyon royall."[79] The Englishness of those expressions, and the numerous references throughout the text to St. George being "our patron," suggest that Silene actually stands in for England in Barclay's *Life*. Furthermore, after the Sileneans convert to Christianity, dispose of the dragon's remains, and build their church, St. George has some parting advice for them about how to organize their society (which is present in Mantuan, but far more developed in Barclay):

ye that are comons / obey your kynge and lorde
Obserue vnto hym / love and fydelyte
Auoyde Rebellyon / for certaynely discorde
Is rote and mother of carefull pouerte ...
No man presume / more hye than is degre
A lowest place : is oft moste sure and stable
Abyde in vertue / be neuer chaungeable
Namely be true / to god your heuynly lorde ...

ye ryche helpe them / whiche haue necessyte
Eche socour other / suche way is charytable
... suche of you / as are in hye degre
Set all your myndes / and chefe intencyon
To se the pore / haue right and equyte
Rather with fauour / than wronge extorcyon

And ye that are kynge / hede of the regyon
Se that eche man / in maners lyie and do
After the degre / whiche he is callyd to do ...
And lyke as your rowme / is moste of excellence ...
So ought your lyfe / be clennest from offence ...
A vycyous prynce / is as a plage mortall
And foule example / to all his comonte

And ye that are mynystres / to god omnipotent
Informe ye other / to walke the path of grace
But se your owne lyfe / be pure and innocent.[80]

This advice is a fair encapsulation of late-medieval socio-political theory. It is remarkable because it encompasses *all* the estates of the kingdom, with specific rights and duties prescribed for each one. This contrasts with the saint's advice in the *Golden Legend*, which is directed at the king alone, and offers three instructions on the stewardship of the church, and one on the care of the poor. St. George, who has restored the king's dignity, is

79   Barclay, *Life of St. George*, 31, 35, 53.
80   Barclay, *Life of St. George*, 57–59.

thus projected as the king's patron, but a king who is the head of a community of the realm in which everyone has a proper role to play. The exhortation to the youth of England to follow the example of their patron's "manly doughtiness" and to avoid their own "thriftless game," to the benefit of the commonwealth, underlines this participatory aspect of St. George's national patronage. The notion that such things as thrift and mutual goodwill are enough to ensure a harmonious and prosperous society strike the modern reader as absurd, of course, but the point is that such platitudes were widely cherished (witness the invective later heaped on Machiavelli's *Prince*) and, in Barclay's work, endorsed (and guaranteed) by St. George, patron of the entire kingdom.

Barclay's *Life* thus represents an apposite culmination of St. George's late-medieval patronage. Chapter 3 dealt with the royal use of St. George, and how that use resonated with the saint's popularity among the barons and knights of England. This had the effect of creating a sense of common purpose among the political class, which bound nobles close to the king, but which could be used against the king if he ever strayed from that purpose. By the early sixteenth century, this sense of common purpose had spread to other people in the kingdom. It never completely colonized popular devotion, and it might have been explicitly hierarchical (more so, for instance, than the Order of the Garter). But even in Barclay's Life, which is quite "regal" (casting discontent against the king, even expressed through Parliament, as a very bad thing), St. George does warn the king, in no uncertain terms, to live a clean life and not to be vicious. The king is also subject to "social control."

This idea of a hierarchical but inclusive political community may not always have been realized, of course. The king did not always rule well, rich did not always protect the poor, and commoners did not always mind their collective station. But it is clear that it existed, helping to provide a further element of stability to the late-medieval English polity, and bestowing St. George's dignity on the nation. By the sixteenth century St. George was so ingrained as a representative of England that he survived the Reformation as a national symbol, a status he retains to this day.

5

St. George's Post-Medieval Career

St. George's career in England since his advent as the national patron in the fourteenth and fifteenth centuries has been varied. The sixteenth century saw the first major shift in that career on account of the English Reformation, which simultaneously denigrated traditional Catholic religion, and strengthened English national identity. Since St. George was a figure of both, it is no surprise that people no longer prayed to him, dedicated churches to him, or commissioned statuary of him for votive purposes. He endured, however, as a figure of chivalry and romance, one that still reflected well on the English. The advent of "Britain" and of the Enlightenment in the eighteenth century diminished his appeal, but he came back into fashion in the nineteenth as a result of neo-medievalism and Imperial pride. Falling out of favor again in the twentieth century, he has enjoyed a modest recent revival as political devolution in the United Kingdom has forced the recovery of a specifically English identity, and its attendant symbolism. For the time being, his English future looks bright.

Renaissance humanism, and the Protestant Reformation that it inspired, were not kind to St. George. The fact that the saint made no appearance in the Bible, now judged to be the chief arbiter of Christian practice, did not help – even worse was the absence of any proper primary source attesting to his origins and career. Worst of all was the fantastic and sentimental story of the dragon, which encapsulated everything humanists and Reformers despised about medieval piety. In 1509, Erasmus of Rotterdam, in his famous polemic *Praise of Folly*, mocked those who believed that gazing upon an image of St. Christopher would protect them from death, or that accosting a statue of St. Barbara with the proper words would allow them to return from battle unharmed. In George, such simpletons have "discovered a new Hercules ... They all but worship George's horse, most religiously decked out in breastplates and bosses, and from time to time oblige him with some little gift. To swear by his bronze helmet is thought to be an oath fit for a king."[1] The Reformer Jean Calvin, in his *Institutes of the Christian Religion,* asserted that since Scripture places the principal part of worship in the invocation of God, it is manifest sacrilege to offer prayer to others, such as "George and Hippolyte, and similar phantoms."[2] Even Pope Clement VII, in response to criticisms such as these, tried to expunge all mention of the dragon from prayers to St. George in breviaries and missals of the church.[3]

These intellectual debates had little apparent effect on the practice of religion in England, however. On the eve of the Reformation, St. George was as popular as ever. In 1521 the parishioners of Bassingbourn, Cambridgeshire, began a large money-raising effort to have a new image of St. George made, which was completed in 1523 by the "George Maker" Robert Jones of Walden.[4] Guilds dedicated to the saint continued to be active and even to be founded through the 1530s, and St. George's Day processions were held into the 1540s. Royal support for the cult continued as well. Henry VIII had a figure of St. George engraved on his armor, was shown kneeling next to St. George in the east window of St. Margaret's parish church in Westminster, and possessed numerous jewels with images of the saint.[5] His George Noble of 1526 was the first English coin to have St. George depicted on it, and in the same year a pageant in Rome celebrating the Holy League had the kings of England and France

---

[1] Desiderius Erasmus, *The Praise of Folly*, trans. Clarence H. Miller (New Haven and London: Yale University Press, 1979), 63.

[2] John Calvin, *Institutes of the Christian Religion*, trans. Henry Beveridge (Grand Rapids, Mich.: Eerdmans, 1989), book III, chap. 20, § 27.

[3] P.J. Hogarth, "St. George: The Evolution of a Saint and his Dragon," *History Today* 30:4 (1980): 17–22, at 20.

[4] Eamon Duffy, *The Stripping of the Altars: Traditional Religion in England, 1400–1580* (New Haven and London: Yale University Press, 1992), 156.

[5] Samuel Rush Meyrick, "Description of the Engravings on a German suit of Armour, made for Henry VIII, in the Tower of London," *Archaeologia* 22 (1829): 106–13; G. Scharf, "On a Votive Painting of St. George and the Dragon," *Archaeologia* 49 (1886): 254; *The Antient Kalendars and Inventories of the Treasury of His Majesty's Exchequer*, ed. Francis Palgrave (London: Public Records Commissioners, 1836), 3: 260, 271–72, 273.

represented by images of St. George and St. Denis.[6] The series of acts that culminated in Henry's break with Rome and the establishment of himself as Supreme Governor of the Church of England in 1534 had no initial effect on the veneration of saints – Henry's church was to be Catholic, just not Roman Catholic. His dissolution of the monasteries proceeded far more from financial greed than any principled opposition to monasticism, and his destruction of the shrine of St. Thomas Becket in 1540 was largely a function of Thomas's political symbolism and not of his status as a saint. Other saints, including St. George, were left untouched.

This situation was to change in the reign of Henry's son and successor Edward VI. Edward had been raised as a Protestant; more importantly, his regency council was dominated by committed Protestants. The six years of young Edward's reign mark the true beginning of the English Reformation, and St. George did not remain unscathed. This was apparent from the very beginning. On his way to his coronation on 19 February 1547, Edward passed through the city of London, where a child richly appareled was ready to pronounce a Latin oration, and a St. George was to have made one in English, "but for lack of time it could not be done, the king made such speed."[7] Was it lack of time, or were other motives involved? Edward certainly proceeded in this vein: in 1547 his council induced Parliament to pass an act dissolving religious guilds and fraternities, and outlawing religious processions, thus undermining a key feature of the veneration of St. George in England.[8] St. George's status as a national saint did serve to counter somewhat his lack of appearances in the Bible: Thomas Cranmer's first Book of Common Prayer of 1549 listed St. George's Day in red letter in its calendar, although the second prayer book of 1552 demoted the feast to black letter. George was the only non-biblical saint so commemorated, and certainly in opposition to the spirit of the book, which held that:

> some [festivals] at the first were of Godly entent and purpose devised, and yet at length turned to vanitie and superstition: some entered into the church by undiscrete devotion, and such a zeale as was without knowledge: and for because thei were winked at in the beginning, thei

6 British Museum, *Handbook of the Coins of Great Britain* (London: British Museum, 1869–70), no. 406; Sydney Anglo, *Spectacle, Pageantry, and Early Tudor Policy* (New York: Oxford University Press, 1997), 208–09.
7 John Leland, *De rebus britannicis Collectanea* (London: Benjamin White, 1774), 4: 319.
8 A.G. Dickens, *The English Reformation*, 2nd edn. (University Park, Pa.: Penn State Press, 1989), 230–31.

grewe daily to more and more abuses: whiche not onely for their unprofit ablenesse, but also because thei have much blinded the people, and obscured the glory of God, are worthy to be cut awaie, and clene rejected.[9]

It is not surprising, therefore, that in 1552, the Bishop of London declared St. George's Day void.[10] Nor was the Order of the Garter spared. An incident recorded by John Foxe, who heard it from one Edward Underhill, encapsulates the young king's attitude toward the patron of the order. At the Garter feast of 1551, held that year at Greenwich, Edward asked his fellow members:

"My Lords, I pray you what saint is S. George that we heere so honour him?" At which question the other lords being so astonied, the lord treasurer that then was [the marques of Winchester], perceiving this, gave answer and said, "If it please your Majestie, I did never reade in any historie of S. George, but only in Legenda Aurea, where it is thus set downe, that S. George out with his sword, and ran the dragon through with his speare." The King, when he could not a great while speak for laughing, at length said, "I pray you, my lord, and what did he do with his sword the while?" "That I cannot tell your Majestie," said he. And so an end of that question of good S. George.[11]

As early as 1548 a Privy Council ordinance stated that "all such things, as be not conformable and agreeing to his Majesty's Injunctions, Orders, or Reformations, now of late prescribed, should be also in that most Noble Order and the Ceremonies thereof left undone, and reformed."[12] Preliminary suppressions included the requiem Mass for departed knights and the Latin processional, for which was substituted an English one. In 1550 a commission of six knights was appointed to further revise the statutes; the results, published three years later, claimed that the "Old Serpent Satan" had invested the statutes with "many obscure, superstitious, and repugnant opinions." As a consequence, the Order was to be divorced from all association with St. George – it was to be known

---

9 *Book of Common Prayer* (London, 1552), "Of ceremonies," http://justus. anglican.org/resources/bcp/1552/Front_matter_1552.htm (accessed 16 June 2008).

10 *Chronicle of the Grey Friars of London*, Camden Society Old Series 53 (London: Camden Society, 1852), 74.

11 Quoted in Hogarth, "St George," 20.

12 In Roy Strong, *The Cult of Elizabeth: Elizabethan Portraiture and Pageantry* (Berkeley and Los Angeles: University of California Press, 1977), 166.

simply as the Garter, with the simple emblem of a knight on horseback and the motto "Honi Soit Qui Mal Y Pense," and festivities were to be transferred from 23 April to Whitsunday. Edward died, however, before these new statutes could be put into effect,[13] and his Roman Catholic successor Mary had no interest in upholding them. Indeed, the Garter ceremonies became for her a useful public statement of return to the old religion, with its pre-Reformation masses and processions.[14] Thus it appeared that St. George, as a saint, had been saved for the time being.

The accession of Mary's sister Elizabeth in 1558 caused another religious upheaval. Elizabeth, like Edward, had been raised as a Protestant, and with the Act of Supremacy of 1559 had herself declared the Supreme Governor of the Church of England. The Act of Uniformity of the same year provided a new prayer book for the church, a compromise between the first and second Edwardian prayer books. Elizabeth's actual religious practice, however, was tolerant of Catholic ceremony, and as a consequence she did not revisit Edward's attempted Garter reforms. At the annual Garter ceremony, congruent with the new religious dispensation, a Prayer Book communion service was celebrated, and not in memory of departed Garter knights. However, the association of the Order with St. George remained, along with sumptuous pageantry and feasting. Although the festivities tended to be held at Whitehall and not Windsor, they were held on 23 April, and the Queen's Chapel Closet was decorated as the chapel at Windsor, complete with stalls and banners of the knights, and choristers, chaplains, heralds, and the gentlemen pensioners were all in attendance. An engraving by Marcus Gheerarts the Elder records the 1576 Garter procession – he portrays it as dignified, but in no way plain: all participants were dressed in their robes, with the knights and Elizabeth herself wearing their Garter collars.[15] All this, indeed, was of a piece with Elizabeth's public self-fashioning as queen. In accession day tilts, court masques, and a long series of official portraits, Elizabeth was constantly portrayed as Gloriana, the Virgin Queen, and the object of the chivalric adoration of her courtier knights. Such Elizabethan neo-medievalism certainly helped to preserve the place of St. George in English culture, although not as Edward III would have recognized him: George was now purely a figure of romance and chivalry,

---

13 Strong, *Cult of Elizabeth*, 166; Timothy Hugh Wilson, "Saint George in Tudor and Stuart England," (M.Phil. dissertation, Warburg Institute, 1976), 63.
14 Wilson, "Saint George," 70.
15 See Strong, *Cult of Elizabeth*, 169–71.

whose story writers were free to embellish with all manner of invention, since the Catholic hagiographical tradition of Jacobus de Voragine was no longer relevant.

Three works published in the reign of Elizabeth may serve to illustrate this phenomenon. The first, Edmund Spenser's *Faerie Queene*, appeared in 1590. The author, Elizabeth's Poet Laureate, intended the entire work as a glorification of his patron and her Tudor dynasty. The *Faerie Queene* was to contain twelve books, although Spenser only managed to compose half that number before his death in 1599. Each book, composed of twelve cantos of approximately 50 nine-line "Spenserian" stanzas, is an extended allegory on a particular virtue, such as temperance, chastity, or friendship. The first book, on holiness, contains a novel treatment of the story of St. George, here called the Redcrosse knight on account of the saint's well-known coat of arms. At the start of the book Redcrosse receives a commission from Gloriana, Queen of Fairy Land, to deliver the maiden Una to her parents and to rid their kingdom of the dragon that has been plaguing it. Redcrosse has many adventures along the way, not all of which redound to his credit: he defeats the monster Error, but is then tricked by the magician Archimago into believing that Una is woman of easy virtue. He abandons her and is then beguiled by the witch Duessa, who appears as the beautiful and innocent girl he had thought Una was. Successive encounters with her associates – the Saracen brothers Sansfoy, Sansloy, and Sansjoy; Lucifera, Queen of the House of Pride; and Orgoglio, the arrogant giant – leave Redcrosse debilitated and imprisoned in Orgoglio's dungeon. Meanwhile Una, who has found protection from a lion, a band of satyrs, and a rustic knight, meets a dwarf who tells her about the plight of Redcrosse. They encounter Prince Arthur and beseech his aid; Arthur storms Orgoglio's castle, slays the giant, frees Redcrosse, and exposes Duessa for the imposter she is. Redcrosse returns to his mission with Una, although he almost succumbs to the villain Despair out of his sense of unworthiness and guilt. Una instead leads him to the House of Hope, where he is restored to spiritual and physical health. It is at this point in the narrative that Redcrosse is revealed to be St. George, the dragon-slaying patron of England. They finally reach the land of Una's parents, and after an apocalyptic three-day battle Redcrosse finally overcomes the dragon. The kingdom is freed, and Redcrosse and Una are betrothed.

If the theme of this first book is "holiness" it is not hard to interpret the allegory as a defense of the Protestant Church of England from various evils plaguing it, for the most part associated with Roman Catholicism. Thus do Una, England's "one church," and her champion St. George, suffer the depredations of Roman Catholic Error, of Archimago and Duessa (representing the Pope and Queen Mary, who briefly separated England from the true faith), of those "without faith," "without law" and "without joy," of Pride (and other deadly sins), of Orgoglio (perhaps representing Philip of Spain), and of the dragon (representing Catholicism itself). All this is a long way from the standard narrative running from Jacobus de Voragine to Alexander Barclay – Spenser retains the damsel, her parents, and the dragon, but freely embellishes his narrative with all manner of invented incidents, including the actual betrothal of St. George with the maiden; respect for hagiographical tradition was not at a premium in Protestant England. But St. George, allegedly the worst sort of invented and unbelievable saint, was not so Catholic that he could not be cast as a champion of Protestantism. The chivalry of St. George found a place in the neo-chivalry of Elizabeth's court, and the symbolic open-endedness of his dragon allowed for a new interpretation.

A similar reworking of the St. George legend is available in our second work, Richard Johnson's *Seven Champions of Christendom*, published in two parts in 1596 and 1597. Johnson's seven champions are Saints George, Andrew, David, Patrick, Denis, James, and Anthony, representing England, Scotland, Wales, Ireland, France, Spain and Italy respectively. The book opens with the story of St. George's birth at Coventry. As he emerges from his mother's womb it is discovered that he has on his breast "the liuely forme of a Dragon, vpon his right hand a bloody Crosse, and on his left leg a golden garter."[16] George is immediately stolen by Kalyb, the Lady of the Woods, and kept in captivity throughout his childhood. Eventually George manages to free himself, and have Kalyb enclosed in a rock of stone; he also frees the six other champions whom Kalyb had earlier imprisoned in a Brazen Castle. These other knights render knightly courtesies to George before setting off on their own adventures. St. George's wanderings take him to Egypt, where he slays the burning dragon, and redeems the king's daughter Sabra, but is betrayed by Almidor, the black king of Morocco and sent to the soldan of Persia to be imprisoned. After seven years he escapes, and steals back Sabra from the Moorish king. He then leads the other six champions in jousts at a wedding feast and in battles against the pagans in Portugal, Hungary and Barbary. In Egypt, a necromancer raises spirits to fight against the Christians; the six are enchanted, but freed by St. George. Later, the six are imprisoned by a giant, and again freed by St. George. George also procures food for

---

[16] Richard Johnson, *The Seven Champions of Christendom (1596/7)*, ed. Jennifer Fellows (Aldershot: Ashgate, 2003), 7.

them when they are famished in a wood, and finally he frees them all from imprisonment in the Black Castle. The champions enjoy a round of tourneying at the court of the Grecian Emperor before their respective deaths are related; George himself succumbs to the sting of a dragon's tail. But they are all resurrected for one final battle against the Pagans, which they naturally win.

It is clear that *Seven Champions* was quite popular. The second part was prompted by the public's "kind acceptance of my first part" the previous year.[17] The two parts were reissued in 1608 with minor changes, and again in 1616 with more substantial changes, including the addition of seven new chapters, a version that was reprinted several times throughout the seventeenth century, in an age in which romances are generally thought to have been passé (the story, at any rate, with its long-winded and unsubtle narrative, is not the most inspired example of the genre). But *Seven Champions* is certainly in keeping with the times. Apart from his connection to a dragon and a maid, the St. George of Johnson's romance bears little resemblance to medieval hagiography (nor do the stories of any of the other champions, for that matter) – instead, the story of St. George here is largely indebted to the Middle English romance *Sir Bevis of Hampton*. Unlike the *Faerie Queene*, *Seven Champions* is not an elaborate allegory of the defense of the Church of England from Roman Catholicism, but a celebration of a rather jejune English nationalism. St. George is the foremost of the champions: the story opens with him, the only one of the champions who has his birth and childhood (which is located specifically in England) related. Throughout, George remains paramount: he has most of the narrative expended on him, is clearly the leader of the champions, and is the one who rescues them from dangerous situations or inspires them to achieve greater things. *Seven Champions* thus represents a lowbrow version of the *Faerie Queene*, a reinterpretation of the legend of St. George for nationalistic purposes, in this case to cast the English as the most important people in Europe, and its natural leaders. St. George evidently enjoyed a continued appeal as a national symbol beyond the court.

A third literary use of St. George during the reign of Elizabeth is Gerrard De Malynes's *Saint George for England, Allegorically Described* (1601). De Malynes, a merchant and sometime government advisor, was uninterested in any narratives, traditional or otherwise, about the saint, but did find his conflict with the dragon to be useful on two counts. The first appears in the preface to Thomas Edgerton, Lord Keeper of the Great Seal:

---

[17] Johnson, *Seven Champions*, xxiii.

The inuented historie of S. *George* … may conveniently be applied to these dayes of her Maiesties most happy gouernement, wherin the beames of the Orientall starre of Gods most holy word appeare vnto vs most splendent and transparent, to the singular comfort of all faithfull. For wheras vnder the person of the noble champion Saint GEORGE our Sauiour Christ was prefigured, deliuering the Virgin (which did signifie the sinfull soules of Christians) from the dragon or diuels power: So her most excellent Maiesty by aduancing the pure doctrine of CHRIST IESVS in all truth and sincerity, hath (as an instrument appointed by diuine prouidence) bene vsed to perform the part of a valiant champion, deliuering an infinite number out of the diuel's power, whereunto they were tied with the forcible chaines of darknesse.[18]

De Malynes notes that the St. George legend has been "abused," but following Spenser it may still be interpreted in accord with Protestant values: here St. George is a type of Christ, a savior of souls. Unlike in the *Faerie Queene*, however, Queen Elizabeth is not cast in a distant, supervisory role, but as St. George himself! Her active choice of Protestantism for England saved it, as St. George saved the damsel in distress. But De Malynes was much less concerned with religion than with what he called "political usury." The text of the book is an extended meditation on the evils of this practice, which De Malynes imagines as a dragon capable of great and varied destruction. Fortunately, St. George, representing the "king's authority," may be able to rescue the damsel (the "king's treasure") from this wicked creature. This argument is strangely anachronistic and somewhat at odds with his praise of Elizabeth's Protestantism (it is the medieval Catholic church that was so set against usury, after all) but it is unsurprising that when De Malynes offered advice on the protection of what he considered the national interest, he chose the metaphor of St. George and the dragon, now thoroughly a part of the national mythology.

But this Elizabethan neo-chivalric moment was not to last. Although the early Stuart monarchs made much use of Garter ceremonial,[19] their dynasty also saw increased political discord that eventually broke out into civil war between king and parliament in the 1640s. Since the latter was dominated by Puritans, most of whom held Calvin's opinions about saints, St. George reverted to being a royal symbol and not a national one. Gone were the days when he served as a rebuke to kings for not ruling well; instead, he became emblematic of the decadence of the court itself. This

---

[18]   Gerrard De Malynes, *Saint George for England, Allegorically Described* (London: Richard Field, 1601), A2r–A2v.
[19]   Wilson, "Saint George," 105–06.

opinion was greatly aided by a new interpretation of St. George's legend first published in 1596 by John Rainolds, at the time dean of Lincoln cathedral. Rather than take issue with the invented dragon story, Rainolds offered a far more devastating critique: St. George was in fact identical with George of Cappadocia, the sycophantic and rapacious Arian archbishop of Alexandria, lynched by a mob in 361 – and subsequently venerated by Arians as a martyr, and allegedly introduced into the Catholic calendar upon their conversion to Catholicism![20] Anyone venerating St. George was not merely venerating a phantasm, but a heretic, and a particularly malevolent one at that. After Rainolds, writers on St. George were obliged to take a defensive tone. Tristram White, for instance, in a rhyming hymn in praise of St. George published in 1614, deals briefly with his struggle with the dragon, spends a great deal of time on his martyrdom and the example it provides for Christians, and elaborates on St. George's connection to England through Edward III's foundation of the Order of the Garter. He then closes by stating that:

> If any now of the malignant crew,
> Shall some blinde forlorne paradox renue,
> Denying to us such a Saint as George,
> And not alone against his acts disgorge
> Their causeless rancour, them o Muse beware
> Black be their mouthes, and therefore flye them farre
> Least thy white plumes be stained by their filth
> For evill speech the purest temper spilth.[21]

Similarly, Peter Heylyn's *Historie of that Most Famous Saint and Souldier of Christ Jesus, St. George of Cappadocia*, published in 1631 and dedicated to King Charles I, was written since

> some few of late, on what authority I know not, have tooke upon them to discharge him, both of his place in Heaven, and reputation in the Church ... by the first ranke of them, it is undoubtedly affirmed, that George the Martyr, so much honoured in the Christian world, is but a Counterfeit, a Larva; onely some strange Chimaera, the issue of an idle braine; one that had never any being on the Earth. The others, as unquestionably, have made him in his life, a dangerous and bloudy Hereticke: and since his death, a wretched Soule amongst the damned.[22]

---

20 John Rainolds, *De Idolatria Ecclesiae Romanae* (Oxford, 1596).
21 Tristram White, *The Martyrdom of Saint George of Cappadocia: Titular Patron of England, and of the most Noble Order of the Garter* (London: William Barley, 1614), [no page numbers].
22 Peter Heylyn, *The Historie of that Most Famous Saint and Souldier of Christ Jesus*,

Heylyn firmly believed that St. George *did* exist and that he was *not* identical with the Arian George, and spent much of his 350-page work attempting to prove it, and thereby rescue the dignity of his realm and its king. Unfortunately, it was not enough to prevent King Charles's loss of the Civil War to Parliament, and of his life.

One further problem with St. George began under the Stuarts, and that is that they were monarchs of Scotland as well as England. This complicated somewhat St. George's relationship with the king. Although the two countries retained their separate governments, they increasingly shared things emanating from the political center. The King James Bible (1611), authorized for both the Church of England and the Church of Scotland, was one such. Another was a royal navy, for which James I ordered, in 1606, that all vessels "shall beare in their mainetoppe the Red Crosse, commonly called St George's Crosse, and the White Crosse commonly called S Andrew's Crosse, joyned together according to a forme made by our heralds."[23] This first version of the Union Jack became a powerful emblem of the Union, in which the Stuarts were deeply invested. The Union Jack was not without its flaws, however. Although supposedly illustrating the uniting of St. George with St. Andrew, of England with Scotland, many Scots found it unsatisfactory since St. George's cross overlaid St. Andrew's, making it appear more important. Such a problem is inherent in the graphic placement of any two symbols to represent two different things: as long as "up" is better than "down," "over" than "under," or (from the viewer's perspective) "left" than "right," one of the symbols will always appear to be more important than the other. Indeed, separate symbols lend themselves too well to expressing contrast and mutual antagonism, as did the anonymous Scottish poet who wrote "A Comparison between St. Andrew and St. George" in 1634, praising the former at the expense of the latter.[24]

Instead, there was a clear need for a unified symbol for a new political reality, and the classical figure of Britannia, the personification of the Roman province of the same name, came to fill it. Classical personifications of this type were popular anyway on account of the lasting influence of the Renaissance, but Britannia was also useful politically. Although the

St. George of Cappadocia, Asserted from the Fictions of the middle ages of the Church and opposition of the present (London: Henry Seyle, 1631), A5v.

[23] In Nicholas Groom, *The Union Jack: The Story of the British Flag* (London: Atlantic Books, 2006), 135.

[24] Samantha Riches, *St George*, 189.

Roman province had encompassed only what is now England and Wales and a small part of Scotland, it ultimately bequeathed its name (in the shortened form of "Britain") to the entire island. "Britannia" could therefore represent the Union of England (with Wales) and Scotland, which was co-extensive with the island of Britain. On Roman coinage Britannia had been portrayed as a young woman, in a centurion's helmet and a flowing garment, sitting on a rock and holding a spear and shield. Under the Stuarts she started to reappear in such places as a pageant in London in 1605, as described by Anthony Mundy in his *Triumphs of Reunited Britannia*:

> On a mount triangular, as the island of Britain itself is described to be, we [see] in the supreme place, under the shape of a fair and beautiful nymph, Britannia herself.[25]

In 1672, Britannia appeared on the farthing and halfpenny coins, modeled on King Charles II's mistress, the Duchess of Richmond (figure 12), and in 1694 the governors of the newly founded Bank of England chose to portray Britannia on the bank's seal (despite the fact that they were not governing a Bank of Britain).[26] With Parliamentary union in 1707 her importance grew all the more, and she regularly appeared in artwork and political cartoons throughout the eighteenth century as the embodiment of the new British "nation," often with a Phrygian cap or Corinthian helmet, or hoplite shield bearing the Union Jack. She also might be accompanied by a lion, the royal heraldic beast of both England and Scotland. Later, on account of the increasing importance of British sea power, she was shown holding a trident, or occasionally in a chariot being pulled by seahorses, both attributes of Neptune, the Roman god of the sea.[27] And if Britannia was too classical or feminine for some tastes, another personification of Great Britain appeared in 1712, shortly after parliamentary union, by the London satirist John Arbuthnot. John Bull was not as popular as Britannia, and usually viewed as overly English by the Scots, but he has had a remarkable longevity in both art and literature. Bull is usually depicted as a stocky man with a dark tailcoat, light trousers

---

25   A. Mundy, *The Triumphs of re-united Britania* (London: W. Jaggard, 1605), [7–8].
26   C.V.H. Sutherland, *English Coinage 600–1900* (London: B.T. Batsford, 1973), 179 (plate 101, nos. 711, 712). The seal of the Bank of England was reproduced on a £2 coin to mark the Bank's tercentenary in 1994.
27   See the examples in Linda Colley, *Britons: Forging the Nation 1707–1837* (New Haven and London: Yale University Press, 1992), on pages 10, 70, 78, 89, 96, 98, 133, 141, 209, 267, 311, 341.

or breeches, tall leather boots and a low top hat. He may hold a walking stick and be accompanied by a bulldog, and his waistcoat came to be done up as a Union Jack. He is an earthy figure, with no intellect but full of native wisdom and good humor, preferring the simple pleasures of rural life to the cynical sophistication of the city – very much how many Britons liked to view themselves.[28]

Britannia and John Bull were not empty symbols, prescribed by the political center but finding no resonance in the hinterland. Linda Colley has shown how the idea of Britain, particularly after parliamentary union in 1707, was taken up by many English and Scots as a vehicle for their Protestantism against the hated French, and for the economic opportunities it afforded, both at home and abroad.[29] All this did not mean that the idea of England, and St. George who represented him, were eclipsed entirely in the seventeenth and eighteenth centuries. St. George, however, became somewhat diminished, controversial, and esoteric. Thomas Lowick, for instance, published a rhyming *History of the Life and Martyrdom of St. George, the Titular Patron of England* in 1664 with a dedication to the restored King Charles II:

> For in my judgement never English King
> Had greater cause than You, to honour Him:
> Heroick force and Martial form withal,
> 'Twixt King and Patron were collateral[30]

It was also easy for Lowick to cast the king's father Charles I as St. George: in colloquy with the "tyrant," the tyrant demands to know why George dares to oppose "our great Parliament," a clear reference to Cromwell and his backers.[31] Lowick's work follows the traditional hagiographic script of George's dragon-slaying and martyrdom, and even makes the connection between St. George and England to be the result of papal initiative: Lowick invents a detail about how the pope granted to a king of England a relic of St. George's heart, which served to calm a raging storm on the king's return voyage to England.[32] Thus not only is St. George a partisan royalist figure in Lowick's work, he is also a seeming defender of Roman Catholicism! Lowick proceeds to defend his use of relics by

---

[28] Groom, *Union Jack*, 189.

[29] Colley, *Britons*, 1–9.

[30] Thomas Lowick, *History of the Life and Martyrdom of St. George, the Titular Patron of England* ... (London: William Crook, 1664), [ii].

[31] Lowick, *History*, 24.

[32] Lowick, *History*, 34–35.

citing the scriptural examples of miracles worked by St. Paul's handkerchief, St. Peter's shadow, or the prophet Elisha's bones[33] – but all this comes across as less an attempt to restore St. George as a national figure than to hijack him for a particular agenda.

The Order of the Garter continued to function during the Stuart and Hanoverian eras, maintaining the customary connection between St. George and England. The Garter, indeed, became a favorite topic for antiquarian research, starting with Elias Ashmole's exhaustive *Institution, Laws and Ceremonies of the Order of the Garter* and a third edition of John Selden's *Titles of Honor*, both of which appeared in 1672. Thomas Dawson's *Memoirs of St. George of the Garter* was published in 1714; the work was dedicated to the new king George I and (by Dawson's admission) largely cribbed from the works of Selden and Ashmole. In 1724, John Anstis published an edition of a register of the order of the Garter compiled during the reign of Edward VI (the "Black Book"). Joseph Pote published *The History and Antiquities of Windsor Castle* in 1749, dedicated to Frederick, Prince of Wales, including an updated list of members and officers of the Order. Finally, G.F. Beltz published his *Memorials of the Most Noble Order of the Garter* in 1841, dedicated to the young Queen Victoria. Some of these works contain important and still relevant research, but they generally deal only tangentially with St. George, and had a rather limited audience.

St. George himself did receive some academic attention in the eighteenth century, mostly focusing on the problem of his origins and his connection to England. In 1704, Thomas Salmon proposed the novel idea that the origins of St. George as the patron of England could be found in the person of one George, Bishop of Ostia, who is mentioned in the Anglo-Saxon Chronicle as being a papal legate to Mercia and Northumbria in 786.[34] This argument received little attention. Slightly more attention was garnered by John Byrom, whose *Miscellaneous Poems* appeared in 1773, containing one entitled "On the Patron of England."[35] Byrom asserted in this poem that the true patron of England was in fact Pope Gregory the Great, who sent St. Augustine to convert the Anglo-Saxons; over time, poor scribal transmission had confused "Georgius" for "Gregorius"! If this argument was intended to be a serious one, Samuel Pegge demolished it in a paper read before the Society of Antiquaries in 1777, showing from primary sources that George was indeed known as such in England since

---

33 Lowick, *History*, 35–36.
34 Thomas Salmon, *A New Historical Account of St. George for England, and the Original of the most noble order of the Garter* (London: Nathaniel Dancer, 1704).
35 John Byrom, *Miscellaneous Poems* (Leeds: James Nichols, 1814), 1: 65–68.

Anglo-Saxon times, despite a single mistranscription of "Gregore" for "Georges" in a French chronicle of the sixteenth century.[36] The most attention, however, was earned by Edward Gibbon, whose famous *History of the Decline and Fall of the Roman Empire* (1776–89) endorsed and revived John Rainolds's idea that St. George was in fact George of Cappadocia, the mid-fourth-century Arian archbishop of Alexandria.[37] Over time, wrote Gibbon, that "odious stranger,"

> disguising every circumstance of time and place, assumed the mask of a martyr, a saint, and a Christian hero; and the infamous George of Cappadocia [was] transformed into the renowned St George of England, the patron of arms, of chivalry, and of the garter.[38]

These sentiments fit well with Gibbon's Enlightenment skepticism, itself dominant among many educated people, but they did not go unchallenged. John Milner, a Catholic priest and Fellow of the Society of Antiquaries, published *An Historical and Critical Inquiry into the Existence and Character of Saint George* in 1792, specifically to combat Gibbon. Milner explained that Cappadocia was quite capable of producing two men named George, that St. George was never designated "bishop" in any martyrology (which he surely would have been, if the two figures were identical), and that from the earliest days Christians distinguished between St. George and Archbishop George.[39] Milner's points were all very sound, although they were no match for the popularity of *Decline and Fall*.

St. George also enjoyed a certain amount of popularity outside academic and court circles. As mentioned, Richard Johnson's *Seven Champions of Christendom* enjoyed multiple reprintings in the seventeenth century, and inspired a number of imitations, such as the chapbook *The Life and Death of St George, the Noble Champion of England* (reprinted seven times between 1750 and 1820), or two of the poems in Bishop Percy's *Reliques of Ancient English Poetry* (1765, also much reprinted): "The Birth of St George" and "St George and the Dragon."[40] The eighteenth century has also bequeathed

36 Samuel Pegge, "Observations on the history of St. George, the Patron Saint of England," *Archaeologia* 5 (1779): 1–32.
37 Edward Gibbon, *The Decline and Fall of the Roman Empire* (New York: The Modern Library, n.d.), 1: 790–92.
38 Gibbon, *Decline and Fall*, 792.
39 John Milner, *An Historical and Critical Inquiry into the Existence and Character of Saint George* (London: Debrett, 1792), 46, 51, 56–57.
40 Riches, *St George*, 180; Thomas Percy, *Reliques of Ancient English Poetry* (New York: Dover Publications, 1966), 3: 215–32.

to us the oldest evidence of Mummers' plays, popular dramatic pieces usually performed by groups of young men around Christmastime. E.K. Chambers had collected over one hundred by 1933; a well-known example appears in Thomas Hardy's novel *The Return of the Native* (1878).[41] The plays generally introduce the main characters; a fight ensues between them; one or more of them dies, later to be revived, often by a braggadocio doctor; other peripheral characters enter, and finally a collection is taken. The leading fighter in these plays is often St. George, sometimes called Sir George, and his opponent is called the Turkish knight or some variant of "Beau Slasher." Other characters may include a great variety from history or mythology, including Hector, Alexander, St. Patrick, or later, Bold Bonaparte or Wellington.[42] Such plays, by their very unconcern with historical accuracy, indicate that their named characters enjoyed a certain perennial popular appeal.

St. George, however, was to expand that appeal far beyond folk custom, or court or antiquarian interest, in the nineteenth century, the century that saw the Middle Ages (and chivalry in particular) come back into fashion. Nineteenth-century medievalism, like the Romantic Movement of which it was a part, began as a reaction to the modern world. Eighteenth-century *philosophes* had poured scorn on anything vaguely medieval, and promoted "reason" as a panacea for the ills of humanity. However, as the French Revolution descended into the Terror, and then threw up the world-conquering Napoleon, more than a few people began to wonder whether such "medieval" values as faith, deference, order and tradition did not have some value after all. Certainly Metternich and other European foreign ministers attempted to reconstitute Europe with these ingredients at the Congress of Vienna in 1815. Being a medieval and religious figure, St. George could represent that sort of tradition and stability, at least in England: those in charge of the elaborate Garter ceremonies of 1805, for instance, were instructed to emphasize the antiquity of the ceremony as a

---

41 See also Thomas Hardy, *The Play of St. George, as aforetime acted by the Dorsetshire Christmas Mummers* (Cambridge: Cambridge University Press, 1921), "based on the version in *The Return of the Native*, and completed from other version and from local tradition."

42 See Ronald Hutton, *The Stations of the Sun: A History of the Ritual Year in Britain* (Oxford and New York: Oxford University Press, 1996), 70–80; E.K. Chambers, *The English Folk-Play* (Oxford: Clarendon Press, 1933). See also Arthur Beatty, "The St. George, or Mummers', Plays; a Study in the Protology of the Drama," *Transactions of the Wisconsin Academy of Sciences, Arts and Letters* 15 (2) (October, 1906): 276.

deliberate riposte to the contrived novelties being celebrated across the Channel, such as the Legion d'honneur or Napoleon's self-coronation.[43] Benedetto Pistrucci's famous engraving of St. George (figure 13), which first appeared on sovereign and crown coins in 1817, immediately following the Congress of Vienna, may also be seen as an example of this.

More serious than the revolution in politics was the revolution in industry, which in England stuck closer to home and wrought greater disruption. Steam power and mechanical manufacturing may have vastly increased the strength of the economy, but to many people it seemed to have produced nothing but misery: dangerous, exhausting and alienating work, the despoliation of the landscape, the emergence of vast crime- and disease-ridden slums, shoddy mass-produced goods sold by means of intrusive advertising, and the apparent enthronement of money as the basis for all human relationships. Critics yearned for an organic "medieval" society where none of these conditions prevailed: where people took pride in the work of their hands, where they lived in villages of face-to-face contact and knew and trusted each other, where they deferred to their betters, who in turn looked after their interests.[44] Being medieval and chivalric, St. George became a figure of this critique as well. Good examples may be found in the works of the Pre-Raphaelite Brotherhood, founded in London in 1848. Both in the way that they painted, and in the subject matter they chose, the Pre-Raphaelites resisted the nineteenth century as they perceived it. The name itself referred to the Renaissance artist Raphael Sanzio (1483–1520), the last great artist before (they claimed) painting conventions had grown lifeless and mechanical, and fittingly many Pre-Raphaelites chose to depict medieval themes, including St. George. Dante Gabriel Rossetti, for instance, painted *The Marriage of St George and Princess Sabra* in 1857, *St George and the Princess Sabra* in 1862, and *The Wedding of St George* in 1864. All three of these paintings are based on the poems in Percy's *Reliques* and not on Voragine's *Golden Legend* (i.e. the hero actually gets to marry his princess in the end), but are no less medievalist for it.[45] Others followed suit.

---

[43]   Colley, *Britons*, 216–17; Mark Girouard, *The Return to Camelot: Chivalry and the English Gentleman* (New Haven and London: Yale University Press, 1981), 24.

[44]   See e.g., Alice Chander, *A Dream of Order: The Medieval Ideal in Nineteenth-Century English Literature* (Lincoln, Nebr.: University of Nebraska Press, 1970), 1–5.

[45]   Joseph A. Kestner, "The Pre-Raphaelites, St George and the construction of masculinity," in *Collecting the Pre-Raphaelites: The Anglo-American Enchantment*, ed. Margaretta Frederick Watson (Aldershot: Ashgate, 1997), 149–62, at 151–52.

Although not an official member of the Brotherhood, William Morris, founder of the Arts and Crafts Movement, was closely associated with them, and his company produced two different sets of stained glass windows for country houses in Yorkshire (in 1862 and 1872), and a cabinet in 1862, all featuring various scenes from the St. George legend.[46] Another Pre-Raphaelite associate, Edward Burne-Jones, explored the story in a series of oil paintings for a house at Witley, Surrey done between 1865 and 1867 (now dispersed), and in 1868 and 1877 revisited the subject in paintings now on display at the William Morris Gallery in Walthamstow and at the Wadsworth Atheneum in Hartford, Connecticut (figure 14). This last painting depicts a youthful and somewhat ethereal figure standing over a dragon and bearing a novel shield, showing a nude princess tied up and awaiting her destruction, a memento of his recent heroism.[47] In all of these works it is clear that the romance and chivalry of St. George was what appealed the most to the Pre-Raphaelites, and their followers and clients. In the face of the modern world and all its attendant woes, St. George represented a time, it is thought, when heroism was still possible.

An even more serious use of St. George against industrial society was that of the critic and aesthete John Ruskin. Ruskin hated industrial society and longed for a Britain dominated by agriculture and agrarian values, so much so that he founded a Guild of St. George in 1871 to help bring it about. Guild members were to be known as Companions and contribute 10% of their income to realize its aims, which included the establishment of a sort of agrarian covenant community. In Ruskin's words, the Guild would:

> try to take some small piece of English ground, beautiful, peaceful and fruitful. We will have no steam-engines upon it, and no railroads … We will have no liberty on it, but instant obedience to known law … no equality in it, but recognition of every betterness that we can find, and reprobation of every worseness … We will have plenty … of corn and grass in our fields … We will have music and poetry, and children shall learn to dance and sing to it.[48]

Ruskin's beautiful vision was not as attractive as he hoped. Ruskin himself was the chief determiner of "betterness" and "worseness," and himself

---

[46] Kestner, "Pre-Raphaelites," 150.

[47] Kestner, "Pre-Raphaelites," 153.

[48] Quoted in John D. Rosenberg, *The Darkening Glass: A Portrait of Ruskin's Genius* (New York: Columbia University Press, 1986), 195.

acted as the "known law," a situation with a necessarily limited appeal. Rather than revolutionizing the countryside, therefore, the Guild had only 57 companions by 1885, at which point Ruskin suffered a mental breakdown and withdrew from its affairs. (The Guild still exists, however, its chief duty being to maintain Ruskin's extensive art collection on display in Sheffield.)[49] But even though it was a dissident society, St. George was still an ideal figure as its patron. England's national saint acted as a call for the country to return to its medieval roots. And although the society had little to do with chivalry as such, Ruskin's use of St. George may in fact have been a reference to the saint's occasional patronage of agriculture, something of which the deeply learned Ruskin would have been aware.

The failure of the utopian aspect of the Guild of Saint George, however, should not lead us to believe that medievalism died with it. On the contrary, while Ruskin and the Pre-Raphaelites may have used the Middle Ages as a refuge from bourgeois industrial society, that society was fully capable of absorbing and co-opting the critique.[50] The Victorian concept of the gentleman, for instance, came to be heavily informed by a revived ideal of chivalry. A gentleman was to be true to his word, loyal to his superiors, and protective of women and children. He was to engage in a constant struggle against impure thoughts in himself and injustice in others. This model of behavior, while not completely medieval in origin, was not escapist or revolutionary either, but an ideal to which all men, regardless of occupation or even station in life, could aspire.[51] The applicability of St. George to these ideas does not need to be elaborated. The age of neo-chivalry also coincided with the apogee of the British Empire, something in which most British people took great pride, and St. George also enjoyed a remarkable resurgence as a patriotic icon in the late nineteenth and early twentieth centuries as well. These two aspects were linked: the British liked to believe that their Empire was a force for good, so what better a mascot for it than the chivalric St. George? This

[49] Rosenberg, *Darkening Glass*, 197–98.
[50] Jackson Lears notes that a similar process occurred in America at this time: "in offering temporary escapes to a realm of innocence or wish-fulfillment, or in stressing action as an end in itself, some antimodern impulses revived the modern ethos of achievement even as they recast it in a looser therapeutic mold." See T.J. Jackson Lears, *No Place of Grace: Antimodernism and the Transformation of American Culture, 1880–1920* (New York: Pantheon Books, 1981), 179.
[51] See Girouard, *Return to Camelot*, 281.

desire was so strong that it overcame any objections to a symbol of England representing the United Kingdom (since 1801, also including Ireland) and the Empire itself. If any Scots, Welsh, or Irish (or English for that matter) objected to this casual elision between "England," "Britain," and "Empire" they did not do so in any sustained or systematic way. Of course, the British symbols of the Union Jack, Britannia, John Bull, and Queen Victoria herself were by no means eclipsed, which may have helped. But St. George was certainly on the rise, cherished by government and people alike.

The Royal Society of St. George (RSSG), founded by one Howard Ruff in 1894, is a prime example. The RSSG's aim was "to encourage interest in the English way of life, customs and traditions," and by 1920 had enrolled 20,000 members.[52] English customs and traditions certainly included country life, and in this sense the RSSG was a continuation of Ruskin's Guild of Saint George, but it had no utopian ambitions and in fact acted as a cheerleader for British political interests. A notable occasion for doing so was during the Second Anglo-Boer War (1899–1902), when C.W.B. Clarke's *The True History of Saint George the Martyr, Patron Saint of England* appeared, taking inspiration from the Society and using deliberately archaic language to deliver its invective against the Afrikaners.[53] *True History*, in fact, was one of at least nine short, popular books on St. George to appear between 1885 and 1913 (and one of four connected in some way to the RSSG);[54] clearly, there was a market for knowledge about the saint. Some of these books were competent

52 Riches, *St George*, 200.
53 C.W.B. Clarke, *The True History of Saint George the Martyr, Patron Saint of England* (Cape Town: SA "Electric" Printing and Publishing, 1900).
54 The books are: "Guanon" [Sara Ann Mattson], *St. George and the Dragon: A World-Wide Legend Localised* (London: Wyman & Sons, 1885); Clarke, *True History*; William Fleming, *The Life of St. George, Martyr, Patron of England* (London: R&T Washbourne, 1901); Edward Clapton, *Life of St. George*, 2nd edn. (London: Swan Sonnenschein, 1903 [1901]); Elizabeth Oke Gordon, *Saint George Champion of Christendom and Patron Saint of England* (London: Swan Sonnenschein, 1907); Margaret H. Bulley, *St. George for Merrie England* (London: George Allen and Sons, 1908); Cornelia Steketee Hulst, *St. George of Cappadocia in Legend and History* (London: David Nutt, 1909); H.O.F., comp., *St. George for England: The Life, Legends and Lore of our Glorious Patron*, 2nd edn. (London: F. Edwards & Co., n.d. [c. 1910]); Alice Brewster, *The Life of St. George, the Patron Soldier-Saint of England* (London: Royal Society of Saint George, 1913). The books by Clarke, Clapton, and H.O.F. were dedicated to the RSSG; Brewster's was published by the Society.

popularizations of current academic knowledge;[55] others featured invented connections of the saint to England. Sara Ann Mattson, who wrote under the name "Guanon" in 1885, attempted to place the origin of St. George's legend, including his dragon-fight, in Cornwall, on the basis of some superficial similarities between St. George's legend and local Celtic lore. Edward Clapton wrote about how St. George, while alive, had sailed to Britain and landed in what is now Lancashire (thereby bequeathing his name to the channel between England and Ireland). He proceeded to convert Helena, the wife of Emperor Constantius and mother of Constantine the Great, who was then at York, to Christianity. Upon hearing of Diocletian's persecution, St. George hastened back to his home in Beirut, sold his belongings, and presented himself to the Emperor for martyrdom.[56] Most of the books did not go so far in inventing such historic details, but six of them did contain some reference to "England" or "England's Patron" in their titles, to underline the patriotic appeal.[57]

[55]   E.g. Fleming, *The Life of St. George*; Bulley, *St. George for Merrie England*; Hulst, *St. George of Cappadocia*.

[56]   Clapton, *Life of St. George*, 13–16. He adds that the connection between Beirut and Britain (and thus St. George's memory) was maintained through trade: the oldest coins of Beirut had a trident on them, which can still be seen on the English penny; the names of the two places are also linked etymologically through the Hebrew "Brit," meaning covenant.

[57]   This was also the era of comparative-religious speculation about the origins of St. George. John Hogg thought that the inscription at Shakka, Syria could be dated to 350, thereby antedating the death of Archbishop George by eleven years. This seemingly ended the controversy over St. George's Arian origins; scholars then turned to wondering whether St. George had his origins in the cults of Mithras, Horus, or Tammuz. Could the Gelasian decree's prohibition of his legend, plus the lack of any proper primary source for the saint, plus his immense popularity, be explained by understanding him as a Christianized version of a pagan god? See, inter alia, A. von Gutschmid, "Über die Sage vom heiligen Georg, als Beitrag zur iranischen Mythengischichte," *Berichte über die Verhandlungen der Königlich Sächsischen Gessellschaft der Wissenschaften zu Leipzig, Philologisch-Historische Class* 13 (1861): 175–202; Charles Clermont-Ganneau, "Horus et St. George d'après un bas-relief inedit du Louvre," *Revue archéologique* NS 32 (1876): 196–204, 372–99; Sabine Baring-Gould, *Curious Myths of the Middle Ages*, 2nd edn. (Cambridge: Rivingtons, 1868), 2: 12–25. As all these theories celebrate superficial similarities while ignoring profound differences between cults, they have not stood the test of time. (Neither has Hogg's theory – others have suggested that the inscription dates from the mid-sixth century, congruent with other datable evidence for

A patriotic and chivalric St. George was also prescribed for English children. Clifford Mills and John Ramsey wrote *Where the Rainbow Ends*, a Christmas pantomime first performed at the Savoy Theatre in 1911, which enjoyed a long run. The play concerns a brother and sister, Crispian and Rosamund, who escape from the home of their wicked aunt and uncle and travel on a magic carpet to find their parents, who have been shipwrecked in the land where the rainbow ends. First, however, they must pass through the land of the Dragon King, and when Rosamund mentions that she is "an English maid in danger," St. George appears in a flash of light, and after a talk about Agincourt promises that "I am ever with you – your faithful guardian knight ... God for George, England, and the Right." St. George does rescue them from the depredations of the Dragon King, who had been trying to corrupt the English ("I flung my gold dust in the people's eyes and lulled them into false security"). But St. George calls them to return to their true destiny (to "fight aggression and foul tyranny") and at the end of the play cries out

> Rise, Youth of England, let your voices ring
> For God, for Britain, and for Britain's King.[58]

Audience and cast would then all join in singing the National Anthem. Another children's group with an affinity for St. George was the Boy Scouts, founded in 1907 by the hero of the siege of Mafeking, Lt. Gen. Robert Baden-Powell. Baden-Powell took as his inspiration two American boys' groups, Ernest Seton's Woodcraft Indians and William Forbush's Knights of King Arthur, and combined their themes.[59] In Baden-Powell's *Scouting for Boys* (1908), a series of "camp fire yarns" instructed boys in

---

St. George's cult; see John Hogg, "Supplemental Notes on St. George the Martyr, and on George the Arian Bishop," Transactions of the Royal Society of Literature of the United Kingdom 2nd series 7 (1863): 116–17; Christopher Walter, "The Origins of the Cult of Saint George," *Revue des Études Byzantines* 53 (1995): 316). More lasting scholarship from the era included E. Wallis Budge's edition of a Coptic legend of St. George in 1888, John Matzke's series of articles establishing a stemma of all known Western manuscripts of St. George's Passion (1902–04), P. Michael Huber's *Zur Georgslegende* (Erlangen: Fr. Junge, 1906), Hippolyte Delehaye's chapter on St. George in *Les Légendes grecques des saints militaires* (Paris: A. Picard, 1909), and Johan Aufhauser's *Das Drachenwunder des heiligen George in der griechishen und lateinischen Überlieferung* (Leipzig: B.G. Teubner, 1911).

58 Girouard, *Return to Camelot*, 2.
59 Girouard, *Return to Camelot*, 254.

practical skills like first aid, outdoor cooking, pioneering, and stalking game; other yarns emphasized healthy living, good citizenship, and chivalry to others. This latter yarn in particular extolled the virtues of King Arthur and his Knights of the Round Table and of St. George who, Baden-Powell alleged, had acted as their patron, being one of the few saints who knew anything about horsemanship (figure 15).[60] A later edition of *Scouting for Boys* extended that patronage to the Scouts, who were enjoined to know his story and follow his example:

> When he was faced by a difficulty or danger, however great it appeared – even in the shape of a dragon – he did not avoid it or fear it, but went at it with all the power he could put into himself and his horse. Although inadequately armed for such an encounter, having merely a spear, he charged in, did his best, and finally succeeded in overcoming a difficulty which nobody dared to tackle.[61]

This lesson is accompanied by an illustration of a Boy Scout rolling up his sleeves before a sculpture of St. George, with the caption "Prepared and alert a Scout follows the lead / of our Patron Saint George and his spirited steed." Although the scouting movement very quickly became an international one, in Baden-Powell's original incarnation it was quite British-patriotic. One of Baden-Powell's explicit aims in the Scout movement, indeed, was to raise a generation of young men who would value the Empire and fight to defend it against its enemies, as Baden-Powell himself had done in South Africa ("Don't be disgraced like the young Romans, who lost the Empire of their forefathers by being wishy-washy slackers without any go or patriotism in them").[62] As a patron of the Empire, St. George fit very well with this aspect of scouting too.

It comes as no surprise, therefore, that at the outbreak of World War I in 1914, St. George should have appeared on the side of the British. He was a national saint, and one who fought for good against evil – and the German violation of Belgian neutrality was certainly evil. Thus a well-known poster by the Parliamentary Recruiting Committee featured St. George on horseback slaying a dragon, with the legend "BRITAIN NEEDS

---

[60] Robert Baden-Powell, *Scouting for Boys: The Original 1908 Edition* (Mineola, N.Y.: Dover Publications, 2007), 241–42.

[61] Robert Baden-Powell, *Scouting for Boys* (1951 edn.), "Yarn 20 – Chivalry to Others," http://www.thedump.scoutscan.com/yarn20.pdf (accessed 9 June 2008).

[62] Baden-Powell, *Scouting for Boys: Original Edition*, 314.

YOU AT ONCE (figure 16)." Justin Huntly McCarthy's "The Ghosts at Boulogne," published in the *Daily Chronicle* on 30 August 1914, asked God

> to forge
> A sword to strike the Dragon of the Slime,
> Bidding St. Denis with St. George stand fast
> Against the Worm. St. Denis and St. George![63]

Note how St. George takes the lead in this poem: dragon (or "Worm") slaying is his specialty, which St. Denis must learn by his side – a not entirely accurate metaphor for the events on the ground in France in the autumn of 1914. Similarly, the battle of Agincourt, originally fought against the French, provided a prism through which to see the new war, even if the French were now allies. Arthur Machen's story "The Bowmen," published in the *Evening News* on 29 September 1914, is one example. "The Bowmen" concerns the first major engagement of the British Expeditionary Force at the Battle of Mons (Belgium), on 22–23 August. His position almost overwhelmed, one British soldier remembers and repeats a motto he had once seen on the plates in a "queer vegetarian restaurant in London": *Adsit Anglis Sanctus Georgius* ("May Saint George be a present help to the English"). Immediately the soldier hears "a great voice" with thousands shouting "Array, array, array … St. George! St. George! … Ha! messire; ha! sweet Saint, grant us good deliverance! … St George for merry England … a long bow and a strong bow … Heaven's Knight, aid us!" In front of the trench he sees "a long line of shapes, with a shining about them" – an army of resurrected Agincourt bowmen, who proceed to fell the Germans by the thousands. The German General Staff decided that the English must have used poison gas, as no wounds could be found on many of their dead, but "the man who knew what nuts tasted like when they called themselves steak knew also that St. George had brought his Agincourt Bowmen to help the English."[64] Although Machen was a well-known author of supernatural stories, and never claimed that the story had any basis in fact, it soon took on a life of its own. It was preached from pulpits across the country as proof that God was on the side of the British, and independent witnesses came forth to corroborate

---

63 Justin Huntly McCarthy, "The Ghosts at Boulogne," in *Songs and Sonnets for England in War Time: Electronic Edition*, http://beck.library.emory.edu/greatwar/ poetry/view.php?id=Lane_lane052 (accessed 10 June 2008).

64 Arthur Machen, *The Angels of Mons, The Bowmen, and Other Legends of the War* (New York and London: G.P. Putnam's Sons, 1915), 23–31.

it, including officers who had actually seen St. George and others who had discovered dead Germans with arrow wounds.[65] Later, a wounded member of the Lancashire Fusiliers asked his nurse for a picture of St. George "because he had seen him on a white horse, leading the British at Vitry-le-François, when the Allies turned."[66] Thus did St. George sanctify the British war effort.

Of course, it is not these images that we associate with World War I today. Rather, it is the Remarquean nightmare of constant artillery bombardment, machine guns, barbed wire, poison gas, and trenches filled with mud, rats, lice, and the stench of rotting corpses. Such things are assumed to have killed forever any notions of war as a high-minded or ennobling activity.[67] If the chivalric writing of Justin McCarthy or Arthur Machen represented the war at its outset, the ironic, disillusioned writing of Wilfred Owen or Siegfried Sassoon represented it at the end – and has continued to do so ever since. Certainly, the Great War remains the Great Divide on any number of levels, but more recent work on the public remembrance of the war in the 1920s and 1930s has shown that much of that remembrance was in fact suffused with medievalism. In the search for any meaning to the mass industrial slaughter of the Western Front, many people reached for the familiar pre-war images of the Crusades, chivalry, medieval spirituality, and mythology. Village memorials often took the form of crosses, either Celtic or "Eleanor" (modeled on those constructed by Edward I in the late thirteenth century for his dead queen).[68] In stained glass and statuary the crusading King Richard I was popular, as were different Arthurian characters.[69] But most of all the patriotic and chivalric figure of St. George was employed to ennoble, or at least render comprehensible, the sacrifice of so many men. Perhaps the best-known example is Adrian Jones's Empire Cavalry War Memorial, erected at

---

[65]   Machen, *Angels of Mons*, 11.

[66]   Girouard, *Return to Camelot*, 284.

[67]   See, for example, Paul Fussell, *The Great War and Modern Memory* (New York: Oxford University Press, 1975), and "The Fate of Chivalry, and the Assault upon Mother," in *Thank God for the Atom Bomb and Other Essays* (New York: Summit Books, 1988), 221–48.

[68]   Stefan Goebel, *The Great War and Medieval Memory: War, Remembrance and Medievalism in Britain and Germany, 1914–1940* (Cambridge: Cambridge University Press, 2007), 70, 240.

[69]   Goebel, *Great War*, 116, 193.

Stanhope Gate off Park Lane in London in 1924. Its main feature takes the form of a bronze, life-sized statue of St. George, cast from captured enemy cannon. Clad in plate armor, George raises a sword to the sky, and rides on a horse bestriding a dead, coiled dragon.[70] Other public memorial statues of St. George included examples by Sir George Frampton in Peterborough (unveiled in London in 1921) and H.C. Fehr in Leeds (unveiled in 1922). In the 1920s, St. George appeared in stained glass memorial windows in English parish churches, such as in Oddington, Gloucestershire, or Hadlow, Kent. As before the war, St. George was prescribed as a model for children, as in a tapestry by Mrs. Akers-Douglas at Eton (manufactured by Morris and Co. in 1923) or in a statue by G.P. Hutchinson at Leys School, Cambridge (unveiled in 1922).[71] Also as before the war, St. George was an Imperial icon as well as an English one, appearing as sculpture in such places as Soldiers' Tower at the University of Toronto (completed in 1924), the British Imperial war graves cemetery in Jerusalem,[72] or on a Great War memorial in Pietermaritzburg, South Africa (figure 17). In all these places the war was still cast as an honorable one, with a chivalric and Christian figure conquering a dastardly foe.

Instead, it was World War II that marked a diminution of the patriotic St. George. This is ironic, for this war was much more "honorable" than its predecessor, given that the allies forced an unconditional surrender on an enemy that turned out to be monstrously evil. But this war changed Britain even more than the previous one. Clement Atlee's Labour Party won the General Election of July 1945 on the promise of constructing a Welfare State, in which the government would provide universal cradle-to-grave social services, to be paid for by heavy (and heavily progressive) taxation. In this context of enforced equality the need for "chivalry" as a guarantor of social cohesion began to look rather quaint, as perhaps did St. George. The immense cost of the war, and the maturation of colonial independence movements, also entailed a rapid retreat from the Empire, and thus the loss of a major aspect of St. George's patronage. Baden-Powell would have disapproved, but it is unlikely that any amount of "go" could have kept the Empire together in its prewar form. (The 1951 edition of *Scouting for Boys* admits that "we no longer think of the colonies as places

---

70 Girouard, *Return to Camelot*, 292.
71 Goebel, *Great War*, 201, 191, 92, 88, 57, 250.
72 Goebel, *Great War*, 124.

made for our special benefit or profit" and that "in the past, many mistakes have been made.")[73]

In postwar Britain, therefore, St. George acquired an unsavory reputation for being associated with people who rejected this state of affairs – i.e. those on the extreme political right. They might not have been able to get the Empire back, but they were not about to allow Britain to be taken over by brown-skinned ex-colonials. Such an association with the far right began even during the war, when John Amery recruited a unit of British POWs for the Waffen-SS, officially called the British Free Corps, but also known as the Legion of St. George. This name has recently been revived for a "Rock Against Communism" (i.e., white power) musical act, which sings songs like "White Preservation Society," and has an album entitled *In Defense of the Realm*. Similarly, the Neo-Nazi League of Saint George was founded in 1974, an offshoot of the Action Party, a lineal descendant of Oswald Mosley's British Union of Fascists. The League of St. George claimed a closer adherence to Mosley's ideas, particularly his "Europe a Nation" policy, which sought to unite Europeans against their common enemies (variously Communists or non-Europeans). Accordingly, the League of St. George takes pride in its links to other far-right nationalist groups.[74] But it does not appear that this broad-mindedness helped the reputation of St. George in England, nor has his association with the SS or with racist music, things from which it is rightfully very difficult to recover.

The story, however, does not end there. In the 1990s and current decade St. George has actually enjoyed a modest revival among the English. This has less to do with a renewed Christianity or medievalism, and still less with the popularity of extreme-right politics, than with the recovery of "England" as a category, and thus of its original symbolism. One simple way this has come about has been with the revival of the St. George's cross flag in connection with English sporting events and other specifically English occasions. Most English football fans throughout much of the twentieth century saw nothing anomalous in waving Union Jack flags to express their support for their team – a well-known example being the English football fans depicted in Peter Collinson's 1969 film *The Italian Job*, bedecked in Union Jacks as they visit Turin. According to Nick Groom,

---

[73]   Baden-Powell, *Scouting for Boys* (1951), "Yarn 27 – Our Empire and Commonwealth," http://www.thedump.scoutscan.com/yarn27.pdf (accessed 2 July 2008).

[74]   See *League of St George – the Website of the League of Saint George!*, http://www.leaguestgeorge.com (accessed 18 June 2008).

this situation may have had its roots as far back as the English Civil War, when the Parliamentarians revived St. George's cross as a flag for their armies, not on account of any affinity for the saint, but simply as a contrast to the Union flag of the Stuarts.[75] With the Restoration, St. George may have returned to court in poem and ceremony, but his flag, now associated with Puritan excess, went into long-term abeyance. By the 1990s, however, this connection was long forgotten, and enough objection had been raised (largely by the Scots) to the elision of "England" with "Britain" in flag usage that the plain St. George's cross began to reappear on football terraces. The Euro '96 football tournament, hosted by England, represented the tipping point for this revived usage.[76] Ever since then supporters of the English national football, rugby, and other teams have cheered them on by waving St. George's cross flags or painting St. George's cross on their faces (figure 18), and when the team plays "there is not a taxi or white van in the country that does not carry a strategically placed Cross of St. George."[77] It should be said that this red cross is not merely a signifier for "England" – supporters will occasionally dress up as St. George (the opening ceremonies for Euro '96, indeed, featured a mock battle between St. George and a dragon)[78], while a headline for a preview of the England–Wales quarterfinal match at the Rugby World Cup of 2003 announced that "St. George's men [were] hoping to lance a rejuvenated-looking dragon."[79]

Sport may be dismissed as ephemeral or unserious, and even when one's national team plays it is easy to ignore if one is not a fan. But the extraction of "England" from "Britain" has also been achieved through New Labour's policy of devolution of political power to Wales, Scotland, and Northern Ireland. All of these countries now have national assemblies that have been granted the right to determine specific types of policy. England does not have such an assembly, however, and the fact that Scottish, Welsh and Northern Irish MPs can vote on legislation at Westminster that affects England but does not necessarily affect their own constituents has provoked a "Campaign for an English Parliament"

---

75 Groom, *Union Jack*, 144–45.
76 Groom, *Union Jack*, 297–98.
77 Jim White, "How our modest nation can fly the flag," *Telegraph.co.uk*, 16 January 2006, http://www.telegraph.co.uk/opinion/main.jhtml?xml=/opinion/2006/01/16/do1603.xml, accessed 19 June 2008.
78 See the photograph in Riches, *St George*, 209.
79 "Preview – England v Wales," *Planet Rugby* (http://planet-rugby.com/LATEST_NEWS/story_32463.sthml, accessed 8 November 2003).

(fittingly represented by a St. George's cross flag, with a Tudor double rose at the center).[80] Many English people do not care deeply about this situation, given that (as of 2005) more than 80% of Westminster MPs represent English constituencies anyway. But even if England is simply what is left over from this "break-up of Britain," it has still given a cultural impetus to a revived idea of "Englishness," and a revived St. George. One manifestation of this has been renewed attention to St. George's Day, 23 April. In 1998, *The Sun* newspaper launched a campaign to revive St. George's Day celebrations, and about 50,000 St. George's Day greeting cards are now sold every year.[81] The Royal Society of St. George has managed to reverse its long-term membership decline, and on St. George's Day in 2007 organized a formal march in London, accompanied by English music and dance performances in Covent Garden.[82] Bedford-based brewer Charles Wells Ltd. certainly supports the adoption of St. George's Day as a national holiday, not only to reverse English "apathy and complacency," but also for the sake of the extra £14.1 million of trade, and the millions of happy drinkers, a national holiday would generate.[83] "Apathy and complacency" may be a significant hurdle, in fact, since many English people view brash patriotism as un-English; just as the lack of national assembly is not a real issue, so also is "Englishness" simply to be taken for granted and not made a big thing of.[84] But others lament this situation, and find it hard to keep quiet in the face of a defiant Celtic fringe. Said an East London scaffolder in 2002, "I don't see why Scottish, Irish and Welsh can openly celebrate their national days and we can't."[85] According to

[80]   *Campaign for an English Parliament,* http://www.thecep.org.uk/wordpress (accessed 18 June 2008).
[81]   Groom, *Union Jack,* 298.
[82]   Philip Johnston, "The day that dare not speak its name," *Telegraph.co.uk,* 23 April 2007, http://www.telegraph.co.uk/opinion/main.jhtml?xml=/opinion/2007/04/23/do2302.xml (accessed 19 June 2008).
[83]   "The Campaign," *The Value of St George campaign,* http://www.thevalueofstgeorge.com/index.php?oURL=home%2FThe+Campaign%2FCampaign+Aims (accessed 19 June 2008).
[84]   "We considered our readers' appeal, but felt that making a fuss of St George's Day remains a little un-English." "The English Way," *Telegraph.co.uk,* 24 April 2002, http://www.telegraph.co.uk/opinion/main.jhtml?xml=/opinion/2002/04/24/dl2403.xml (accessed 7 July 2008).
[85]   Charles Starmer-Smith, "Flags and Roses for St George's Day," *Telegraph.co.uk,* 24 April 2002, http://www.telegraph.co.uk/news/main.jhtml?xml=/news/2002/04/24/ncarey124.xml (accessed 23 April 2002).

another commentator in 2007:

> The enthusiasm for Englishmen to proclaim St George's Day a national holiday is building. A ground swell of patriotism is returning after years of paying no heed to our avenging paragon while tolerating our Celtic neighbours' over-enthusiasm for nailing up griffins [sic], wearing tartan and the lauding of little green men.[86]

Whether or not 23 April becomes a national holiday, it is clear that the English are much more mindful of it, and of St. George himself, and of "England," than in the past – and are likely to continue to be so.

Is this a good thing? St. George has historically been England's national saint for reasons outlined in this book, but is he an appropriate figure for the twenty-first century? One of the chief concerns about his revival is his recent association with the far right, and whether celebrating him justifies racism and xenophobia. The fact that he was a crusading saint has not helped his reputation among England's growing Muslim population. But the desire to reclaim the saint from such things is strong. Some people, indeed, have attempted to make St. George a figure of the left. The Gloucester Cathedral newsletter for April 2005 mentioned that:

> This month we remember St George – martyred in 303, legend says, for protesting against the persecution of Christians. As Christians, we too are duty bound to speak out against intolerance and injustice and to support all agencies who are committed to alleviating world poverty.[87]

And a report in the Church of England newspaper, for its part, claimed "St. George's Day should become a national day to celebrate the tradition of dissent," since St. George was "originally celebrated for defending the marginalised and challenging the persecution policy of the then Emperor."[88] Time will tell whether these efforts are successful. But it seems that for the vast majority of people St. George's symbolism is neither "right" nor "left," simply English. It is difficult to imagine, for instance, the thousands of fans who welcomed home the English rugby team from its victorious World Cup campaign in 2003, lining the streets of London and enthusiastically waving St. George's cross flags, as racists or

---

86   Adam Edwards, "By George, it's time to raise the flag!" *Telegraph.co.uk*, 21 April 2007, http://www.telegraph.co.uk/global/main.jhtml?xml=/global/2007/04/23/nosplit/ftgeorge20.xml (accessed 19 June 2008).
87   *Gloucester Cathedral Newsletter*, April 2005.
88   In Edwards, "By George."

xenophobes. Even Archbishop George Carey, in a farewell speech in 2002, noted that St. George "had suffered a rather unfair press in recent times" and went on to draw a distinction between the "little Englander" mentality of jingoism and xenophobia, and the "measured pride in the values, achievements and aspirations of a culture and society," which he viewed as a positive thing.[89]

Even still, is St. George the right vehicle for this patriotism? As a chivalric figure, does he endorse social hierarchies, sexist gender relations, and a hypocritical, Manichean view of conflict? Some people certainly believe so, who as a consequence have proposed St. Alban as an alternative national saint. Like George, Alban "spoke truth to power," and was martyred for his faith before the Roman Empire became Christian – furthermore, he actually did these things in what is now England (at Verulamium, now St Albans, north of London).[90] He did not, however, slay any dragons or rescue damsels in distress, sparing us an embarrassing confabulation and its political implications. A campaign among Church of England clergy in 2006 sought to have St. Alban declared the patron of the country at that summer's General Synod, although this does not seem to have made the agenda.[91] But it is unlikely that the English public would follow this lead even if a resolution had passed, and not just because weekly Anglican church attendance now hovers at around 2% of the population. Instead, it is safe to say that people find St. George appealing now for one of the same reasons that they found him appealing in the fifteenth century: his chivalry is not necessarily oppressive, but fun, an adventure that everyone can partake in. Just as medieval chivalry had an appeal beyond the knightly class, and peasant bards told the same sorts of stories, about the same sorts of heroes, as did Homeric bards for their

[89]   George Carey, "Holding Together: Church and Nation in the 21st Century," 2 May 2002, http://www.anglicancommunion.org/acns/news.cfm/2002/5/2/ACNS2976 (accessed 19 June 2008).

[90]   Graham Claydon, "Harry, England, and St Alban!" *Spectator.co.uk*, 24 April 2004, http://www.spectator.co.uk/the-magazine/features/12153/harry-england-and-st-alban.thtml (accessed 19 June 2008). Claydon points out that St. Alban's feast day, 22 June, is usually more clement than 23 April. It is also less likely to conflict with Easter, as did St. George's Day in 2000.

[91]   Steve Doughty, "Will George be slayed as England's patron saint?" *Mail Online*, 2 July 2006, http://www.dailymail.co.uk/news/article-393651/Will-George-slayed-Englands-patron-saint.html (accessed 19 June 2008).

[92]   See M.I. Finley, *The World of Odysseus*, rev. edn. (New York: Viking Press, 1965), 120.

aristocratic patrons, so also does chivalry retain its perennial attraction far beyond the court and peerage.[92] "Chivalry" may no longer be a general principle of behavior as it was in the late-Victorian and Edwardian eras, but the recent success of, say, Peter Jackson's *Lord of the Rings* trilogy, or J.K. Rowling's *Harry Potter* franchise, indicates that the idea of a quest in the service of good shows remarkable staying power. St. George, who did just that, continues to reflect well on the English.

Although Gordon Brown has attempted to reverse somewhat his predecessor's policy of devolution by promoting "Britishness,"[93] St. George's future in England looks bright. Both his flag and his day are once again part of the national fabric, and the figure itself receives new artistic treatment, which is as dramatic as it has ever been.[94] This St. George is not a militaristic saint, still less a crusading or a fascist one, and he does not intercede in heaven on behalf of the English nation. Instead, he is simply one of the many characteristics of "Englishness" that have enjoyed a varied but continuous career from the Middle Ages to the present.

[93] "Brown speech promotes Britishness," *BBC News*, 14 January 2006, http:// news.bbc.co.uk/2/hi/uk_news/politics/4611682.stm (accessed 7 July 2008).
[94] See, for instance, Timothy Noad's rendition of St. George and the dragon, used on gold sovereigns for 2005.

Appendix: Records of St. George in Medieval England

Table 1: Pre-Reformation church dedications to St. George in England, from Frances Arnold-Forster's *Studies in Church Dedications.*[1]

No.	Place	Confirmation [date of earliest mentioning]
1	Arreton, Hampshire	
2	Barton in Fabis, Notts.	
3	Beckenham, Kent	
4	Benenden, Kent	
5	Bicknoller, Somerset	
6	Bourton, Dorset*	
7	Bradfield St. George, Suffolk	Norman Scarfe, *Suffolk in the Middle Ages* (Woodbridge, Suffolk: Boydell, 1986), 78 [1186–91]
8	Bradley, Linconshire	David Hickman, ed., *Lincoln Wills, 1532–34* (Woodbridge, Suffolk: Boydell, 2001), 360 [1534]
9	Brailes, Warwickshire	
10	Brede, Sussex	
11	Brinsop, Herefordshire	
12	Brockworth, Gloucestershire	
13	Great Bromley, Essex	
14	Burrington, Herefordshire	
15	Cam, Gloucestershire	
16	Camberwell, Surrey	
17	Canterbury, Kent	*Letters and Papers, Reign of Henry VIII*, vol. 18 (London: HMSO, 1902), 2: 309 [1541]
18	Chesham Bois, Bucks.*	
19	Church Gresley, Derbyshire†	Alison Binns, *Dedications of Monastic Houses in England and Wales 1066–1216* (Woodbridge, Suffolk: Boydell, 1989), 129 [temp. King Stephen] *[table*

---

[1]   Frances Arnold-Forster, *Studies in Church Dedications* (London, Skeffington and Sons, 1899), 3: 361–63, 351–52, 353, 354.

No.	Place	Confirmation [date of earliest mentioning]
1 cont.]		
20	North Clifton, Nottinghamshire	BL Add. MS 7966a, f. 28v [1306]
21	Clun, Shropshire	
22	Clyst, Devon	Nicholas Orme, *English Church Dedications with a survey of Cornwall and Devon* (Exeter: University of Exeter Press, 1996), 147 [by 1327]
23	Crowhurst, Surrey	
24	Crowhurst, Sussex	
25	South Damerham, Wiltshire	Possible confirmation due to twelfth cent. sculptured tympanum
26	Dean Prior, Devonshire	Orme, *English Church Dedications*, 153 [1479]
27	Didbrook, Gloucestershire	
28	Dittisham, Devonshire	Orme, *English Church Dedications*, 154 [1363]
29	Doncaster, Yorkshire	Possible confirmation due to twelfth cent. sculptured tympanum
30	Donington Wood, Shropshire*	
31	Eastergate, Sussex	
32	Easton-in-Gordano, Somerset	
33	Edington, Somerset	
34	Edworth, Bedfordshire	
35	Esher, Surrey	
36	Evenly, Northamptonshire	
37	Exeter, Devonshire	Orme, *English Church Dedications*, 160 [c. 1215]
38	Falfield, Gloucestershire*	
39	Fingringhoe, Essex	
40	East Fordington, Dorset	Possible confirmation due to twelfth cent. sculptured tympanum
41	Fovant, Wiltshire	
42	Gayton le Marsh, Lincolnshire	
43	Georgeham, Devonshire	Orme, *English Church Dedications*, 164 [1323]
44	Gooderstone, Norfolk	
45	Gravesend, Kent	
46	West Grinstead, Sussex	
47	Halstead, Essex	
48	Ham, Kent	
49	Hampnett, Gloucestershire	
50	Hanworth, Middlesex	
51	Hardingham, Norfolk	
52	West Harnham, Wiltshire	

No.	Place	Confirmation [date of earliest mentioning]

[table 1 cont.]

No.	Place	Confirmation [date of earliest mentioning]
53	Hatford, Berkshire	
54	Hatley, Cambridgeshire	
55	Hethe, Oxfordshire†	
56	Hindolveston, Norfolk	
57	Hinton St. George, Somerset	A.D. Mills, *A Dictionary of English Place-Names* (Oxford and New York: Oxford University Press, 1991), 173 [1246]
58	Hulme, Lancashire*	
59	Ivychurch, Kent	
60	Kelmscott, Oxfordshire	
61	Kencott, Oxfordshire	
62	King's Stanley, Gloucestershire	
63	Langton-Maltravers, Dorset	
64	Littleport, Cambridgeshire	
65	London (Boltolph Lane)	
66	Manchester, Lancashire†	
67	Methwold, Norfolk	
68	Middleton, Durham	
69	Milson, Shropshire	
70	Minsterworth, Gloucestershire	
71	Modbury, Devonshire	Binns, *Dedications*, 101. [1140]
72	Monkleigh, Devonshire	Orme, *English Church Dedications*, 184 [1519]
73	Morebath, Devonshire	Orme, *English Church Dedications*, 185 [1526]
74	Nantwich, Cheshire†	
75	Newbold Pacey, Warwickshire	
76	Norwich (Colegate), Norfolk	Possible confirmation since urban churches needed to be distinguished from each other
77	Norwich (Tombland), Norfolk	Possible confirmation since urban churches needed to be distinguished from each other
78	Nympton, Devonshire	
79	Ogbourne, Wiltshire	Binns, *Dedications*, 102 [1133]
80	Orcheston, Wiltshire	*Liber Quotidianus*, 34 [1300]
81	Orleton, Herefordshire	
82	Oxford, Oxfordshire	Royal Commission on Historical Monuments, *Oxford* (London: HMSO, 1939), 156 [1074]
83	Pontesbury, Shropshire	David Knowles and R. Neville Hadcock, *Medieval Religious Houses: England and Wales* (New York: Longman, 1971), 435 [pre-1066]

No.	Place	Confirmation [date of earliest mentioning]
[table 1 cont.]		
84	Portland, Dorset	
85	Poynton, Cheshire†	
86	Preshute, Wiltshire	
87	Redditch, Worcestershire*	
88	Rodington, Shropshire	
89	Rollesby, Norfolk	
90	Ruishton, Somerset	
91	Saham Toney, Norfolk	
92	Sampford-Brett, Somerset	
93	Sandcroft, Suffolk	
94	Semington, Wiltshire	
95	Sevenoaks-Weald, Kent*	
96	Shillingford, Devonshire	Orme, *English Church Dedications*, 199 [1398]
97	Shimpling, Norfolk	
98	Shimplingthorne, Suffolk	
99	Southacre, Norfolk	
100	Springthorpe, Lincolnshire†	
101	Old Stalybridge, Lancashire	
102	Stamford, Lincolnshire	London, BL Stowe MS 594 [1420–49]
103	Stow, Cambridgeshire	
104	Stowlangtoft, Suffolk	
105	Thetford, Norfolk	F. Blomefield, *Essay Towards a Topographical History of the County of Norfolk* (London: William Miller, 1805), 2: 74 [971]
106	Thrushelton, Devonshire	Possibly confirmed; Orme, *English Church Dedications*, 209.
107	Thwaite, Suffolk	Peter Northeast, ed., *Wills of the Archdeaconry of Sudbury, 1439–1461: Wills from the Register 'Baldwyne' Part I: 1439–1461* (Woodbridge, Suffolk: Boydell, 2001), 241 [1449]
108	Toddington, Bedfordshire	
109	Tredington, Gloucestershire	
110	Trotton, Sussex	Possible confirmation – canons of Dureford Abbey to present a candle to Trotton church on St. George's Day. See W.H. Blaauw, "Dureford Abbey – Its Fortunes and Misfortunes," *Sussex Archaeological Collections* 8 (1856): 60

No.	Place	Confirmation [date of earliest mentioning]

[table 1 cont.]

111	Wembdon, Somerset	E.H. Bates, "Dedications of the Churches of Somersetshire," *Proceedings of the Somersetshire Archaeological and Natural History Society* 51 (1905): 134 [1530]
112	Whatley, Somerset	
113	Whitwick, Leicestershire*	
114	Wilton, Somerset	Bates, "Dedications," 134 [1190] 115
	New Windsor, Berkshire*	*CPR 1350–54*, 127 [1348]
116	Woolhope, Herefordshire	
117	Wooton, Northamptonshire	
118	Wrotham, Kent	
119	Wyverstone, Suffolk	
120	York, Yorkshire	

* = chapelry
† = joint dedication with other saint(s)

Table 2: Churches, chapels, and hospitals of St. George in England by known century of earliest mentioning.

10th–11th	12th	13th	14th	15th	16th
Dunster	Bradfield	Ashcombe	Broadclyst	Beckington	Beaford
Oxford	Ch. Gresley	Exeter	Clifton	Bodmin	Looe
Thetford	Modbury	Hinton	Clyst	Cockington	Monkleigh
Pontesbury	Ogbourne	Nympton	Cogges	Dean Prior	Morebath
	Shrewsbury	Orcheston	Dittisham	Manaton	Wembdon
	Southwark	Tealeburgh	Georgeham	Stamford	Canterbury
	Wilton	Treneglos	Seaton	Truro	Bradley
			Shillingford	Wynbunbury	
			Tolverne	Yeovil	
			Windsor	Thwaite	

Table 3: Number of Pre-Reformation dedications to St. George by county.

Dedications	County
19	Devonshire
12	Somerset
11	Cornwall
11	Norfolk
7	Gloucestershire
7	Kent
7	Wiltshire
6	Suffolk
5	Oxfordshire
5	Shropshire
5	Sussex
4	Herefordshire
4	Lincolnshire
3	Cambridgeshire
3	Cheshire
3	Cumberland
3	Dorset
3	Essex
3	London and Middlesex
3	Surrey
2	Bedfordshire
2	Berkshire
2	Lancashire
2	Northamptonshire
2	Nottinghamshire
2	Warwickshire
2	Yorkshire
1	Derbyshire
1	Durham
1	Hampshire
1	Westmorland
0	Buckinghamshire
0	Hertfordshire
0	Huntingdonshire
0	Leicestershire
0	Northumberland
0	Rutland
0	Staffordshire
0	Worcestershire

Table 4: Relative popularity of the top 20 Pre-Reformation dedications in England.[2]

Rank	Dedication	Tally	%
1	Virgin Mary	1938	18.33
2	All Saints	1044	9.88
3	Peter alone	739	6.99
4	Michael	611	5.78
5	Andrew	577	5.46
6	John the Baptist	446	4.22
7	Nicholas	385	3.64
8	James the Great	327	3.09
9	Peter and Paul	275	2.60
10	Trinity	238	2.25
11	Margaret	230	2.18
12	Laurence	220	2.08
13	Mary Magdalene	172	1.63
14	Leonard	156	1.48
15	Martin	151	1.43
16	Bartholomew	147	1.39
17	Giles	144	1.36
18	Helena	113	1.07
19	George	106	1.00
20	John the Evangelist	103	0.97

[2] Arnold-Forster, *Studies*, 3: 1–26. George's total is 106 because Arnold-Forster omits both chapelries and churches of multiple dedication in her total. The percentages were calculated by dividing the number of pre-Reformation dedications for each saint by 10,571, the total number of all pre-Reformation dedications in Arnold-Forster. This number is slightly more than the number of parishes usually estimated to have been in existence at the time of the English Reformation (Gervase Rosser claims 8,000 or 9,000; Christopher Haigh 9,500. See Gervase Rosser, "Going to the Fraternity Feast: Commensality and Social Relations in Late Medieval England," *Journal of British Studies* 33 [1994]: 431, n. 3; Christopher Haigh, *The English Reformations* [Oxford: Clarendon Press, 1993], 5).

Table 5: Medieval stained glass images of St. George in England.

Stained glass images almost invariably show George standing, dressed in armor and in a surcoat of his arms, killing a dragon at his feet with a lance through its mouth. Exceptions and other details are noted.

Location	Century/date	Notes*
Aldwinkle, Northamptonshire	14th	no dr. but shield of arms; with Christopher
Bampton, Devonshire	16th	
Besthorpe, Norfolk	15th	paired with a bishop or abbot; opposite Michael
Binfield, Berkshire		no surcoat or shield of arms, but definitely G. Nr. Christopher
Bowness-on-Windermere, Westmd.	14th–15th	
Brinsop, Herefordshire		no dr. but shield of arms as well as surcoat
Bristol, Gloucestershire	14th?	no dr., but shield and pennoncel as well as surcoat
Broughton, Staffordshire	late 15th	no surcoat or shield of arms, but definitely G.
Compton Vernay, Warwickshire	16th	G. one of eight saints, incl. Barbara, Christopher, Anne, Margaret, Dominic
Coughton, Warwickshire	15th–16th	
Doddiscombleigh, Devonshire	15th	mounted. Between bishop-saint and Andrew; but reconstructed
Edworth, Bedfordshire		no dr., but shield of arms as well as surcoat
Egmanton, Nottinghamshire	14th	no dr. or surcoat, but shield of arms
Gloucester Abbey, Gloucestershire	14th	no dr., but shield of arms as well as surcoat. One of approx. 70 figures in E. window
Great Malvern Priory, Worcs.		
Kelmscott, Oxfordshire	15th–16th	mounted
Ketteringham, Norfolk	15th–16th	
Haddon Hall, Derbyshire (Chapel)	early 15th	w. Michael and Anne
Hereford, Herefordshire	14th	no dr. or surcoat, and shield of arms bears light cross on dark shield, but label "St. Georgius"

Location	Century/date	Notes*
[table 5 cont.]		
Heydour, Lincolnshire	c. 1380	no dr. but shield of arms; w. Ed. Conf. and Edm.
Himbelton, Worcestershire	15th	w. shield but no arms; labeled "Sanctus Georgius"
Ludlow, Shropshire	15th	
Peterborough Abbey, Hunts.	15th	no dr. or arms but label "Georgii." Shown with 5 other warrior saints incl. Michael, Alban
St. Neot's, Cornwall	early 16th	12-window cycle of legend incl. dr.
Stamford, Lincolnshire	15th	in same window as Katherine, Anne, Paul. There was also a cycle of the life of G.; see ch. 2
Trull, Somerset	15th	w. Michael and Margaret, each killing dr.
Wells, Somerset	14th	no dr., but shield of arms as well as surcoat
West Hallam, Derbyshire	14th	mirroring Michael
West Harling, Norfolk	15th	
Wimbledon, Surrey	c. 1360	no dr., but shield and pennoncel of arms
Wrangle, Lincolnshire		no dr., but shield of arms as well as surcoat
Woolley, Yorkshire		no surcoat but flag on pennon
York, Holy Trinity, Goodramsgate	c. 1472	mirrors Christopher
York, St. John's Mickelgate		nr. Christopher
York, St. Martin-le-Grand, Coney St.	15th	
York, St. Michael, Spurriergate		
York, St. Michael-le-Belfrey	15th	with a noble, a bishop, and Christopher

* G. = George; dr. = dragon

Table 6: Mural paintings of St. George in England[3]

Location	Date	Notes
Amney St. Mary, Gloucestershire		* (very fragmentary)
Arlington, Sussex		
Arundel, Sussex		
Astbury, Cheshire	15th	* scene includes G., pr., charger, George kneels before BVM and child
Bartlow, Cambridgeshire	15th	* only dr. remaining. C.
Barton, Cambridgeshire	14th	* (indistinct)
Baulking, Berkshire	15th	*
Bedale, Yorkshire	c. 1470	* mounted G., killing dr.
Bletsoe, Bedfordshire	late 15th	* scene includes mounted G., dr., pr., K.&Q.
Bovey Tracey, Devonshire		
Boxgrove, Sussex	c. 1400	*
Bradfield Combust, Suffolk	c. 1410	* mounted G., killing dr. C.
Bramfield, Suffolk		included horse
Bradwinch, Devonshire		
Braughing, Hertfordshire		
Broughton, Buckinghamshire	c. 1450	* includes mounted G., dr., pr., lamb
Broughton, Oxford	15th	C.
Calstock, Cornwall	15th	* princess leading dr. w. girdle; mounted G. follows
Canterbury Cathedral, Kent		
Cheddar, Somerset		
Chellesworth, Suffolk	15th	included dr. and two figures watching from a tower

3   Sources: Lewis André, "Saint George the Martyr in Legend, Ceremonial, Art, Etc.", *Archaeological Journal* 57 (1900): 204–23, 218; A. Caiger-Smith, *English Medieval Mural Paintings* (Oxford: Clarendon Press, 1963), 132–36, 150, 158, 165–66, 168, 171–73; 175, 178, 180, 182; E.W. Tristram, *English Wall Painting of the fourteenth century* (London: Routledge and Kegan Paul, 1955), 300; Ethel Carleton Williams, "Mural Paintings of St. George in England," *Journal of the British Archaeological Association*, 3rd series 12 (1949): 30–36. The bulk of Table 6 comes from Williams; Lewis André, Caiger-Smith, and Tristram confirm some of her findings while adding Bovey Tracey, Devonshire, Bradwinch, Devonshire and Slapton, Suffolk (Lewis André), Broughton, Oxfordshire, and Lydiard Tregoze, Wiltshire (Caiger-Smith), and Silk Willoughby, Linconshire (Tristram). Information about St. Christopher is derived from Lewis André.

Location	Date	Notes
[table 5 cont.]		
Chippenham, Cambridgeshire from		* G. kills dr., K.&Q. watch city walls
Conington, Huntingdonshire	early 16th	*
Croydon Old Church, Surrey	c. 1390	G. mounted, pr. watching. C.
Darenth, Kent		
Dartford, Kent	c. 1470	
Devizes, Wiltshire		C.
Drayton, Norfolk		G. stood piercing dr. C.
Dunsford, Surrey	late 13th	
Earl Stonham, Suffolk		*
East Wellow, Hampshire		* G. meets pr.
Evenley, Northamptonshire		
Eversden, Cambridgeshire		G. on north wall, C on south
Farleigh Hungerford, Somerset	late 15th	* G. on foot
Finchley, Middlesex		
Fring, Norfolk		*
Fritton, Norfolk	15th	* mounted G., dr., pr. C.
Gawsworth, Cheshire	c. 1420	mounted G., pr. w. lamb, K.&Q. C.
Great Bedwyn, Wiltshire		G. w. John Baptist
Great Berkhampstead, Hertfordshire		
Hadleigh, Essex		mounted G., pr., K.&Q. from castle
Hardham, Sussex	c. 1135	* dragon slaying, scenes from G.'s martyrdom
Hargrave, Northamptonshire	15th	C.
Haughton, Staffordshire	15th	
Heath, Shropshire		* mounted G. killing dr.
Hereford Cathedral (chapter house)		
Horley, Oxfordshire		* "only the horse's leg remains"
Hornchurch, Essex		
Hornton, Oxfordshire (two images)	both 15th	* G. mounted; * G. on foot
Houghton Conquest, Bedfordshire		
Kersey, Suffolk	15th	* G. and pr.
Kingston, Cambridgeshire	15th	* mounted G. killing dr., pr. watching. C.
Kirtlington, Oxfordshire	15th	* mounted G. killing dr., pr. watching
Lavenham, Suffolk (private house)		* mounted G. killing dr.
Linkinhorne, Cornwall		G. and dr.
Little Kimble, Buckinghamshire	c. 1320	* no dr. but label GEORGIUS.
Lydiard Tregoze, Wiltshire	15th	C.
Mid Lavant, Sussex	1485–1509	
Mobberly, Cheshire	late 15th	* mounted G. killing dr., pr. watching. C.

Location	Date	Notes
[table 5 cont.]		
Nether Wallop, Hampshire	c. 1460	* mounted G. killing dr.
North Wingfield, Derbyshire		G and dr.
Norwich, St. Gregory	late 15th	* mounted G. killing dr., pr. and lamb, K&Q.
Norwich, St. John Maddermarket	15th	
Nunney, Somerset		*
Oakwood, Surrey	late 15th	G. killing dr.
Pickering, Yorkshire	c. 1460	* mounted G. killing dr. C.
Pickhill, Yorkshire		
Pitton, Wiltshire		
Preston, Suffolk (two depictions)		both G. and dr. One over chancel arch with C.
Raunds, Northamptonshire	early 15th	* mounted G. C.
St. Just in Penwith, Cornwall	15th	* mounted G., dr.
Salisbury, St. Thomas		G. and dr.
Shorthampton, Oxfordshire	c. 1400	*
Shouldham Thorpe, Norfolk		
Silk Willoughby, Lincolnshire	14th	G and dr.
Slapton, Northamptonshire	15th	* mounted G. killing dr., pr. and lamb, K.&Q.
Slapton, Suffolk		C.
South Burlingham, Norfolk	15th	* palimpsest underneath C.
South Newington, Oxfordshire		mounted G. painted over martyrdom of Thos. Beck.
Sproughton, Suffolk		G. and dr. C.
Stedham, Sussex		mounted G. on north wall, C. on south
Stotfold, Bedfordshire		mounted G. killing dr.
Stratford, Holy Cross chapel		
Sutton Courtenay, Berkshire	c. 1450	mounted G. killing dr.
Troston, Suffolk (two depictions)	13th, 15th	* both mounted G killing dr. One with C.
Trotton, Sussex	late 15th	mounted G.
Warborough, Oxfordshire	14th	mounted G., pr.
Westfield, Sussex		
Westmeston, Sussex	c. 1150	G. before Datianus
Whimple, Devon		C.
Willingham, Cambridgeshire	14th	mounted G. killing dr.
Wilsford and Mere, Wiltshire		G. and dr.
Witton, Norfolk	early 15th	mounted G. killing dr. C.
Worsted, Norfolk		

* = extant painting; pr. = princess; K.&Q. = king and queen; C. = St. Christopher depicted nearby; G. = George; dr. = dragon.

Table 7: Guilds to St. George in Cornwall.[4]

Place	Dedication	Earliest date recorded
Lostwithiel	George	1414
Launceston, St. Mary Magdalene Church	George	1467
North Petherwin Church	George	1493
Lanteglos-by-Fowley	George	1502
Golant, St. Samson Church	George	1509
Liskeard Church	George	1544
South Petherwin Church	George	1544
Antony	George	1545–47

---

[4] Source: Orme, *Saints of Cornwall*, 125–26.

Table 8: Guilds of the 1388 Return dedicated to St. George.[5]

Place	Dedication	Date
Littleport, Cambridgeshire	St. George	1378
Lincoln, Lincolnshire	St. George	1377
Springthorpe, Lincolnshire	St. George	–
Lynn, Norfolk, Parish of St. Margaret	St. George	1376
Lynn, Norfolk, chapel of St. Nicholas	SS. Mary and George	–
Norwich, Norfolk	St. George	1385
Great Yarmouth, Norfolk, charnel house next St. Nicholas Church	St. George the Martyr	–
Great Yarmouth, Norfolk, in chapel of St. George, St. Nicholas's Church	St. George the Martyr	1377–78
Bury St. Edmunds, Norfolk	St. George	c. 1369
Warwick, Warwickshire	St. George	1377–89

5   Source: Herbert F. Westlake, *The Parish Gilds of Medieval England* (London: Society for Promoting Christian Knowledge, 1918), 144, 170, 177, 194, 197, 203, 218, 227, 232.

Table 9: Late Medieval English guilds dedicated to St. George not included in Westlake's *Parish Guilds* or Orme's *Saints of Cornwall*.[6]

Place	Dedication	Date
Chichester, Sussex	George	1368
London, St. Giles Cripplegate parish	George	1368
Salisbury, Wiltshire	George	1376 (perhaps 1306)
York, Yorkshire	George and Christopher	1394 (merger in 1460s)
Totnes, Devonshire	George	1415
Coventry, Taylors and Shearmen	George	1425
Dublin, Ireland	George	1448
London, Armorers guild	George	1452
Nottingham, St. Peter's	George	1459
Northampton, Northants.	George the Martyr	1473
Exeter, Devon, Holy Trinity parish	George	by 1482
Exeter, Devon, Guildhall	George	by 1486
Peterborough, Northants	George and James	by 1495
Banwell, Somerset	George	1518
Bridgewater, Somerset	George	dissolved 1548
Dunster, Somerset	George	dissolved 1548
Boston, Lincolnshire	George	1533
Morton, Lincolnshire	George	1534
Leicester, Leicestershire	George	pre-Reformation
Chagford, Devonshire	George	pre-Reformation
Braunton, Devonshire	John and George	pre-Reformation
Stratton, Devonshire	George	pre-Reformation
Little Walsingham, Norfolk	George	pre-Reformation

[6] Sources: L.F. Salzman, ed., *The Victoria History of the County of Sussex* (London: Institute for Historical Research, 1935), 3: 92; George Unwin, *The Gilds and Companies of London* (London: Methuen, 1908), 369; Elizabeth Crittall, ed., *The Victoria History of the County of Wiltshire* (London: Institute for Historical Research, 1962), 6: 97; Eileen White, *The St Christopher and St George Guild of York* (York: Borthwick Institute, 1987), 2, 5; Hugh R. Watkin, *The History of Totnes Priory and Medieval Town, Devonshire* (Torquay: the author, 1917), 2: 332; W.B. Stephens, ed., *A History of the County of Warwick* (London: Institute for Historical Research, 1969), 8: 331–32; Steven G. Ellis, "Brotherhood of St. George," in *The Oxford Companion to Irish History*, ed. S.J. Connolly (Oxford: Oxford University Press, 1998), 60; *CPR 1452–61* (London: HMSO, 1910), 105; R.F.B. Hodgkinson, trans., *The Account Books of the Gilds of St. George and St. Mary in the Church of St. Peter, Nottingham* (Nottingham: Thomas Forman and Sons, 1939), 17; Dorothy Edwards, et al., eds., *Early Northampton Wills Preserved in the Northampton Record Office* (Northampton: Northampton Record Society, 2005), 50 et passim; Nicholas Orme, personal communication, referencing Exeter, Devon Record Office,

Holy Trinity Exeter, PW 2–3, and ED/M/941; W.T. Mellows, ed., *Peterborough Local Administration: Churchwardens' Accounts 1467–1573*, (Peterborough: Northampton Record Society, 1939), xxxvii; Katherine L. French, *People of the Parish: Community Life in a Late Medieval English Diocese* (Philadelphia: University of Pennsylvania Press, 2001), 211, 213, 217; David Hickman, ed., *Lincoln Wills, 1532–34* (Woodbridge, Suffolk: Boydell, 2001), 195, 370; William Kelly, *Notices Illustrative of the Drama, and other Popular Amusements ... of the Borough of Leicester* (London: John Russel Smith, 1865), 36–38; Robert Whiting, *The Blind Devotion of the People: Popular Religion and the English Reformation* (Cambridge: Cambridge University Press, 1989), 107 (Chagford), 112 (Braunton), 110; David Galloway and John Wasson, eds., *Records of Plays and Players in Norfolk and Suffolk, 1330–1642* (Oxford: Malone Society, 1980), 74, 76.

Bibliography

Manuscript sources

London, National Archives (Public Record Office)

C 47	Chancery, miscellaneous accounts
E 36	Treasury, miscellaneous accounts
E 101	Exchequer, miscellaneous accounts
E 403	Exchequer, issue rolls and receipts

British Library

Additional 4712
Additional 6113
Additional 7966a
Additional 7965
Additional 38126
Arundel 341
Arundel 406
Cotton Nero C VIII
Edgerton 3510
Harley 642
Royal French 20.B.IX
Royal French 20.D.VI
Royal Latin 9.A.XIV
Sloane 2471
Sloane 2565
Sloane 2633
Sloane 2683
Stowe 594

London, Courtauld Institute

Catalogue of medieval stained glass

Minneapolis, University of Minnesota

Z 822 N 81

Oxford, Bodleian Library

Douce 231

Facsimile editions

London, Lambeth Palace Library

209 (published London: Harvey Miller, 1997)

Printed sources

*The Account Books of the Gilds of St. George and St. Mary in the Church of St. Peter,
Nottingham*. Translated by R.F.B. Hodgkinson. Thoroton Society Record Series
7. Nottingham: Thomas Forman and Sons, 1939.

Acta Sanctorum quotquot tota orbe coluntur. In process. Paris: V. Palmé, 1863–.

Adalbertus. *Vita Henrici II*. In *Monumenta Germaniae Historica, Scriptores* 4.
Hannover: Hahnsche Buchhandlung, 1841.

Adamnan. *De Locis Sanctis*. Edited by Denis Meehan. Scriptores Latini Hiberniae
3. Dublin: Dublin Institute for Advanced Studies, 1958.

Aelfric of Eynsham. *An Anglo-Saxon passion in the Cambridge University Library*.
Edited and translated by C. Hardwick. London: The Percy Society, 1850.

—— *Aelfric's Lives of the Saints: Being a Set of Sermons on Saints' Days formerly observed
by the English Church, edited from Manuscript Julius E. VII in the Cottonian
Collection, with Various Readings from other Manuscripts*. Edited by W.W. Skeat.
2 vols. Early English Text Society 76, 82; 94, 114. London: EETS, 1881–85,
1890–1900.

Aelred of Rievaulx. *Vita Sancti Aedwardi Confessoris*. In *Patrologiae Latina* 195, cols.
769–70.

Ambroise. *The Crusade of Richard the Lionheart*. Translated by Merton Jerome
Hubert. New York: Octagon Books, 1976.

Anderson, J.J. *The Records of Early English Drama: Newcastle upon Tyne*. Toronto
and Buffalo: University of Toronto Press and Manchester: Manchester
University Press, 1982.

Annales Monastici. Edited by H.R. Luard. 5 vols. Rolls Series 36. London: Longman,
1846–69.

Annali Genovesi di Caffaro e de' suoi Continuatori. Edited by Luigi Tommaso Belgrano.
Fonti per la Storia d'Italia 11. Genoa: Istituto Sordo-Muti, 1890.

The Antient Kalendars and Inventories of the Treasury of His Majesty's Exchequer. Edited
by Francis Palgrave. 3 vols. London: Public Records Commissioners, 1836.

Baden-Powell, Robert. *Scouting for Boys: The Original 1908 Edition*. Mineola, N.Y.:
Dover Publications, 2007.

—— *Scouting for Boys*. 1951 Edition. At http://www.thedump.scoutscan.com/
s4b.html.

Barclay, Alexander. *The Life of St. George.* Early English Text Society 230. London: EETS, 1955.

Bartholomew Anglicus. *Medieval Lore: An Epitome of the Science, Geography, Animal and Plant Folk-Lore and Myth of the Middle Age.* Edited by Robert Steel. London: Elliot Stock, 1893.

The Book of Common Prayer. London, 1552.

The Book of the Pontiffs. Edited by Raymond Davis. 2nd edn. Liverpool: Liverpool University Press, 2000.

Brooks, E.W. "Acts of S. George." *Museon* 38 (1925): 67–115.

Brown, Carleton, ed. *Religious Lyrics of the XVth Century.* Oxford: Clarendon Press, 1939.

"Brown speech promotes Britishness." *BBC News,* 14 January 2006. At http://news.bbc.co.uk/2/hi/uk_news/politics/4611682.stm.

The Brut, or the Chronicles of England. Edited by Friedrich W.D. Brie. 2 vols. Early English Text Society Extra Series 131, Original Series 136. London: EETS, 1906–08.

Budge, E.A.W. *The Martyrdom and Miracles of St. George of Cappadocia.* London: D. Nutt, 1888.

—— *George of Lydda, the Patron Saint of England: A Study of the Cultus of St. George in Ethiopia.* London: Luzac and Co., 1930.

Byerly, Benjamin F. and Catherine Ridder Byerly, eds. *Records of the Wardrobe and Household 1286–89.* London: HMSO, 1986.

Byrom, John. *Miscellaneous Poems.* 3 vols. Leeds: James Nichols, 1814.

Calendar of Charter Rolls, 1226–57. London: HMSO, 1903.

Calendar of Charter Rolls, 1341–1417. London: HMSO, 1916

Calendar of Close Rolls, 1251–53. London: HMSO, 1927.

Calendar of Liberate Rolls, 1240–1244. London: HMSO, 1930.

Calendar of Liberate Rolls, 1251–60. London: HMSO, 1959.

Calendar of Patent Rolls, 1348–50. London: HMSO, 1905.

Calendar of Patent Rolls, 1350–54. London: HMSO, 1907.

Calendar of Patent Rolls, 1381–85. London: HMSO, 1897.

Calendar of Patent Rolls, 1385–89. London: HMSO, 1900.

Calendar of Patent Rolls, 1388–92. London: HMSO, 1902

Calendar of Patent Rolls, 1391–96. London: HMSO, 1905

Calendar of Patent Rolls, 1452–61. London: HMSO, 1910.

Calvin, John. *Institutes of the Christian Religion.* Translated by Henry Beveridge. Grand Rapids, Mich.: Eerdmans, 1989.

"The Campaign." *The Value of St George campaign.* At http://www.thevalueofstgeorge.com/index.php?oURL=home%2FThe+Campaign%2FCampaign+Aims.

Campaign for an English Parliament. At http://www.thecep.org.uk/wordpress.

Campbell, William, ed. *Materials for a History of the Reign of Henry VII.* 2 vols. Rolls Series 60. London: Longman, 1877.

Capgrave, John. *Liber de Illustribus Henricis.* Edited by Francis Charles Hingeston. Rolls Series 7. London: Longman, 1858.

Carey, George. "Holding Together: Church and Nation in the 21st Century," 2

May 2002. At http://www.anglicancommunion.org/acns/news.cfm/2002/ 5/2/ACNS2976.

Caxton, William. *The Golden Legend or Lives of the Saints as Englished by William Caxton.* 7 vols. London: J.M. Dent, 1900.

The Chronicle of Adam Usk 1377–1421. Edited and translated by Christopher Given-Wilson. Oxford Medieval Texts. Oxford: Clarendon Press, 1997.

Chronicle of the Grey Friars of London, Camden Society Old Series 53. London: Camden Society, 1852.

Chronicle of the Third Crusade: A Translation of the Itinerarium et Gesta Regis Ricardi. Translated by Helen J. Nicholson. Crusade Texts in Translation 3. Aldershot, Hants. and Brookfield, Vt.: Ashgate, 1997.

Chronicles and Memorials of the Reign of Richard I. Edited by W. Stubbs. 2 vols. Rolls Series 38. London: Longman, 1864.

Chronicles of the Reigns of Edward I and Edward II. Edited by W. Stubbs. 2 vols. Rolls Series 76. London: Longman, 1882.

Chronicon Henrici Knighton. Edited by J.R. Lumby. Rolls Series 92. London: Longman, 1895.

Chronicque de la traison et mort de Richard deux roy d'Engleterre. Edited by Benjamin Williams. London: English Historical Society, 1846.

The Church Book of St. Ewen's, Bristol, 1454–1584. Edited by Betty R. Masters and Elizabeth Ralph. Bristol: Bristol and Gloucestershire Archaeological Society, 1967.

The Churches and Monasteries of Egypt and some Neighbouring Countries attributed to Abu Salih, the Armenian. Translated by B.T.A. Evetts. Oxford: Clarendon Press, 1895.

Claydon, Graham. "Harry, England, and St Alban!" *Spectator.co.uk,* 24 April 2004. At http://www.spectator.co.uk/the-magazine/features/12153/harry-england-and-st-alban.thtml.

Cole, Charles Augustus, ed. *Memorials of Henry the Fifth, King of England.* Rolls Series 11. London: Longman, Brown, Green, 1858.

Concilia Magnae Britanniae et Hiberniae. Edited by D. Wilkins. 4 vols. London: s.n., 1737.

Dalton, O.M. *Catalogue of the Early Christian Antiquities and Objects from the Christian East in the Department of British and Mediaeval Antiquities and Ethnography of the British Museum.* London: British Museum, 1901.

Davies, Reginald Thorne, ed. *Medieval English Lyrics: A Critical Anthology.* London: Faber, 1966.

Dawes, Elizabeth and Norman H. Baynes. *Three Byzantine Saints: Contemporary Biographies translated from the Greek.* Oxford: Basil Blackwell, 1948.

Delehaye, Hippolyte. "Une version nouvelle de la Passion de Saint Georges." *Analecta Bollandiana* 27 (1908): 373–83.

De Malynes, Gerrard. *Saint George for England, Allegorically Described.* London: Richard Field, 1601.

Detlefsen, D. "Über einen griechishen Palimpsest der k.k. Hofbibliothek mit Bruchstücken einer Legende vom heil. Georg." *Sitzungsberichte der Kaiserlichen*

Akademie der Wissenschaften. Philosophish-Historische Classe 27 (1858): 383–404.

Dobson, R.B., ed. *The Peasants' Revolt of 1381*. History in Depth. London: Macmillan, 1970.

Doughty, Steve. "Will George be slayed as England's patron saint?" *Mail Online*, 2 July 2006. At http://www.dailymail.co.uk/news/article–393651/Will-George-slayed-Englands-patron-saint.html.

The Early South English Legendary or Lives of the Saints. Edited by Carl Horstmann. Early English Text Society 87. Millwood, N.Y.: Kraus Reprint, 1987.

Edwards, Adam. "By George, it's time to raise the flag!" *Telegraph.co.uk*, 21 April 2007. At http://www.telegraph.co.uk/global/main.jhtml?xml=/global/2007/04/23/ nosplit/ftgeorge20.xml.

Edwards, Dorothy, ed. *Early Northampton Wills Preserved in the Northampton Record Office*. Northamptonshire Record Society 42. Northampton: NRS, 2005.

"The English Way." *Telegraph.co.uk*, 24 April 2002. At http://www.telegraph.co.uk/opinion/main.jhtml?xml=/opinion/2002/04/24/dl2403.xml.

Erasmus, Desiderius. *The Praise of Folly*. Translated by Clarence H. Miller. New Haven and London: Yale University Press, 1979.

Eusebius. *The History of the Church from Christ to Constantine*. Translated by G.A. Williamson. Harmondsworth: Penguin, 1965.

—— *The Life of Constantine the Blessed Emperor*. Greek Ecclesiastical Historians 1. London: Samuel Bagster and Sons, 1845.

Fredegarii et aliorum Chronica. Vitae Sanctorum. Edited by Bruno Krusch. In *Monumenta Germaniae Historica, Scriptores rerum Merovingicarum* 2. Hannover: Hahnsche Buchhandlung, 1888.

Froissart, Jean. *Oeuvres de Froissart*. Edited by Kervyn de Lettenhove. 25 vols. in 26. Brussels: Victor Devaux, 1867–77.

Gairdner, James, ed. *Memorials of the Reign of King Henry VII*. Rolls Series 10. London: Longman, 1858.

—— *Three Fifteenth-Century Chronicles*. Camden Society New Series 28. London: Camden Society, 1880.

—— and R.H. Brodie, eds. *Letters and Papers, Foreign and Domestic of the Reign of Henry VIII*. 21 vols. in 37. Vaduz: Kraus Reprint, 1965.

Galloway, David and John Wasson, eds. *Records of Plays and Players in Norfolk and Suffolk, 1330–1642*. Collections of the Malone Society 11. Oxford: Malone Society, 1980.

Geoffrey Malaterra. *De Rebus Gestis Rogerii*. Edited by E. Pontieri. Rerum Italicarum Scriptores 5. Bologna: Zanichelli, 1926.

Geoffrey of Monmouth. *History of the Kings of Britain*. Translated by Lewis Thorpe. Harmondsworth: Penguin, 1966.

Gervase of Canterbury. *The Historical Works of Gervase of Canterbury*. Edited by W. Stubbs. 2 vols. Rolls Series 73. London: Longmans, 1880.

Gesta abbatum fontanellensium. Edited by S. Loewenfeld. In *Monumenta Germaniae Historica, Scriptores rerum Germanicarum* 18. Hannover: Hahnsche Buchhandlung, 1886.

Gesta Francorum et aliorum Hierosolimitanorum. Edited by R. Hill. Medieval Texts.

London: Thomas Nelson, 1962.

Gesta Henrici Quinti: The Deeds of Henry the Fifth. Edited by Frank Taylor and John
S. Roskell. Oxford: Clarendon Press, 1975.

Gloucester Cathedral Newsletter. April 2005.

The Great Chronicle of London. Edited by A.H. Thomas and I.D. Thornley. London:
Corporation of the City of London, 1938.

Greene, Richard Leighton. *The Early English Carols.* 2nd edn. Oxford: Clarendon
Press, 1935.

—— *A Selection of English Carols.* Clarendon Tudor and Medieval Studies. Oxford:
Clarendon Press, 1962.

Gregory of Tours. *Glory of the Martyrs.* Translated by Raymond van Dam.
Liverpool: Liverpool University Press, 1988.

Hammond, E.P. "Two Tapestry Poems by Lydgate." *Englische Studien* 43 (1910):
10–26.

Hardy, Thomas. *The Play of St. George as Aforetime Acted by the Dorsetshire Christmas
Mummers.* Cambridge: Cambridge University Press for Florence Emily Hardy,
1921.

Hardyng, John. *The Chronicle of John Hardying.* London: Henry Ellis, 1812.

Heylyn, Peter. *The Historie of that Most Famous Saint and Souldier of Christ Jesus, St.
George of Cappadocia, Asserted from the Fictions of the Middle Ages of the Church
and Opposition of the Present.* London: Henry Seyle, 1631.

Hickman, David, ed. *Lincoln Wills, 1532–34.* Woodbridge, Suffolk: Boydell, 2001.

*Historie of the Arrivall of Edward IV. in England and the Finall Recouerye of his
Kingdomes from Henry VI. A.D. M.CCCC.LXXI.* Edited by John Bruce. London:
Camden Society, 1838.

Horae Eboracensis: The Prymer or Hours of the Blessed Virgin Mary. Edited by Canon
Wordsworth. Publications of the Surtees Society 132. Durham: The Society,
1920.

Ingram, R.W. *Records of Early English Drama: Coventry.* Toronto: University of
Toronto Press, 1981.

Itinera Hierosolymitana Saeculi IIII–VIII. Edited by Paul Geyer. Corpus Scriptorum
Ecclesiasticorum Latinorum 39. New York and London: Johnson Reprints,
1964.

Jacobus de Voragine. *The Golden Legend: Readings on the Saints.* Translated by
William Granger Ryan. 2 vols. Princeton: Princeton University Press, 1993.

Jalabert, Louis and René Mouterde. *Inscriptions grecques et latines de la Syrie.* 21
vols. so far. Paris: Paul Guenther, 1929-.

*Johannes de Trokelowe et Henrici de Blaneforde, monachorum S. Albani, necnon
quorundam anonymorum, Chronica et Annales.* Edited by H.T. Riley. 3 vols. Rolls
Series 28. London: Longman, 1866.

*Johannes Monachus, Liber de Miraculis. Ein neuer Beitrag zu mittelalterlichen
Mönchsliteratur.* Edited by P. Michael Huber. Sammlung mittellateinischer
Texte 7. Heidelberg: Carl Winters Universitätsbuchhandlung, 1913.

Johnson, Richard. *The Seven Champions of Christendom (1596/7).* Edited by Jennifer
Fellows. Aldershot: Ashgate, 2003.

Johnston, Philip. "The day that dare not speak its name." *Telegraph.co.uk*, 23 April 2007. At http://www.telegraph.co.uk/opinion/main.jhtml?xml=/opinion/2007/04/23/ do2302.xml.

Joyce, Sally L. and Evelyn S. Newlyn, eds. *Records of Early English Drama: Cornwall*. Toronto and Buffalo: University of Toronto Press, 1999.

Kelly, William. *Notices Illustrative of the Drama, and other Popular Amusements ... of the Borough of Leicester*. London: John Russel Smith, 1865.

League of St George – the Website of the League of Saint George! At http://www.leaguestgeorge.com.

Leland, John. *De rebus britannicis Collectanea*. 6 vols. London: Benjamin White, 1774.

Liber Quotidianus Contrarotulatoris Garderobae anno regni regis Edwardi primi vicesimo octavo. London: Society of Antiquaries, 1787.

The Life of King Edward who rests at Westminster attributed to a monk of Saint-Bertin. Edited by Frank Barlow. 2nd edn. Oxford: Clarendon Press, 1992.

The Lives of the Eighth-Century Popes. Edited by Raymond Davis. Liverpool: Liverpool University Press, 1992.

The Lives of the Ninth-Century Popes. Edited by Raymond Davis. Liverpool: Liverpool University Press, 1995.

Louis, Cameron, ed. *The Records of Early English Drama: Sussex*. Toronto and Buffalo: University of Toronto Press, 2000.

Lowick, Thomas. *The History of the Life & Martyrdom of St. George, the titular patron of England with his conversion of Arabia by killing of a dreadful dragon, and delivering the kings daughter*. London: J. Best for William Crook, 1664.

Ludovicus II. *Diplomata*. In *Monumenta Germaniae Historica, Diplomata Karolinorum* 4. Munich: MGH, 1994.

Lydgate, John. *The Minor Poems of John Lydgate*. Edited by Henry Noble MacCracken. 2 vols. Early English Text Society Extra Series 107, Early English Text Society 192. London: EETS, 1911–34.

Machen, Arthur. *The Angels of Mons, The Bowmen, and Other Legends of the War*. New York and London: G.P. Putnam's Sons, 1915.

Matthew Paris. *Chronica Majora*. 3 vols. Rolls Series 57. London: Longmans, 1876.

McCarthy, Justin Huntly. "The Ghosts at Boulogne." In *Songs and Sonnets for England in War Time: Electronic Edition*. At http://beck.library.emory.edu/greatwar/poetry/view.php?id=Lane_lane052.

Migne, J.-P., ed. *Patrologiae Cursus Completus ... Series Latina*. 221 vols. Paris: 1844–64.

The Miracles of King Henry VI. Edited by Ronald Knox and Shane Leslie. Cambridge: Cambridge University Press, 1923.

Miracula S. Georgii. Edited by Johann B. Aufhauser. Leipzig: B.G. Teubner, 1913.

Mirk, John. *Mirk's Festial: A Collection of Homilies*. Edited by Theodore Erbe. Early English Text Society Extra Series 96. London: EETS, 1905.

Monumenta Juridica: The Black Book of the Admiralty. Edited by Travers Twiss. 4 vols. Rolls Series 55. London: Longman, 1871–76.

Mundy, A. *The Triumphs of Re-united Britania*. London: W. Jaggard, 1605.

Munro, Dana C., ed. "Speech of Urban II at the Council of Clermont." In *Translations and Reprints from the Original Sources of European History* 1: 2 (1895): 1–8.

Myers, A.R., ed. *English Historical Documents* 4 1327–1485. London: Eyre and Spottiswoode, 1969.

Les Œuvres de Simund de Freine. Edited by John E. Matzke. Société des Anciens Textes Français 59. Paris: Firmin-Didot, 1909.

Orderic Vitalis. *The Ecclesiastical History*. Edited by Marjorie Chibnall. 6 vols. Oxford: Clarendon Press, 1972.

Parker, R.E. "A northern fragment of *The Life of St. George*." *Modern Language Notes* 38 (1923): 97–101.

A Parisian Journal 1405–1449. Translated by Janet Shirley. Oxford: Oxford University Press, 1968.

Passiones Vitaeque Sanctorum aevi Merovingici. Edited by Bruno Krusch. *Monumenta Germaniae Historica, Scriptores rerum Merovingicarum* 3. Hannover: Hahnsche Buchhandlung, 1888.

Paul the Deacon. *History of the Langobards*. Translated by William Dudley Foulke, edited by Edward Peeters. Philadelphia: University of Pennsylvania Press, 1974.

Pearl, Cleanness, Patience and Sir Gawain: Reproduced in Facsimile from the Unique MS Cotton Nero A.x in the British Museum. Edited by Israel Gollancz. Early English Text Society 210. London: EETS, 1923.

Peeters, Paul. "Une Passion arménienne de S. Georges." *Analecta Bollandiana* 28 (1909): 249–271.

Peterborough Local Administration: Churchwardens' Accounts 1467–1573. Edited by Mellows. Northamptonshire Record Society 9. Peterborough: NRS, 1939.

Pilkinton, Mark C. *Records of Early English Drama: Bristol*. Toronto, Buffalo and London: University of Toronto Press, 1997.

Political Poems and Songs relating to English History composed during the period from the accession of Edward III to that of Richard III. Edited by Thomas Wright. 2 vols. Rolls Series 14. London: Longman, Green, 1859.

"Preview – England v Wales." *Planet-Rugby*, 8 November 2003. At http://planet-rugby.com/LATEST_NEWS/story_32463.sthml.

Procopius of Caesarea. *Buildings*. Volume VII of *Procopius*. Translated by H.B. Dewing. Loeb Classical Library. London: William Heinemann and Cambridge: Harvard University Press, 1921.

Psellus, Michael. *Fourteen Byzantine Rulers*. Translated by E.A.W. Sawyer. Harmondsworth: Penguin, 1966.

Rainolds, John. *De Idolatria Ecclesiae Romanae*. Oxford, 1596.

The Records of the Gild of Saint George in Norwich, 1389–1547: A Transcript with an Introduction. Edited by Mary Grace. Norfolk Record Society 9. Norwich: NRS, 1937.

The Register of Henry Chichele, Archbishop of Canterbury, 1414–1443. Edited by E.F. Jacob. 4 vols. Canterbury and York Society 46. Oxford: Oxford University Press, 1937–47.

The Register of Thomas Langley, Bishop of Durham 1416–1437. Edited by R.L. Storey. 6 vols. Surtees Society 169. Durham and London: Surtees Society, 1956–1970.

Rituale Ecclesiæ Dunelmensis. Edited by J. Stephenson. Surtees Society 10. London: J.B. Nichols, 1840.

Robbins, Rossell Hope, ed. *Historical Poems of the XIVth and XVth Centuries.* New York: Columbia, 1959.

—— *Secular Lyrics of the Fifteenth Century.* 2nd edn. Oxford: Clarendon Press, 1955.

Roger of Wendover. *The Flowers of History.* Edited by Henry G. Hewlett. 3 vols. Rolls Series 84. London: HMSO for Eyre and Spottiswoode, 1886–89.

Rotuli Parliamentorum. Edited by J. Strachey. 6 vols. London: s.n. 1783.

Rous, John. *Historia Regum Angliae.* Edited by Thomas Hearn. Oxford: J. Fletcher, 1745.

The St. Albans Chronicle 1406–1420. Edited by V.H. Galbraith. Oxford: Clarendon Press, 1937.

Schwartz, Eduard. *Kyrillos von Skythopolis.* Texte und Untersuchungen zur Geschichte der altchristlichen Literatur 49: 2. Leipzig: J.C. Heinrichs Verlag, 1939.

Scriptores Originum Constantinopolitanarum. Edited by Theodore Preger. New York: Arno Press, 1975.

The Siege of Carlaverock. Edited by N.H. Nicolas. London: J.B. Nichols, 1828.

Speculum Sacerdotale. Edited by Edward H. Weatherly. Early English Text Society 200. London: EETS, 1936.

Starmer-Smith, Charles. "Flags and Roses for St George's Day." *Telegraph.co.uk*, 24 April 2002. At http://www.telegraph.co.uk/news/main.jhtml?xml=/news/2002/04/24/ncarey124.xml.

Sutton, Anne F. and P.W. Hammond. *The Coronation of Richard III: The Extant Documents.* Gloucester: Alan Sutton and New York: St. Martin's Press, 1983.

Testamenta Vetusta. Edited by N.H. Nicolas. London: Nichols and Son, 1826.

Toulmin Smith, [Joshua], and Lucy Toulmin Smith, eds. *English Gilds: The Original Ordinances of More than One Hundred Early English Gilds.* Early English Text Society 40. London: EETS, 1870.

The treatise of Walter De Milemete de Nobilitatibus, sapientiis, et prudentiis regum, reproduced in facsimile from the unique manuscript preserved at Christ Church, Oxford. Edited by M.R. James. Oxford: Roxburghe Club, 1913.

Usk, Adam. *Chronicon Adae de Usk AD 1377–1421.* Edited by E.M. Thompson. 2nd edn. London: Henry Froude, 1904.

Venantius Fortunatus. *De basilica S. Georgi.* In *Monumenta Germaniae Historica, Auctorum Antiquissimorum* 4:1. Berolini: Weidmann, 1881.

La Vie de la Vierge Marie de Maitre Wace: publiée d'après un manuscrit inconnu aux prémiers éditeurs, suivie de La vie de Saint George: poème inedit du même trouvère. Edited by Victor Luzarche. Tours: J. Bouserez, 1859.

Waddington, William H. *Inscriptions Grecques et Latines de la Syrie.* Rome: "L'Erma" di Bretschneider, 1968.

Warkworth's Chronicle of the First Thirteen Years of the Reign of King Edward the Fourth. Edited by James Orchard Halliwell. London: Camden Society, 1839.

The Westminster Chronicle, 1381–1394. Edited by L.C. Hector and Barbara F. Harvey. Oxford: Clarendon Press, 1982.

White, Eileen. *The St Christopher and St George Guild of York.* Borthwick Papers 72. York: Borthwick Institute, 1987.

White, Jim. "How our modest nation can fly the flag." *Telegraph.co.uk,* 16 January 2006. At http://www.telegraph.co.uk/opinion/main.jhtml?xml=/opinion/2006/01/16/ do1603.xml.

White, Tristram. *The Martyrdom of Saint George of Cappadocia: Titular Patron of England, and of the most Noble Order of the Garter.* London: William Barley, 1614.

Wickham Legg, Leopold G. *English Coronation Records.* Westminster: Archibald Constable, 1901.

The Will of King Henry VII. Edited by Thomas Astle. London: T. Payne and B. White, 1775.

Worcestre, William. *Itineraries.* Edited by John H. Harvey. Oxford Medieval Texts. Oxford: Clarendon Press, 1969.

Wynnere and Wastoure. Edited by S. Trigg. Early English Text Society 297. Oxford: EETS, 1990.

Zarncke, Friedrich. "Eine zweite Redaction der Georgslegende aus dem 9. Jahrhundert." *Berichte über die Verhandlungen der Königlich Sächsischen Gesellschaft der Wissenschaften zu Leipzig. Philologisch-Historische Class* 27 (1875): 256–277.

Secondary sources

Abel, P.M. "Le tombeau de l'higoumène Cyriaque à Jericho." *Revue Biblique* 8 (1911): 286–89.

Allmand, Christopher. *The Hundred Years War: England and France at War, c. 1300–c. 1450.* Cambridge: Cambridge University Press, 1989.

Anderson, Benedict. *Imagined Communities: Reflections on the Origin and Spread of Nationalism,* 2nd edn. London: Verso, 1991.

André, J. Lewis. "Saint George the Martyr, in Legend, Ceremonial, Art, Etc." *Archaeological Journal* 57 (1900): 204–23.

Anglo, Sydney. *Spectacle, Pageantry, and Early Tudor Policy.* New York: Oxford University Press, 1997.

Anstis, J., ed. *The Register of the Most Noble Order of the Garter, called the Black Book.* London, 1724.

Arnold-Forster, Frances. *Studies in Church Dedications, or England's Patron Saints.* 3 vols. London: Skefington and Son, 1899.

Ashley, Kathleen and Pamela Sheingorn, eds. *Interpreting Cultural Symbols: Saint Anne in Late Medieval Society.* Athens and London: University of Georgia Press, 1990.

Ashmole, Elias. *The Institution, Laws & Ceremonies of the Most Noble Order of the Garter.* London: Printed by J. Macock, for Nathanael Brooke, 1672.

Aufhauser, Johann B. *Das Drachenwunder des heiligen George in der griechischen und lateinischen überlieferung*. Byzantinisches Archiv 5. Leipzig: B.G. Teubner, 1911.

Backhouse, Janet. "Devotions and Delights." In *Age of Chivalry*, edited by Nigel Saul, 76–89. New York: St. Martin's Press, 1992.

Barber, Richard. *Edward Prince of Wales and Aquitaine: A Biography of the Black Prince*. New York: Charles Scribner's Sons, 1978.

Baring-Gould, Sabine. *Curious Myths of the Middle Ages*. 2nd edn. 2 vols. London, Oxford and Cambridge: Rivingtons, 1868.

Barlow, Frank. *Edward the Confessor*. English Monarchs. Berkeley and Los Angeles: University of California Press, 1970.

Barron, Caroline. "The Quarrel of Richard II with London, 1392–97." In *The Reign of Richard II: Essays in Honour of May McKisack*, edited by F.R.H. DuBoulay and Caroline M. Barron, 173–201. London: Athalone Press, 1971.

Barrow, Julia. "Athelstan to Aigublanche, 1056–1268." In *Hereford Cathedral: A History*, edited by Gerald Aylmer and John Tiller, 21–47. London and Rio Grande: Hambledon Press, 2000.

Bates, E.H. "Dedications of the Churches of Somersetshire." *Proceedings of the Somersetshire Archaeological and Natural History Society* 51 (1905): 105–35.

Beatty, Arthur. "The Saint George, or Mummers', Plays; a Study in the Protology of Drama." *Transactions of the Wisconsin Academy of Sciences, Arts, and Letters* XV 2 (October 1906): 273–324.

Beaune, Colette. *The Birth of an Ideology: Myths and Symbols of Nation in Late-Medieval France*. Edited by Frederic L. Cheyette, translated by Susan Ross Huston. Berkeley, Calif., and Oxford: University of California Press, 1991.

Begent, Peter J. and Hubert Chesshyre. *The Most Noble Order of the Garter: 650 Years*. London: Spink, 1999.

Beltz, George Frederick. *Memorials of the Most Noble Order of the Garter, from its Foundation to the Present Time*. London: William Pickering, 1841.

Bengtson, Jonathan. "Saint George and the Development of English Nationalism in the Late Middle Ages." M.Phil. thesis, Oxford University, 1994.

—— "Saint George and the Formation of English Nationalism." *Journal of Medieval and Early Modern Studies* 27:2 (1997): 317–40.

Bibliotheca Hagiographica Graeca. 3rd edn. 3 vols. Subsidia Hagiographica 8. Edited by F. Halkin. Brussels: Société des Bollandists, 1957.

Bibliotheca Hagiographica Latina Antiquae et Mediae Aetatis. 3 vols. Brussels: Société des Bollandists, 1898–1911.

Binns, Alison. *Dedications of Monastic Houses in England and Wales 1066–1216*. Studies in the History of Medieval Religion. Woodbridge, Suffolk: Boydell Press, 1989.

Blaauw, W.H. "Dureford Abbey—Its Fortunes and Misfortunes." *Sussex Archaeological Collections* 8 (1856): 41–96.

Blomefield, F. *Essay Towards a Topographical History of the County of Norfolk*. 5 vols. London: William Miller, 1805.

Boase, T.S.R. *Kingdoms and Strongholds of the Crusaders*. London: Thames and Hudson, 1971.

Bond, Francis Edgerton. *Dedications and Patron Saints of English Churches: Ecclesiastical Symbolism, Saints and their Emblems.* London and New York: Humphrey Milford, Oxford University Press, 1914.

Bond, Maurice F. *The Inventories of St. George's Chapel.* Historical Monographs Relating to St. George's Chapel, Windsor Castle 7. Windsor: Oxley and Son, 1947.

Boulton, D'Arcy Jonathan Dacre. *The Knights of the Crown: The Monarchical Orders of Knighthood in Later Medieval Europe.* Revised edn. Woodbridge, Suffolk: Boydell and New York: St Martin's Press, 2000.

Brewster, Alice. *The Life of St. George, the Patron Soldier-Saint of England.* London: Royal Society of Saint George, 1913.

Brieger, Peter. *English Art 1216–1307.* The Oxford History of English Art 4. Oxford: Clarendon Press, 1957.

British Museum, *Handbook of the Coins of Great Britain.* London: British Museum, 1869–70.

Britnell, R.H. and A.J. Pollard, eds. The *Macfarlane Legacy: Studies in Late Medieval Politics and Society.* New York: St. Martin's Press, 1995.

Brooks, E.W. "Acts of S. George." *Museon* 38 (1925): 67–115.

Brown, R. Allen, H.M. Colvin, and A.J. Taylor, eds. *History of the King's Works.* Vols. 1 and 2: *The Middle Ages.* London: HMSO, 1963.

Bulley, Margaret H. *St. George for Merrie England.* London: George Allen and Sons, 1908.

Butler, A.J. *Ancient Coptic Churches of Egypt.* 2 vols. Oxford: Oxford University Press, 1884.

Caiger-Smith, A. *English Medieval Mural Paintings.* Oxford: Clarendon Press, 1963.

Campbell, James. "The Late Anglo-Saxon State: A Maximum View." *Proceedings of the British Academy* 87 (1995): 39–65.

Carlin, Martha. *Medieval Southwark.* London and Rio Grande: Hambledon Press, 1996.

Caviness, Madeline Harrison. *The Windows of Christ Church Cathedral Canterbury.* Corpus Vitrearum Medii Aevii, Great Britain 2. London: British Academy, 1981.

Chambers, E.K. *The English Folk Play.* Oxford: Clarendon Press, 1933.

Chander, Alice. *A Dream of Order: The Medieval Ideal in Nineteenth-Century English Literature.* Lincoln, Nebr.: University of Nebraska Press, 1970.

Cheney, C.R. "Rules for the Observance of Feast Days in Medieval England." *Bulletin of the Institute of Historical Research* 34 (1961): 117–47.

Clanchy, Michael. *From Memory to Written Record: England 1066–1307.* 2nd edn. Oxford and Cambridge, Mass.: Blackwell, 1993.

Clapton, Edward. *Life of St. George.* 2nd edn. London: Swan Sonnenschein, 1903.

Clarke, C.W.B. *The True History of Saint George the Martyr, Patron Saint of England.* Cape Town: The SA "Electric" Printing and Publishing Co., 1900.

Clarke, M.V. "The Wilton Diptych." In *Fourteenth Century Studies*, edited by L.S. Sutherland and M. McKisack, 272–92. Oxford: Clarendon Press, 1937.

Clermont-Ganneau, Charles. "Horus et St. George d'après un bas-relief inedit du

Louvre." *Révue archéologique* NS 32 (1876): 196–204, 372–99.

Colley, Linda. *Britons: Forging the Nation 1707–1837.* New Haven and London: Yale University Press, 1992.

Collins, Hugh E.L. *The Order of the Garter, 1348–1461: Chivalry and Politics in Later Medieval England.* Oxford: Clarendon Press, 2000.

Cosgrove, Art. *Medieval Ireland 1169–1534. A New History of Ireland 2.* Oxford: Clarendon Press, 1993.

Coss, Peter. "Knighthood, Heraldry and Social Exclusion in Edwardian England." In *Heraldry, Pageantry and Social Display in Medieval England,* edited by Maurice Keen and Peter Coss, 39–68. Woodbridge, Suffolk and Rochester, N.Y.: Boydell, 2002.

Cross, F.L. and Livingstone, E.A. eds. *Oxford Dictionary of the Christian Church.* 3rd edn. Oxford: Oxford University Press, 1997.

Dalton, J.N. *The Manuscripts of St. George's Chapel.* Historical Monographs Relating to St. George's Chapel, Windsor Castle 11. Windsor: Oxley and Son, 1957.

Dawson, Thomas. *Memoirs of St. George, the English patron, and of the most noble Order of the Garter.* London: H. Clements, 1714.

Dean, Christopher. *Arthur of England: English Attitudes to King Arthur and the Knights of the Round Table in the Middle Ages and the Renaissance.* Toronto, Buffalo and London: University of Toronto Press, 1987.

Delehaye, Hippolyte. *Les Légends grecques des saints militaires.* Paris: A. Picard, 1909.

—— "Loca sanctorum." *Analecta Bollandiana* 48 (1930): 5–64.

—— *Les Origines du culte des martyrs.* 2nd edn. Subsidia Hagiographica 20. Brussels: Société des Bollandistes, 1933.

Dickens, A.G. *The English Reformation.* 2nd edn. University Park, Pa.: Penn State Press, 1989.

Doubleday, H. Arthur; William Page; L. F. Salzman; W. B. Stephens, eds. *The Victoria History of the County of Warwick.* 8 vols. London: Institute for Historical Research, 1904–69.

DuBoulay, F.R.H. and Caroline M. Barron, eds. *The Reign of Richard II: Essays in Honour of May McKisack.* London: Athalone Press, 1971.

Duffy, Eamon. *The Stripping of the Altars: Traditional Religion in England 1400–1580.* New Haven and London: Yale University Press, 1992.

—— *The Voices of Morebath: Reformation and Rebellion in an English Village.* New Haven and London: Yale University Press, 2001.

Echerd, Arthur Reeves, Jr. "Canonization and Politics in Late Medieval England: The Cult of Thomas of Lancaster." Ph.D. dissertation, University of North Carolina, 1983.

Elder, Isabel Hill. *George of Lydda: Soldier, Saint and Martyr.* London: Covenant Publishing, 1949.

Elliott, Dyan. *Spiritual Marriage: Sexual Abstinence in Medieval Wedlock.* Princeton: Princeton University Press, 1993.

Epstein, Stephen. *Genoa and the Genoese, 958–1528.* Chapel Hill and London: University of North Carolina Press, 1996.

Erdmann, Carl. *The Origin of the Idea of Crusade*. Translated by Marshall W. Baldwin and Walter Goffart. Princeton: Princeton University Press, 1977.

Evans, Joan. "The Wilton Diptych Reconsidered." *Archaeological Journal* 105 (1948): 1–5.

—— *English Art 1307–1461*. Oxford History of English Art 5. Oxford: Clarendon Press, 1949.

Farmer, David Hugh. *The Oxford Dictionary of Saints*. 3rd edn. Oxford and New York: Oxford University Press, 1992.

Fellows, Jennifer. "St. George as Romance Hero." *Reading Medieval Studies* 19 (1993): 27–54.

Ferris, Sumner. "The Wilton Diptych and the Absolutism of Richard II." *Journal of the Rocky Mountain Medieval and Renaissance Association* 8 (1987): 33–66.

Finley, M.I. *The World of Odysseus*. Revised edn. New York: Viking Press, 1965.

Finucane, Ronald C. *Miracles and Pilgrims: Popular Beliefs in Medieval England*. New York: St. Martin's Press, 1977.

Fleming, William. *The Life of St. George, Martyr, Patron of England*. London: R&T Washbourne, 1901.

Forde, Simon; Lesley Johnson; and Alan V. Murray, eds. *Concepts of National Identity in the Middle Ages*. Leeds: Leeds University Press, 1995.

Frazer, J.G. *The Golden Bough*. 3rd edn. 15 vols. New York: Macmillan, 1935.

French, Katherine L. *People of the Parish: Community Life in a Late Medieval English Diocese*. Philadelphia: University of Pennsylvania Press, 2001.

Frend, William H.C. "Fragments of a version of the *Acta S. Georgii* from Q'asr Ibrim." *Jahrbuch für Antike und Christentum* 32 (1989): 89–104.

Fussell, Paul. *The Great War and Modern Memory*. New York: Oxford University Press, 1975.

—— "The Fate of Chivalry, and the Assault upon Mother." In *Thank God for the Atom Bomb and Other Essays*, 221–48. New York: Summit Books, 1988.

Geary, Patrick. *Furta Sacra*. Revised edn. Princeton: Princeton University Press, 1990.

—— *The Myth of Nations: The Medieval Origins of Europe*. Princeton: Princeton University Press, 2002.

Gellner, Ernest. *Nations and Nationalism*. Ithaca: Cornell University Press, 1983.

Gibbon, Edward. *The Decline and Fall of the Roman Empire*. 3 vols. New York: The Modern Library, n.d.

Gillingham, John. *The English in the Twelfth Century: Imperialism, National Identity and Political Values*. Woodbridge, Suffolk: Boydell, 2000.

Girouard, Mark. *The Return to Camelot: Chivalry and the English Gentleman*. New Haven and London: Yale University Press, 1981.

Goebel, Stefan. *The Great War and Medieval Memory: War, Remembrance and Medievalism in Britain and Germany, 1914–1940*. Cambridge: Cambridge University Press, 2007.

Good, Jonathan and Nicholas Orme. "Edward I and the Churches of Devon, 1297." *The Devon Historian* 67 (October 2003): 3–9.

Good, Jonathan. "*Argent, a Cross Gules*: The Origins and English Use of the Arms of Saint George." *The Coat of Arms* 213 (Spring 2007): 9–18.

—— "Richard II and the Cults of Saints George and Edward the Confessor." In *Translatio, or the Transmission of Culture in the Middle Ages and Renaissance*, edited by Laura Hollengreen, 161–78. Turnhout: Brepols, 2008.

Gordon, Dillian. "A new discovery in the Wilton Diptych." *Burlington Magazine* 134 (1992): 662–67.

—— Lisa Monnas, and Caroline Elam, eds. *The Regal Image of Richard II and the Wilton Diptych*. London: Harvey Miller, 1997.

Gordon, Elizabeth Oke. *Saint George Champion of Christendom and Patron Saint of England*. London, 1907.

Graham, T.H.B. and W.G. Collingwood. "Patron Saints of the Diocese of Carlisle." *Transactions of the Cumberland and Westmorland Antiquarian and Archaeological Society* N.S. 25 (1925): 18–23.

Graves, Robert. *The Greek Myths*. 2 vols. Harmondsworth: Penguin, 1960.

Greenfeld, Liah. *Nationalism: Five Roads to Modernity*. Cambridge, Mass.: Harvard University Press, 1992.

Groom, Nicholas. *The Union Jack: The Story of the British Flag*. London: Atlantic Books, 2006.

Guanon [Sara Ann Mattson]. *St. George and the Dragon: A World-Wide Legend Localised*. London: Wyman & Sons, 1885.

Gutschmid, A. von. "Über die Sage vom heiligen Georg, als Beitrag zur iranischen Mythengeschichte." *Berichte über die Verhandlungen der Königlich Sächsische Gesellschaft der Wissenshaften zu Leipzig. Philologisch-Historische Class* 13 (1861): 175–202.

Haigh, Christopher. *The English Reformations*. Oxford: Clarendon Press, 1993.

Halkin, F. "Inscriptions grecques relatives à la hagiographie." *Analecta Bollandiana* 67 (1949): 87–108.

Hanawalt, Barbara A. "Keepers of the Lights: Late Medieval English Parish Gilds." *Journal of Medieval and Renaissance Studies* 14:1 (Spring 1984): 21–38.

Harriss, G.L. *Shaping the Nation: England 1360–1461*. Oxford and New York: Oxford University Press, 2005.

Harvey, I.M.W. "Was there Popular Politics in Fifteenth-Century England?" In *The Macfarlane Legacy: Studies in Late Medieval Politics and Society*, edited by R.H. Britnell and A.J. Pollard, 155–74. New York: St. Martin's Press, 1995.

Harvey, John H. "The Wilton Diptych: A Re-examination." *Archaeologia* 98 (1961): 1–24.

Haskins, Charles. *The Ancient Trade Guilds and Companies of Salisbury*. Salisbury: Bennet Brothers, 1912.

Hastings, Adrian. *The Construction of Nationhood: Ethnicity, Religion and Nationalism*. Cambridge: Cambridge University Press, 1996.

Haubrichs, Wolfgang. *Georgslied und Georgslegende im frühen Mittelalter: Text und Rekonstruktion*. Theorie, Kritik, Geschichte 13. Königstein: Scriptor, 1979.

Hewitt, H.J. *The Organization of War under Edward III 1338–1362*. Manchester: Manchester University Press, 1966.

Hill, George Francis. *Saint George the Martyr*. London: Medici Society, 1915.

Hobsbawm, Eric and Terence Ranger, eds. *The Invention of Tradition.* Cambridge: University Press, 1983.

Hobsbawm, Eric. *Nations and Nationalism since 1780: Programme, Myth, Reality.* Cambridge: University Press, 1990.

H.O.F., comp. *St. George for England: The Life, Legends and Lore of our Glorious Patron.* 2nd edn. London: F. Edwards & Co., n.d. [c. 1910].

Hogarth, P.J. "St. George: The Evolution of a Saint and his Dragon." *History Today* 30:4 (1980): 17–22.

Hogg, John. "Supplemental notes on St. George the Martyr, and on George the Arian Bishop." *Transactions of the Royal Society of Literature of the United Kingdom* 2nd series, 7 (1863): 106–36.

Huber, P. Michael. "Zur Georgslegende." In *Zeitschrift zum 12 Allgemeinen Deutschen Neuphilologentage in München, Pfingsten 1906,* 175–235. Erlangen: Verlag von Fr. Junge, 1906.

Hulst, Cornelia Steketee. *St. George of Cappadocia in Legend and History.* London: David Nutt, 1909.

Hutton, Ronald. *Stations of the Sun: A History of the Ritual Year in Britain.* Oxford: Oxford University Press, 1996.

James, M.R. *A Descriptive Catalogue of the Manuscripts in the Fitzwilliam Museum.* Cambridge: Cambridge University Press, 1895.

—— *A Descriptive Catalogue of the Second Series of Fifty Manuscripts (Nos. 51–100) in the Collection of Henry Yates Thompson.* Cambridge: Cambridge University Press, 1902.

Jerphanion, Guillaume de. *Une Nouvelle province de l'art byzantine: Les églises rupestres de Cappadoce.* 7 vols. Paris: Paul Geuthner, 1936.

Kedourie, Elie. *Nationalism.* 4th edn. Oxford and Cambridge, Mass.: Blackwell, 1994.

Keen, Maurice. *The Laws of War in the Late Middle Ages.* Toronto: University of Toronto Press and London: Routledge and Kegan Paul, 1965.

—— *Chivalry.* New Haven and London: Yale University Press, 1984.

—— and Peter Coss, eds. *Heraldry, Pageantry and Social Display in Medieval England.* Woodbridge, Suffolk: Boydell, 2002.

Keeney, Barnaby C. "Military Service and the Development of Nationalism in England, 1272–1327." *Speculum* 22 (1947): 534–49.

Kestner, Joseph A. "The Pre-Raphaelites, St George and the construction of masculinity." In *Collecting the Pre-Raphaelites: The Anglo-American Enchantment,* edited by Margaretta Frederick Watson, 149–62. Aldershot: Ashgate, 1997.

Keyser, Charles E. *A List of Norman Tympana and Lintels.* 2nd edn. London: Elliot Stock, 1927.

Kirschbaum, Engelbert, Günter Bandmann and Wofgang Braunfels, eds. *Lexikon der Christlichen Ikonographie.* 8 vols. Rome: Herder, 1968–76.

Knapp, Peggy. "Chaucer Imagines England (in English)." In *Imagining a Medieval English Nation,* edited by Kathy Lavazzo, 131–60. Medieval Cultures 37. Minneapolis and London: University of Minnesota Press, 2004.

Knowles, David and R. Neville Hadcock. *Medieval Religious Houses: England and*

Wales. New York: Longman, 1971.

Kumar, Krishan. *The Making of English National Identity.* Cambridge: Cambridge University Press, 2003.

Laborderie, Olivier de. "Richard the Lionheart and the birth of a national cult of St George in England: origins and development of a legend." *Nottingham Medieval Studies* 39 (1995): 37–53.

Lassus, Jean. *Sanctuaires Chrétiens de Syrie.* Paris: Paul Guenther, 1947.

Lavezzo, Kathy, ed. *Imagining a Medieval English Nation.* Medieval Cultures 37. Minneapolis and London: University of Minnesota Press, 2004.

Le Goff, Jacques. "Ecclesiastical Culture and Folklore in the Middle Ages: Saint Marcellus of Paris and the Dragon." In *Time, Work and Culture in the Middle Ages,* translated by Arthur Goldhammer, 159–88. Chicago and London: University of Chicago Press, 1980.

Lears, T.J. Jackson. *No Place of Grace: Antimodernism and the Transformation of American Culture, 1880–1920.* New York: Pantheon Books, 1981.

Lewis, Katherine. *The Cult of St Katherine in Late Medieval England.* Woodbridge, Suffolk: Boydell, 2000.

—— "Becoming a Virgin King: Richard II and Edward the Confessor." In *Gender and Holiness,* edited by S.J.E. Riches and Sarah Salih, 86–100. London and New York: Routledge, 2002.

Lewis, N.B. "The Last Medieval Summons of the English Feudal Levy, 13 June 1385." *English Historical Review* 73 (1958): 1–26.

Lloyd, Simon. "'Political Crusades' in England, c. 1215–17 and c. 1263–5." In *Crusades and Settlement: Papers read a the First Conference of the Society for the Study of the Crusades and the Latin East and presented to R.C. Smail,* edited by Peter Edbury, 113–120. Cardiff: University College of Cardiff Press, 1985.

Loomis, R.S. "Edward I: Arthurian Enthusiast." *Speculum* 28 (1953): 114–27.

Louda, Jirí. *European Civic Coats of Arms.* London: Paul Hamlyn, 1966.

Lyon, Bryce. *A Constitutional and Legal History of Medieval England.* New York: Harper and Row, 1960.

MacGregor, James B. "Praying to Saint George in Fifteenth-Century England." Paper presented at the 42nd International Congress on Medieval Studies, Western Michigan University, Kalamazoo, Michigan, 8 May 2007.

Maddicott, J.R. *Thomas of Lancaster 1307–1322: A Study in the Reign of Edward II.* Oxford: University Press, 1970.

Marcus, G.J. *Saint George of England.* London: Williams and Norgate, 1929.

Marks, Richard. *Image and Devotion in Late Medieval England.* Stroud, Glos.: Sutton, 2004.

Matzke, J.E. "Contributions to the History of the Legend of Saint George, with Special Reference to the Sources of the French, German and Anglo-Saxon Metrical Versions." *Proceedings of the Modern Language Association* 17 (1902): 464–535; 18 (1903): 99–171.

—— "The Legend of Saint George: Its development into a roman d'aventure." *Proceedings of the Modern Language Association* 19 (1904): 449–78.

McClendon, Muriel C. "A Moveable Feast: Saint George's Day Celebrations and

Religious Change in Early Modern England." *Journal of British Studies* 38 (January 1999): 1–27.

McRee, Benjamin R. "Religious Gilds and Civic Order: The Case of Norwich in the Late Middle Ages." *Speculum* 67 (1992): 69–97.

—— "Unity or Division? The Social Meaning of Guild Ceremony in Urban Communities." In *City and Spectacle in Medieval Europe*, edited by Barbara A. Hanawalt and Kathryn L. Reyerson, 189–207. Minneapolis and London: University of Minnesota Press, 1994.

Meyrick, Samuel Rush. "Description of the Engravings on a German suit of Armour, made for Henry VIII, in the Tower of London." *Archaeologia* 22 (1829): 106–13.

Micklethwaite, John Thomas. "Notes on the Imagery of Henry the Seventh's Chapel, Westminster." *Archaeologia* 47 (1883): 361–80.

Millar, Oliver. *Catalogue of the Tudor, Stuart and Early Georgian Pictures in the Collection of Her Majesty the Queen*. 2 vols. London: Phaidon, 1963.

Mills, A.D. *A Dictionary of English Place Names*. Oxford Paperback Reference. Oxford and New York: Oxford University Press, 1991.

Milner, John. *An Historical and Critical Inquiry into the Existence and Character of Saint George, Patron of England*. London: J. Debrett, 1792.

Mitchell, Shelagh. "Richard II: Kingship and the Cult of Saints." In *The Regal Image of Richard II and the Wilton Diptych*, edited by Dillian Gordon, Lisa Monas and Caroline Elam, 115–24. London: Harvey Miller, 1997.

Morgan, David A.L. "The Cult of Saint George c. 1500: National and International Connotations." In *L'angleterre et les pays bourguignons: relations et comparisons XVe-XVIe siècles*, edited by Jean-Marie Cauchies, 151–62. Neuchatel: Centre européen d'études bourguignonnes (XIVe-XVIe s.), 1995.

—— "The Banner-Bearer of Christ and Our Lady's Knight: How God became an Englishman Revisited." In *St George's Chapel Windsor in the Fourteenth Century*, edited by Nigel Saul, 51–62. Woodbridge, Suffolk: Boydell, 2005.

Morgan, Nigel. *The Lambeth Apocalypse: Manuscript 209 in the Lambeth Palace Library*. London: Harvey Miller, 1997.

—— "The Signification of the Banner in the Wilton Diptych." In *The Regal Image of Richard II and the Wilton Diptych*, edited by Dillian Gordon, Lisa Monas and Caroline Elam, 179–88. London: Harvey Miller, 1997.

Newman, Gerald. *The Rise of English Nationalism: A Cultural History 1740–1830*. Revised edition. New York: St. Martin's Press, 1997.

Nicolas, Nicholas Harris. *History of the Battle of Agincourt*. 2nd edn. London: Johnson and Co., 1832.

Orme, Nicholas. "Sir John Speke and his Chapel in Exeter Cathedral." *Devonshire Association Transactions* 118 (1986): 25–41.

—— *English Church Dedications, with a Survey of Cornwall and Devon*. Exeter: University of Exeter Press, 1996.

—— *The Saints of Cornwall*. Oxford and London: Oxford University Press, 2000.

—— and Margaret Webster. *The English Hospital, 1070–1570*. New Haven and London: Yale University Press, 1995.

Ormrod, W.M. "The Personal Religion of Edward III." *Speculum* 64 (1989): 849–77.

—— *The Reign of Edward III: Crown and Political Society in England 1327–1377.* New Haven and London: Yale University Press, 1990.

—— "For Arthur and St George: Edward III, Windsor Castle and the Order of the Garter." In *St George's Chapel Windsor in the Fourteenth Century*, edited by Nigel Saul, 13–34. Woodbridge, Suffolk: Boydell, 2005.

Orwell, George. "England Your England." In *A Collection of Essays by George Orwell*, 257–83. Garden City, N.Y.: Doubleday, 1954.

Pächt, Otto and J.J.G. Alexander. *Illuminated Manuscripts in the Bodleian Library.* 3 vols. Oxford: Clarendon Press, 1966–73.

Pastoureau, Michel. *Armorial des chevaliers de la table ronde.* Paris: Léopard d'Or, 1983.

—— *Traité d'héraldique.* 3rd edn. Paris: Picard, 1997.

Pearsall, Derek. *John Lydgate (1371–1449): A Bio-bibliography.* English Literary Studies Monograph Series 71. Victoria, B.C.: University of Victoria, 1997.

—— "The idea of Englishness in the fifteenth century." In *Nation, Court and Culture: New Essays on Fifteenth-Century English Poetry.* Edited by Helen Cooney. Dublin: Four Courts Press, 2001.

Pegge, Samuel. "Observations on the history of St. George, the Patron Saint of England." *Archaeologia* 5 (1779): 1–32.

Pollard A.J. *Late Medieval England, 1399–1509.* Harlow: Pearson, 2000.

Prestwich, Michael. *Edward I.* English Monarchs. 2nd edn. New Haven and London: Yale University Press, 1997.

Pringle, Denys. *The Churches of the Crusader Kingdom of Jerusalem.* Cambridge: Cambridge University Press, 1998.

Pugh, Ralph Berard; Elizabeth Crittall, and D.A. Crowley, eds. *The Victoria History of the County of Wiltshire.* 16 vols. London: Institute for Historical Research, 1953–99.

Renouard, Yves. "L'ordre de la Jarretière et l'ordre de l'Etoile." In *Etudes d'histoire médievale*, 93–106. Bibliothèque générale de l'école pratique des hautes études, VIe section. Paris: SEVPEN, 1968.

Reynolds, Susan. *Kingdoms and Communities in Western Europe 900–1300.* 2nd edn. Oxford: Clarendon Press, 1997.

Riches, Samantha. *St George: Hero, Martyr and Myth.* Stroud, Glos.: Sutton, 2000.

Ridyard S.J. *The Royal Saints of Anglo-Saxon England.* Cambridge: Cambridge University Press, 1988.

Rosenberg, John D. *The Darkening Glass: A Portrait of Ruskin's Genius.* New York: Columbia University Press, 1986.

Ross, Charles. *Edward IV.* English Monarchs. London and New Haven: Yale University Press, 1997.

Rosser, Gervase. "Going to the Fraternity Feast: Commensality and Social Relations in Late Medieval England." *Journal of British Studies* 33 (1994): 430–46.

Rouse, Robert Allen. *The Idea of Anglo-Saxon England in Middle English Romance.* Cambridge: D.S. Brewer, 2005.

Rowe, B.J.H. "The Clovis Miniature and the Bedford Portrait." *Journal of the Archaeological Association* 3rd series 25 (1962): 56–65.

Royal Commission on Historical Monuments. *An Inventory of the historical monuments of the City of Oxford.* London: HMSO, 1939.

Rubin, Miri. *Corpus Christi: The Eucharist in Late Medieval Culture.* Cambridge: Cambridge University Press, 1991.

Runciman, Stephen. *A History of the Crusades.* 3 vols. Harmondsworth: Pelican, 1971.

Russell, Josiah Cox. "The Canonization of Opposition to the King in Angevin England." In *Anniversary Essays in Medieval History by Students of Charles Homer Haskins,* edited by C.H. Taylor and J.L. La Monte, 279–90. New York and Boston: Houghton Mifflin, 1929.

Salmon, Thomas. *A New Historical Account of St. George for England and the original of the most noble Order of the Garter.* London: N. Dancer, 1704.

Salzman, L.F., ed. *The Victoria History of the County of Sussex.* Volume 3. London: Institute for Historical Research, 1935.

Saul, Nigel, ed. *Age of Chivalry.* New York: St. Martin's Press, 1992.

Saul, Nigel. *Richard II.* English Monarchs. New Haven and London: Yale University Press, 1997.

—— ed. *St George's Chapel Windsor in the Fourteenth Century.* Woodbridge, Suffolk: Boydell, 2005.

Scanlon, Larry. "King, Commons and Kind Wit: Langland's National Vision and the Rising of 1381." In *Imagining a Medieval English Nation,* edited by Kathy Lavezzo, 191–233. Medieval Cultures 37. Minneapolis and London: University of Minnesota Press, 2004.

Scharf, G. "On a Votive Painting of St. George and the Dragon." *Archaeologia* 49 (1886): 243–300.

Scholz, Bernhard W. "The Canonization of Edward the Confessor." *Speculum* 36 (1961): 38–60.

Schwetman, John. "The Appearance of Saint George above the English Troops at Agincourt: The Source of a Detail in the Historical Record." *Notes and Queries* 239 (Sept. 1994): 304–07.

Segal, J.B. *Edessa, 'The Blessed City.'* Oxford: Clarendon Press, 1970.

Sharp, Thomas. *A Dissertation on the Pageants or Dramatic Mysteries anciently performed at Coventry.* Totowa, N.J.: Rowman and Littlefield, 1973.

Smith, Anthony D. *The Ethnic Origins of Nations.* Oxford and New York: Basil Blackwell, 1986.

—— *Nationalism and Modernism.* London: Routledge, 1998.

Smyth, Alfred P. "The Emergence of English Identity, 700–1000." In *Medieval Europeans: Studies in Ethnic Identity and National Perspectives in Medieval Europe,* edited by A.P. Smyth, 24–52. Houndmills, Hants.: Macmillan, and New York: St. Martin's Press, 1998.

Stevenson, J.H. *Heraldry in Scotland.* Glasgow: James Maclehose and Sons, 1914.

Strong, Roy C. "Queen Elizabeth and the Order of the Garter." *Archaeological Journal* 119 (1962): 245–69.

—— *The Cult of Elizabeth: Elizabethan Portraiture and Pageantry*. Berkeley and Los Angeles: University of California Press, 1977.

Sumption, Jonathan. *Pilgrimage: An Image of Medieval Religion*. Totowa, N.J.: Rowman and Littlefield, 1975.

Sutherland, C.V.H. *English Coinage 600–1900*. London: B.T. Batsford, 1973.

Thiselton-Dyer, T.F. *British Calendar Customs, Past and Present*. London: George Bell and Sons, 1876.

Tout T.F. *Chapters in the Administrative History of Mediaeval England*. 6 vols. Manchester: Manchester University Press, 1920–33.

Tristram, E.W. *English Wall Painting of the Fourteenth Century*. London: Routledge and Kegan Paul, 1955.

Tugene, J. Georges. *L'image de la nation anglaise dans l'"Histoire écclesiastique" de Bède le Vénérable*. Strasbourg: Presses Universitaires de Strasbourg, 2001.

Turner, Ralph. *Men Raised from the Dust: Administrative Service and Upward Mobility in Angevin England*. Philadelphia: University of Pennsylvania Press, 1988.

Turville-Petre, Thorlac. *England the Nation: Language, Literature, and National Identity, 1290–1340*. Oxford: Clarendon Press, 1996.

—— "Afterword." In *Imagining a Medieval English Nation*, edited by Kathy Lavezzo, 340–46. Medieval Cultures 37. Minneapolis and London: University of Minnesota Press, 2004.

Unwin, George. *The Gilds and Companies of London*. Antiquaries Books. London: Methuen, 1908.

Vailhé, Siméon. "Une inscription byzantine de Jéricho." *Échos d'Orient* 14 (1911): 231–32.

Vale, Juliet. *Edward III and Chivalry: Chivalric Society and its Context 1270–1350*. Woodbridge, Suffolk: Boydell, 1982.

Vale, Malcolm. *The Origins of the Hundred Years War: The Angevin Legacy 1250–1340*. Oxford: Clarendon Press, 1996.

Van Caenegem R.C. *The Birth of the English Common Law*. Cambridge: Cambridge University Press, 1973.

Waddington, Raymond. "Elizabeth I and the Order of the Garter." *Sixteenth Century Journal* 24 (1993): 97–113.

Wagner, Anthony. *Heraldry in England*. Harmondsworth: Penguin, 1946.

Walker, John. *The National Gallery of Art, Washington*. Revised edn. New York: Harry N. Abrams, 1984

Walter, Christopher. "The Origins of the Cult of Saint George." *Revue des Études Byzantines* 53 (1995): 295–326.

—— *The Warrior Saints in Byzantine Art and Tradition*. Aldershot: Ashgate, 2003.

Warner, G.F. and J.P. Gilson. *Catalogue of Western Manuscripts in the Old Royal and King's Collections in the British Museum*. 4 vols. London: British Museum, 1921.

Watkin, Hugh R. *The History of Totnes Priory and Medieval Town, Devonshire*. 2 vols. Torquay: By the author, 1917.

Weinfurter, Stephan. *Heinrich II. (1002–1024): Herrscher am Ende der Zeiten*. Regensburg: Friedrich Pustet, 1999.

Westlake, Herbert F. *The Parish Gilds of Medieval England*. London: Society for

Promoting Christian Knowledge, 1918.

White, Eileen. *The Saint Christopher and Saint George Gild of York*. Borthwick Papers 72. York: University of York, 1987.

Whiting, Robert. *The Blind Devotion of the People: Popular Religion and the English Reformation*. Cambridge: Cambridge University Press, 1989.

Wilkinson, John. *Jerusalem Pilgrims before the Crusades*. Warminster: Aris and Phillips, 1977.

Williams, Ethel Carleton. "Mural Paintings of St. George in England." *Journal of the British Archaeological Association* 3rd series 12 (1949): 19–38.

Wilson, Stephen, ed. *Saints and their Cults: Studies in Religious Sociology, Folklore and History*. Cambridge: Cambridge University Press, 1983.

Wilson, Timothy Hugh. "Saint George in Tudor and Stuart England." M.Phil. thesis, Warburg Institute, 1976.

Windemuth, Marie-Luise. *Das Hospital als Träger der Armenfürsorge im Mittelalter*. Sudhoffs Archiv Beihefte 36. Stuttgart: Franz Steiner Verlag, 1995.

Winstead, Karen. *John Capgrave's Fifteenth Century*. Philadelphia: University of Pennsylvania Press, 2007.

Withington, Robert. *English Pageantry*. 2 vols. Cambridge, Mass.: Harvard University Press, 1918–20.

Wolffe, Bertram. *Henry VI*. English Monarchs. London: Eyre Methuen, 1981.

Wood, Charles T. "Richard II and the Wilton Diptych." In Charles T. Wood, *Joan of Arc and Richard III: Sex, Saints, and Government in the Middle Ages*, 75–90. New York and Oxford: Oxford University Press, 1984.

Wormald, Francis. "The Wilton Diptych." *Journal of the Warburg and Courtauld Institutes* 17 (1954): 191–203.

Wormald, Patrick. "*Engla Lond*: the Making of an Allegiance." *Journal of Historical Sociology* 7 (1994): 1–24.

Wright, A.R. *British Calendar Customs*. Edited by T.E. Lones. 3 vols. London: Folk-Lore Society, 1936–40.

Wulff, Oskar. *Altchristliche und Mittelalterliche Bildwerke*. 2 vols. Berlin: Reimer, 1909–11.

Wylie, James Hamilton and William Templeton Waugh. *The Reign of Henry the Fifth*. 3 vols. Cambridge: Cambridge University Press, 1929.

Wyon, Alfred. *The Great Seals of England from the Earliest Period to the Present Time*. London: Elliot Stock, 1887.

Index

198 INDEX

Printed and bound by CPI Group (UK) Ltd, Croydon, CR0 4YY

09/06/2025

14685710-0001